P9-DVS-650

CHINA'S INTERNATIONAL BEHAVIOR

Activism, Opportunism, and Diversification

Evan S. Medeiros

Prepared for the United States Air Force

Approved for public release; distribution unlimited

PROJECT AIR FORCE

The research described in this report was sponsored by the United States Air Force under Contract FA7014-06-C-0001. Further information may be obtained from the Strategic Planning Division, Directorate of Plans, Hq USAF.

Library of Congress Cataloging-in-Publication Data

Medeiros, Evan S.
    China's international behavior : activism, opportunism, and diversification /
Evan S. Medeiros.
      p. cm.
    Includes bibliographical references.
    ISBN 978-0-8330-4709-0 (pbk. : alk. paper)
    1. China—Foreign relations—21st century. 2. National security—China.
3. China—Economic polcy—21st century. 4. China—Foreign relations—United
States. 5. United States—Foreign relations—China. I. Title.

JZ1730.A5M435 2009
327.51—dc22

                      2009026441

The RAND Corporation is a nonprofit research organization providing objective analysis and effective solutions that address the challenges facing the public and private sectors around the world. RAND's publications do not necessarily reflect the opinions of its research clients and sponsors. **RAND®** is a registered trademark.

Cover design by Carol Earnest.

© Copyright 2009 RAND Corporation

Permission is given to duplicate this document for personal use only, as long as it is unaltered and complete. Copies may not be duplicated for commercial purposes. Unauthorized posting of RAND documents to a non-RAND Web site is prohibited. RAND documents are protected under copyright law. For information on reprint and linking permissions, please visit the RAND permissions page (http://www.rand.org/publications/permissions.html).

Published 2009 by the RAND Corporation
1776 Main Street, P.O. Box 2138, Santa Monica, CA 90407-2138
1200 South Hayes Street, Arlington, VA 22202-5050
4570 Fifth Avenue, Suite 600, Pittsburgh, PA 15213-2665
RAND URL: http://www.rand.org/
To order RAND documents or to obtain additional information, contact
Distribution Services: Telephone: (310) 451-7002;
Fax: (310) 451-6915; Email: order@rand.org

Preface

The expanding scope of China's international activities is one of the newest and most important trends in global affairs. China is increasingly present and involved in many parts of the world, including in regions once only marginal to Beijing's interests. China's global activism has arisen so rapidly and has so many dimensions that it immediately and naturally raises questions about China's intentions and the implications for U.S. security interests. U.S. policymakers and strategists would like to understand more fully how China defines its international objectives, how it is pursuing them, how effective it has been, and whether it seeks to undermine U.S. power and influence.

To address these issues, this monograph analyzes the content, character, and execution of China's international behavior. It examines how China views its security environment, how it defines its foreign policy objectives, how it is pursuing these objectives, and the consequences for U.S. economic and security interests. The breadth and the rapidity of change in China's international activities are daunting to analyze, let alone to understand. This monograph aims to make such assessments more accessible and meaningful.

This research is relevant for U.S. policymakers and strategists who are focused on managing U.S.-China relations, on shaping Chinese diplomacy, and on ensuring that China's global activism does not undercut U.S. foreign policy goals. This research also helps identify opportunities for the United States and China to broaden and deepen bilateral cooperation.

This monograph is part of a substantial and growing body of RAND Corporation research that examines the security implications for the United States of China's growing power and influence—both as a military and as a diplomatic power. The research reported here was conducted by the Strategy and Doctrine Program of RAND Project AIR FORCE and was sponsored by the U.S. Air Force's Director of Operational Plans and Joint Matters (AF/A5X) and the Combatant Commander of the Pacific Air Forces (PACAF/CC) for a study entitled "The U.S.-China Security Relationship: Taiwan and Beyond." It builds on previous RAND Project AIR FORCE work, including the following:

- Evan S. Medeiros, Keith Crane, Eric Heginbotham, Norman D. Levin, Julia F. Lowell, Angel Rabassa, and Somi Seong, *Pacific Currents: The Responses of U.S. Allies and Security Partners in East Asia to China's Rise*, MG-736-AF, 2008.
- Roger Cliff, Mark Burles, Michael Chase, Derek Eaton, and Kevin Pollpeter, *Entering the Dragon's Lair: Chinese Anti-Access Strategies and Their Implications for the United States*, MG-524-AF, 2007.
- Roger Cliff and David A. Shlapak, *U.S.-China Relations After Resolution of Taiwan's Status*, MG-567-AF, 2007.
- Evan S. Medeiros, Roger Cliff, Keith Crane, and James C. Mulvenon, *A New Direction for China's Defense Industry*, MG-334-AF, 2005.
- Keith Crane, Roger Cliff, Evan S. Medeiros, James C. Mulvenon, and William H. Overholt, *Modernizing China's Military: Opportunities and Constraints*, MG-260-AF, 2005.

RAND Project AIR FORCE

RAND Project AIR FORCE (PAF), a division of the RAND Corporation, is the U.S. Air Force's federally funded research and development center for studies and analyses. PAF provides the Air Force with independent analyses of policy alternatives affecting the development, employment, combat readiness, and support of current and future aerospace forces. Research is conducted in four programs: Force Modernization and Employment; Manpower, Personnel, and Training; Resource Management; and Strategy and Doctrine.

Additional information about PAF is available on our Web site: http://www.rand.org/paf/

Contents

CHAPTER SEVEN
Challenges Facing Chinese Diplomacy

CHAPTER EIGHT
Conclusions

Figures

Tables

Summary

China is now a global actor of significant and growing importance. It is involved in regions and on issues that were once only peripheral to its interests, and it is effectively using tools previously unavailable. It is no longer necessary to emphasize integrating China into the existing constellation of norms, rules, and institutions of the international community; by and large, China is already there. It is influencing perceptions, relationships, and organizations all over the world. China's international behavior is clearly altering the dynamics of the current international system, but it is not transforming its structure.

China's global activism is driven by an identifiable set of *perceptions*, *objectives*, and *policies*—some are long-standing and others are more current. Both China's foreign policy objectives and its policies have evolved in the last decade but with more change in the latter than the former. In this sense, China has a distinct foreign policy strategy, to the extent that any nation has one. China's strategy is best understood as comprising multiple layers, each adding to an understanding of the totality of it. This monograph analyzes these layers, assesses the challenges for China in implementing its strategy, and evaluates the implications for U.S. interests and U.S. policy.

China's Foreign Policy Outlook

China's international behavior is influenced by at least three historically determined lenses that color and shade its perceptions of its security environment and its role in global affairs. First, China is in the process of *reclaiming* its status as a major regional power and, eventually, as a great power—although the latter goal is not well defined or articulated. Chinese policymakers and analysts refer to China's rise as a "revitalization" and a "rejuvenation." Second, many Chinese view their country as a victim of "100 years of shame and humiliation" at the hands of Western and other foreign powers, especially Japan. This victimization narrative has fostered an acute sensitivity to coercion by foreign powers and especially infringements (real or perceived) on its sovereignty. Third, China has a defensive security outlook that stems from historically determined fears that foreign powers will try to constrain and coerce it by exploiting its internal weaknesses.

China's international behavior is also informed by the long-standing diplomatic priorities of protecting its sovereignty and territorial integrity, promoting economic development, and generating international respect and status. These three priorities have been collectively driving China's foreign and security policy since the founding of the People's Republic of China in 1949. Yet, the policy manifestations of these three strategic priorities and the leadership's relative emphasis on them have differed over the last 30 years. (See pp. 7–18.)

Chinese Perceptions of the International Security Environment

China's view of its security environment has two overarching dimensions. The first is a widely held belief that China's success is inextricably linked to the international community, more so than ever before. The second is the pervasive uncertainty about the range and severity of threats to China's economic and security interests. For some, China has never been so secure and, for others, the numbers and types of security threats are growing, motivating deep concerns about the future.

On balance, Chinese leaders have concluded that their external security environment is favorable and that the next 15 to 20 years represent a "strategic window of opportunity" for China to achieve its leading objective of national revitalization through continued economic, social, military, and political development. Chinese policymakers seek, to the extent possible, to extend this window of opportunity through diplomacy.

China's view of its security environment includes six mainstream perceptions:

- **No Major Power War:** There is a low probability of large-scale war among major powers, and thus the next 15 to 20 years is a unique period for China to continue to develop and modernize.
- **Globalization:** Globalization has redefined interstate economic and political interactions, bolstering China's global economic importance and enhancing interdependence among states. Globalization has imposed some constraints on China.
- **The Global Power Balance:** Multipolarity is rapidly emerging; although the United States remains a predominant power in the world, it is declining gradually and in relative terms. The United States is both a potential threat to China's revitalization as a great power and a central partner in China's realization of this goal.
- **Nontraditional Security Challenges:** China faces a variety of such challenges, including terrorism, weapons proliferation, narcotics and human trafficking, environmental degradation, the spread of infectious diseases, and natural disasters. These are redefining China's relations with major powers in Asia and globally, including by creating opportunities for tangible cooperation.
- **Energy Insecurity:** China defines energy security in terms of two issues: price volatility and security of delivery. China feels vulnerable on both fronts. Such perceptions are increasingly driving its efforts to gain access to crude oil and natural gas resources, especially in the Middle East and Africa.
- **China's Rise:** Chinese policymakers see the "rise of China" as an influential factor in global economic and security affairs. China is increasingly confident in its diplomatic reach and influence and feels it has succeeded in dampening fears of a "China threat," especially in Asia. (See pp. 19–44.)

China's Foreign Policy Objectives

Chinese policymakers have crafted a foreign policy strategy that seeks to accomplish five specific objectives: economic growth and development, reassurance, countering constraints, resource diversification, and reducing Taiwan's international space. This list of diplomatic objectives has expanded in the last decade as China became more integrated into the international community.

First, China seeks to maintain a stable international environment to facilitate continued reform and development at home—as Chinese policymakers have reiterated for decades. This domestic focus has a growing variety of external manifestations: China actively uses its diplomacy to expand access to markets, investment, technology, and natural resources. Second, China seeks to reassure Asian states and the international community that its growing capabilities will not undermine other countries' economic and security interests. Third, Chinese diplomacy, especially in Asia, seeks to reduce the ability or willingness of other nations, singularly or collectively, to contain, constrain, or otherwise hinder China's revitalization. Fourth, China is building political relationships to diversify its access to energy and other natural resources, with a focus on Africa, the Middle East, and Latin America. Energy security encompasses diversifying both suppliers and supply routes. Fifth, China seeks to reduce Taiwan's international space and limit other nations' ability to confer legitimacy on Taiwan. (See pp. 45–60.)

China's Foreign Policy Actions

China has developed and deployed a bevy of new and effective ways to pursue its five foreign policy objectives. It has also been more confident, flexible, creative, and assertive in using these new tools. China has established "strategic partnerships" with developed and developing countries alike and has initiated high-level "strategic dialogues" with several major powers. China has embraced multilateral institutions, in every region and on several functional issues. China's expansion of its role in existing regional organizations and its formation of new ones have become staples of its diplomacy. China's use of economic diplomacy is robust and multifaceted, including not only bilateral trade but also outward direct investment, financial arrangements, development aid, and free trade agreements to advance both economic *and* political objectives. China's military diplomacy now incorporates extensive participation in United Nations peacekeeping activities, high-level defense exchanges, joint exercises, and joint training and education; reassurance is a major goal of these enhanced efforts. (See pp. 61–192.)

Challenges Facing Chinese Diplomacy

Beijing confronts several challenges that will constrain its ability to meet its diplomatic objectives and perhaps also skew the ability to understand China's intentions. First, as China's global presence and influence grow, China's neighbors and other states will expect more of Beijing. It is unclear whether China is prepared to respond to these demands, fearing an accumulation of too many burdens; this is already raising questions about China's predictability and its reliability. Second, China's approach to the Taiwan question, which can be inflexible and aggressive at times, undermines its ability to appear moderate and benign. Third, China's myriad and acute governance challenges limit the government's ability to manage internal problems that could spill over onto its neighbors. This governance deficit complicates Beijing's ability to comply fully with its commitments, making China appear as an unreliable actor. A fourth challenge involves weaknesses in China's decisionmaking system. The problems of excessive secrecy and the lack of coordination across the civilian, intelligence, and military bureaucracies hinder China's ability to respond rapidly and effectively to crises with international dimensions. (See pp. 193–200.)

Key Findings about China's International Behavior

China has been largely working within—indeed, deftly leveraging—the current international system to accomplish its foreign policy objectives. It sees more opportunities than constraints in using the current system to advance its interests. China's international behavior is not ideologically driven, and China is not pursuing a revolutionary foreign policy that seeks to acquire new territory, forge balancing coalitions, or advance alternative models of economic development or global security. China is not trying to tear down or radically revise the current constellation of global rules, norms, and institutions. Rather, it has been seeking to master them to advance its interests—an approach that, to date, has proven quite productive for Beijing.

China is also dissatisfied with certain attributes of the current status quo, such as the undetermined status of Taiwan and U.S. global predominance in both security *and* economic affairs. Beijing's response has been to work within the system to address its concerns; this has included attempts to reduce the relative power and influence of the United States, especially U.S. actions directly affecting Chinese interests. China does not currently seek to confront the United States to erect a new international order. But China does challenge some U.S. interests, particularly in Asia. On balance, China has been occasionally assertive but seldom aggressive in pursuing this and other objectives. China's approach has been geared toward attracting and binding others, rather than directly challenging their interests: It is more gravitational than confrontational. It seeks to create an environment in Asia in which states are drawn to, reliant on, and thereby deferential to Beijing, as a way to minimize constraints and maximize its freedom of action.

In part by design and in part by default, China is diversifying its sources of prosperity, security, and status—a trend that holds major implications for China's global influence and U.S.-China relations. China is using its diplomacy to expand its access to markets, investment, technology, and resources to fuel domestic development. It is developing new diplomatic relationships and expanding existing ones with numerous power centers including global and regional institutions. It is also diversifying its sources of international status and legitimacy, to broaden China's appeal.

Chinese leaders continue to approach their foreign policy and foreign relations through the prism of internal affairs, to use foreign policy to assist the increasingly complex tasks of economic and social development at home. This does not mean that China is an insular nation that just wants to be left alone or that Chinese leaders view external affairs as a secondary concern. The reality of China's international behavior could not be further from that.

For China, acting locally now requires that it think globally. The links between domestic and international affairs for China have become stronger and have assumed new dimensions in the last decade, but it is this linkage that will continue to drive China's international behavior. China's twin goals of maintaining economic growth and domestic stability (and, thus, the continued rule of the Chinese Communist Party) remain the prevailing motivations for its external behavior.

As China's global profile grows, China wants a "seat at the table" to play a greater role in shaping global rules, norms, and institutions. This is most evident in China's multilateral diplomacy: China has created new organizations and expanded its participation in existing ones. China's role as an agenda- and rule-setter will only become a more prominent feature of its diplomacy in the coming years. However, China's actual record in such rule-making is quite limited. Although China clearly wants to be part of such processes, it is unclear what new rules or norms it seeks to advance, aside from a greater voice for itself. To date, Beijing has promoted few genuinely new ideas and the institutions it has created are not meant to compete with or replace existing ones. Also, other Asian powers remain wary of China's diplomatic activism and have sought to limit China's attempts to extend its influence through participation in such organizations.

Furthermore, China's international behavior is a deeply transitional phenomenon. China's perceptions, objectives and policies are fixed for now but they are also evolving. Chinese policymakers clearly have objectives in mind, but they are groping their way forward with newfound power, influence, responsibilities, expectations, and constraints. China's international behavior is increasingly driven, as well as constrained, by both domestic imperatives and a dynamic global security environment. Chinese foreign policy reflects a precarious balancing of competing internal and external demands, which are growing in number and variety. These demands, ultimately, will determine the content and character of China's future international behavior—contributing, at times, to seemingly contradictory or inconsistent behaviors. (See pp. 201–207.)

Implications for U.S. Security Interests

China does not seek to displace the United States as the predominant global power. Its elites do not currently want China to be a global leader on par with the United States—a peer competitor. They view their domestic challenges as too great to assume the risks and responsibilities associated with such a role, and they recognize that they lack the material resources to do so. They also fear that such a global role would divert much needed resources from national development and could foster regional backlashes against China. To be sure, Chinese leaders welcome a more multipolar world, one in which multilateralism reigns and U.S. power is constrained. Chinese leaders also want China to be eventually recognized as a great power—although that aspiration has very general attributes and is not well defined. Chinese leaders aspire to such a status as external validation of China's achievements, but they are also wary of the burdens and costs associated with it.

Some of China's foreign policy actions are directed at eroding relative U.S. influence in certain regions and institutions. Russia has been a useful Chinese partner in this effort. However, relations between the two countries remain complex, and they do not currently constitute a united front against the United States. The most competitive aspects of China's foreign policy are evident in the Asia-Pacific, which China views as its strategic periphery. China is not now trying to push the United States out of this region; Chinese leaders recognize the high costs and likely failure of such an effort. Some Chinese policymakers recognize the stability provided by U.S. security commitments. Rather, China seeks to constrain the U.S. ability to constrain China; that is, China seeks to maximize its freedom of action and leverage as a way to counter perceived U.S. efforts to limit Chinese choices. Thus, China seeks to challenge U.S. influence when it directly touches Chinese interests (especially core ones), but China does not seek to confront the United States or expel it from the region.

Furthermore, China's diversification strategy is altering the conduct of U.S.-China relations. As the sources of China's prosperity, security, and status have broadened (and during a period in which China perceives that the United States is in relative decline), Beijing is becoming less willing to accommodate U.S. preferences and more able to resist pressure from Washington, and even to generate countervailing forces. The traditional U.S. approach of relying largely on bilateral diplomacy to shape China's international behavior faces new limitations.

China's ascendance in the Asia-Pacific region is changing the nature of U.S. relations with its allies and partners in the region. As China becomes more relevant to their economic, financial, and military affairs, the needs of U.S. allies and partners and their demands on Washington will change. In some cases, this makes U.S. policy and U.S. commitments more relevant, allowing Asian nations to engage China with more confidence. At the same time, none of these nations wants to choose between the United States and China; none wants the United States to leave the region; none wants China to dominate the region; and none wants to be drawn into an effort to contain China. As China looms larger in their economic development and regional security planning, this will complicate Washington's ability to set exclusively the terms of interaction and cooperation with allies, partners, and others in the Asia-Pacific region and likely beyond. (See pp. 208–220.)

Acknowledgments

This monograph benefited enormously from the assistance of numerous RAND colleagues who aided with its researching, editing, and formatting. Jianglai Zhang and Matt Southerland provided invaluable assistance gathering, processing, and analyzing large amounts of data on numerous aspects of Chinese foreign policy. The breadth of this monograph owes much to their diligence. Beth Hague provided valuable inputs to various sections. RAND colleagues Eric Heginbotham, David Shlapak, and Sarah Harting read several drafts and helped to refine the argumentation and the clarity of the writing.

Numerous Chinese officials and scholars provided invaluable insights into the peculiar art of interpreting "the real meaning" of official slogans about foreign affairs and offered their analysis of the drivers of China's international behavior. I am grateful for the time and insights of these Chinese interlocutors, but all discussions were conducted on the basis of anonymity.

The initial draft of this monograph benefited greatly from formal reviews by Michael Swaine and Norman Levin; Paul Heer provided invaluable insights on the initial draft report as well. Megan Katt and Jessica Hart helped to proofread, format, and finalize various versions of this monograph. Patricia Bedrosian did yeoman's service copy editing the entire document, producing a much tighter read. All mistakes are, of course, my own.

Abbreviations

ACD	Asian Cooperation Dialogue
APEC	Asia Pacific Economic Cooperation
ARF	ASEAN Regional Forum
ASEAN	Association of Southeast Asian Nations
b/d	barrels per day
BFA	Boao Forum for Asia
CACF	China-Africa Cooperation Forum
CCP	Chinese Communist Party
CD	Conference on Disarmament
CEPA	Closer Economic Partnership Arrangement [China-Taiwan]
CSTO	Collective Security Treaty Organization
EAC	East Asian Community
EAS	East Asia Summit
EU	European Union
FBIS	Foreign Broadcast Information Service
FDI	foreign direct investment

FTA	free trade agreement
GCC	Gulf Cooperation Council
GDP	gross domestic product
GMS	Greater Mekong Subregion
IADB	Inter-American Development Bank
IAEA	International Atomic Energy Agency
MES	market-economy status
MINURSO	Mission for the Referendum in Western Sahara
NATO	North Atlantic Treaty Organization
NPC	National People's Congress
NPT	Treaty on the Nonproliferation of Nuclear Weapons
OAS	Organization of American States
ODA	official development assistance
ODI	outward direct investment
OECD	Organisation for Economic Cooperation and Development
OSC	Open Source Center
PLA	People's Liberation Army [People's Republic of China]
PRC	People's Republic of China
RMB	renminbi [China]
SAARC	South Asian Association for Regional Cooperation
SCO	Shanghai Cooperation Organization
UK	United Kingdom
U.N.	United Nations

UNAMIS	U.N. Advance Mission in the Sudan
UNMIS	U.N. Mission in the Sudan
UNPKO	U.N. peacekeeping operations
UNSC	U.N. Security Council
U.S.	United States
WMD	weapons of mass destruction
WTO	World Trade Organization

CHAPTER ONE

Introduction

China's economic and diplomatic interests now span the globe, having gradually moved beyond the Asia-Pacific region in the last decade. China is active on issues and in regions that were previously only peripheral to Beijing's calculations, notably, Latin America and the Middle East. Its diplomacy is affecting the conduct of international relations at virtually all levels of the global system, and its decisions are influencing international perceptions, relationships, institutions, and processes. China has become central to managing, if not resolving, many of the traditional and nontraditional security issues facing the international community.[1] Within Asia, China's strategic periphery, it has become a preeminent power, deeply involved in all aspects of economic and security affairs. China has become a fulcrum of change in the regional order, further ensuring that its pivotal role in Asia will deepen in the future.

These trends beg the following questions: What are China's objectives as a regional power and as a global actor? How is it pursuing them and to what effect on the respective regions? Where is China's interna-

---

[1] Avery Goldstein, *Rising to the Challenge: China's Grand Strategy and International Security*, Stanford, Calif.: Stanford University Press, 2005; Robert G. Sutter, *China's Rise in Asia: Promise and Perils*, Oxford, UK: Rowman & Littlefield, 2005; David Shambaugh, ed., *Power Shift: China and Asia's New Dynamics*, Berkeley, Calif.: University of California Press, 2006. For Chinese assessments of their national goals, see Yan Xuetong, *Guoji Zhengzhi yu Zhongguo* [International Politics and China], Beijing, China: Beijing Daxue Chubanshe, 2005.

Yet some U.S. scholars, such as Robert Sutter, argue that China's regional and global influence has been overstated. Robert G. Sutter, "China's Rise in Asia—Promises, Prospects and Implications for the United States," Occasional Paper Series, Honolulu, Hawaii: Asia-Pacific Center for Security Studies, February 2005.

tional behavior headed? How might its external interests and foreign policy change as its economic and military capabilities expand? And, ultimately, are China's foreign policy objectives consistent with U.S. economic and security interests?

To some extent, China's leaders have articulated answers to these important queries. Chinese policymakers talk about "peace, development, and cooperation" as the main features of China's diplomacy, and they argue that China's foreign policy seeks "to foster a stable and peaceful international environment that is conducive to building a well off society in an all around way." More recently, China's leaders claim to adhere to an international strategy of "peaceful development" in building a "harmonious world."[2]

These and other mantras are ubiquitous in the Chinese government's public discussions of its diplomacy. But such slogans and policies are decidedly unsatisfying, prompting confusion and worry among many external observers. It is not that such Chinese goals are patently untrue or a clever prevarication about Beijing's *real* intentions, a common refrain in the United States; rather, they are insufficient to explain the multiplicity of Chinese interests and actions. China's official characterizations of its foreign policy understate the various layers of perceptions, motivations, and policies that collectively constitute China's international behavior. In doing so, they fail to capture the dynamism of China's foreign affairs, which, in turn, obscures external understandings of Chinese behaviors. Therefore, to answer questions about China's current and future intentions, analysts must turn to the analytical enterprise of weaving together Chinese statements, analyses, and actions (and the motivations implied by all of these) to assess its objectives as a regional power and as a global actor.

---

[2] A summary of all the official Chinese Communist Party (CCP) lexicon on Chinese foreign policy can be found in Yang Jiechi, "Gaige Kaifang Yilai de Zhongguo Waijiao" [China's Diplomacy Since Reform and Opening], *Qiushi* (online), No. 18, September 16, 2008. On peaceful development, see *China's Peaceful Development Road*, Beijing, China: State Council Information Office, December 2005. For an analysis of this latter approach, see Bonnie Glaser and Evan S. Medeiros, "The Changing Ecology of Foreign Policy Decision-making in China: The Ascension and Demise of the Theory of 'Peaceful Rise,'" *China Quarterly*, Vol. 190, June 2007, pp. 291–310.

To this end, this monograph examines China's current and future "international behavior," which is a collective term encompassing both China's foreign *relations* (bilateral and multilateral) and the foreign *policies* it uses to pursue the former. How China conceives of its regional and global interests and the strategies and policies it uses to pursue such interests have direct implications for stability and security in Asia and globally. Moreover, an understanding of the perceptions, strategies, and tools underlying China's diplomacy will illuminate the future directions of China's international behavior.

This monograph argues that China's international behavior is best understood as comprising multiple layers with each one adding to the understanding of China's current actions and future direction. The layers are (1) the historically determined "lenses" through which Chinese policymakers view the world and China's role in it, (2) China's perceptions of its current international security environment, (3) China's foreign policy objectives, and (4) China's specific foreign policy actions in pursuit of its objectives (Figure 1.1). Given the breadth and rapidity of change in China's international behavior, this approach is meant to provide an analytic framework, a model of sorts, for assessing China's current and future intentions and the implications for the United States. It is not meant to be a comprehensive treatment of all aspects of Chinese foreign and national security policy. For example, this monograph does not address Chinese military modernization and Chinese military operations in East Asia, as these topics are independent research projects themselves and thus beyond the scope of the present analysis.[3]

To research China's international behavior, this monograph used Chinese open-source writings extensively, as well as those of Western analysts. These textual sources were complemented by a series of interviews in China in 2005, 2006, 2007, and 2008 with officials, analysts, and scholars involved in research and policymaking on China's foreign and national security affairs.

---

[3] This monograph does address Chinese military diplomacy because it is a relatively new and important part of China's effort to shape its external security environment (Chapter Five).

Figure 1.1
Graphical Depiction of China's International Behavior

Foreign
policy
actions

Foreign
policy
objectives

Perceptions of the
international security
environment

Foreign policy outlook

Historical experiences

Long-term diplomatic priorities

RAND *MG850-1.1*

This monograph is composed of an introduction, six substantive sections, and a chapter containing conclusions. Following the introduction, Chapter Two examines the various lenses through which Chinese policymakers and analysts contemplate China's role in global affairs. These lenses, which are largely derived from Chinese history as well as its long-standing national priorities, both reflect and inform Chinese biases that pervade its foreign policymaking. These are presented as enduring features of China's international behavior. Chapter Three explores China's perceptions of its current international security environment with a specific focus on the perceived challenges it confronts. Chapters Four, Five, and Six then detail China's current diplomatic *objectives* as an international actor and the specific *policies* Beijing has adopted in pursuit of them. The meaning and relevance of China's international actions are interpreted using the context of the previous chapters.

Drawing on Chapters Two through Six, Chapter Seven highlights the multiple challenges China faces in pursuit of both its long-term goals and its current objectives. The study's conclusions (Chapter Eight) distill the monograph's numerous arguments down to several analytic judgments about the current and future content of China's international behavior. That chapter then assesses the consequences of these claims for U.S.-China relations with a focus on the degree of convergence and divergence in U.S. and Chinese global interests.

CHAPTER TWO

China's Foreign Policy Outlook

China's international behavior is influenced by three historically determined "lenses" of perception that color and shade how Chinese policymakers view China's external environment, think about China's role in international affairs, and implement policy actions. These lenses reflect Chinese biases and prejudices about the international system and China's place in it. These lenses are all broad notions related to China's national-role concept and are not commonly articulated by officials, nor do they appear in government documents. Rather, these ideas pervade Chinese research, analysis, and policymaking about Chinese foreign relations and foreign policy.[1]

The Three Lenses

National Revitalization

First, there is a pervasive belief in China that it is in the process of reclaiming its lost status as a "great power" (*da guo* 大国). Chinese

---

[1] To understand the historical influences on Chinese foreign policy, see Niu Jun, *From Yan'an to the World: The Origin and Development of Chinese Communist Foreign Policy*, in Steven I. Levine, ed. and trans., Norwalk, Conn.: Eastbridge Books, 2005; John Garver, "The Legacy of the Past," *Foreign Relations of the People's Republic of China*, Englewood Cliffs, N.J.: Prentice Hall, 1993, pp. 2–30; Michael H. Hunt, *The Genesis of Chinese Communist Foreign Policy*, New York: Columbia University Press, 1996; Lowell Dittmer and Samuel S. Kim, eds., *China's Quest for National Identity*, Ithaca, N.Y.: Cornell University Press, 1993, especially Chapter Eight; and John K. Fairbank, "A Preliminary Framework," in John K. Fairbank, ed., *The Chinese World Order: Traditional China's Foreign Relations*, Cambridge, Mass.: Harvard University Press, 1968, pp. 1–19.

policymakers, analysts, and the media describe China's current rise as a "revitalization" (*fuxing* 复兴) or "rejuvenation" (*zhenxing* 振兴) of China's rightful place in the world as a great power. They commonly refer to China's substantial global influence during the Han, Tang, and late Ming/early Qing dynasties—even though China had very limited contact during these periods with ancient Greece, the Roman Empire, Byzantium, or India.[2] In the words of a *Global Times* commentary, "China is in the midst of the historical process of 'a major country becoming stronger' (*da er qu qiang* 大而趋强)."[3] For many Chinese, the current rise is actually the fourth such instance in Chinese history; they point out that during past dynasties, China was a highly advanced, culturally sophisticated, technologically developed society that contributed significantly to the global economy and, by virtue of this position, was internationally revered and respected.[4]

In referring to these earlier periods, Chinese policymakers and analysts maintain that China was never a hegemonic ruler that relied on force and coercion (a concept known as *badao* 霸道) but rather was a benign and benevolent great power (a concept known as *wangdao* 王道) that attracted other countries by virtue of its moral goodness, cultural richness, economic wealth, and technological sophistication. For many Chinese, China is currently returning to this past role as a benevolent great power, and in doing so it is correcting the historical

---

[2]   For a brief history of China's history as a great power, see Michael D. Swaine and Ashley J. Tellis, *Interpreting China's Grand Strategy: Past, Present and Future*, Santa Monica, Calif.: RAND Corporation, MR-1121-AF, 2000, pp. 21–96.

[3]   "Daguo de Fuze yu Daguo de Xintai" [The Responsibility and Mentality of a Major Power], *Huanqiu Shibao* [Global Times], August 15, 2005.

[4]   Yan Xuetong, "The Rise of China and Its Power Status," *Chinese Journal of International Politics*, Vol. 1, No. 1, 2006, pp. 5–33; Wang Gungwu, "The Fourth Rise of China: Cultural Implications," *China: An International Journal*, Vol. 2, No. 2, September 2004, pp. 311–322; and John K. Fairbank, ed., *The Chinese World Order: Traditional China's Foreign Relations*, Cambridge, Mass.: Harvard University Press, 1968.

aberration of China's decline over the last 150 years since the Opium War of the 1840s.[5]

Moreover, current Chinese conceptions of being a "great power" are very general and not well defined by policymakers or scholars. Chinese conceptions seem to coalesce around the notion of being involved in (indeed, having Chinese views solicited on) any major international decision affecting China's interests (as China defines them). Deference to China by other major powers is a consistent feature of Chinese discussions of what it means to be a great power in the international system. Chinese commentaries, to date, have discussed little about what China would do with its position as a great power aside from preventing coercion by other states and expanding its comprehensive national power.

Chinese arguments about its country's past behavior as a benign hegemon are not solely nationalist rhetoric (although they are part of that discourse) but rather are mainstream perceptions that pervade Chinese attitudes about its global role and the rights entailed in such a position. Common manifestations of this perception can be found in Chinese arguments that China should currently be considered a great power by virtue of its large population, its long history and rich cultural traditions, its large and globally integrated economy, its position as a permanent member on the United Nations Security Council (UNSC), and its possession of nuclear weapons. Importantly, this image of China's past "greatness" contributes to a strong entitlement mentality regarding China's current ascension in international affairs

---

[5] Yan Xuetong, "The Rise of China in Chinese Eyes," *Journal of Contemporary China*, Vol. 10, No. 25, February 2001, pp. 33–39; Huang Renwei, *Zhongguo Jueqi de Shijian he Kongjian* [Time and Space for China's Rise], Shanghai, China: Shanghai Shekeyuan Chubanshe, 2002; Men Honghua, *Zhongguo: Daguo Jueqi* [The Rise of Modern China], Hangzhou, China: Zhejiang Renmin Chubanshe, 2004; and Hu Angang, *Daguo Zhanlue: Liyi yu Shiming* [Great Power Strategy: Interests and Missions], Liaoning, China: Liaoning Renmin Chubanshe, 2000. Also see Swaine and Tellis, 2000.

On the past four rises of China, see Wang Gungwu, 2004. For an analysis of Chinese views on hegemony, see David Shambaugh, "Chinese Hegemony over East Asia by 2015," *Korean Journal of Defense Analysis*, Summer 1997, pp. 7–28.

and the expected treatment of China by other nations. In the words of Qinghua University scholar Yan Xuetong,

> The rise of China is granted by nature . . . [the Chinese] believe that China's decline is a historical mistake that should be corrected . . . the Chinese regard their rise as regaining China's lost international status rather than obtaining something new . . . the Chinese consider the rise of China a restoration of fairness rather than gaining advantages over others.[6]

A Victim Mentality

A second and related view expressed in Chinese writings is that China is a victim of "100 years of shame and humiliation" (*bainian guochi* 百年国耻) at the hands of Western and other foreign powers, especially Japan. Beginning with the Opium War, China was invaded, divided, and weakened by external powers until Mao Zedong unified China and founded the People's Republic of China (PRC) in 1949. This legacy has left a deep impression on the perceptions and national identity of many Chinese; the Communist party has fostered this narrative since its inception, as part of its identity and as a means of fostering its legitimacy. The CCP claims that it will protect China from both *xihua* and *fenhua*—or being split and Westernized by external states.

This victimization narrative has created an acute Chinese sensitivity to potential infringements on China's sovereignty and territorial integrity; it has also contributed to a strong Chinese emphasis in its diplomacy on the principles of equality, mutual respect, and noninterference in the internal affairs of states.[7] These views reinforce the sense of entitlement noted above. Indeed, China's victim mentality and its effort to reclaim lost status are two sides of the same coin that collec-

---

[6]   Yan Xuetong, 2001, p. 35.

[7]   China is not unique in having a vicitimization narrative foster acute sensitivity to sovereignty. South Korea and North Korea hold similar views.

tively shape China's effort to regain its "rightful role" in modern international relations.[8]

This victim mentality has been changing and evolving in recent years. Chinese officials and scholars have discussed the adoption of a "great power mentality" (*daguo xintai* 大国心态) that emphasizes China's substantial accomplishments in developing its economy and its rising status in world affairs. Yet, the victimization theme persists and is common in nationalist rhetoric on China's foreign affairs; it is most readily apparent as a force shaping public opinion and affecting government policy during crises in U.S.-China and U.S.-Japan relations.[9]

Defensive Security Outlook

A defensive security outlook is a third notion that pervades China's thinking on its external affairs. This outlook stems from long-standing and historically determined Chinese fears that foreign powers are trying to constrain China (from rising), could coerce it (in a crisis), or may otherwise exploit its internal weaknesses. These fears have their origins in official CCP histories, which recount the invasion and Westernization of China by foreign powers following the Opium War and, during the Cold War, efforts by the United States and the Soviet Union to frustrate such Chinese goals as developing nuclear weapons and unifying with Taiwan. These historical accounts are used to bolster the legitimacy of the Communist party as the savior of a weak and divided China but also have the follow-on effect of fostering deep insecurities about the intentions of external powers toward China.

---

[8] Peter Hayes Gries, *China's New Nationalism: Pride, Politics, and Diplomacy*, Berkeley, Calif.: University of California Press, 2004; Swaine and Tellis, 2000, pp. 9–20; and Hunt, 1996, pp. 3–28.

[9] On the issue of a "great power mentality" see Jin Xide, "Zhongguo Xuyao Daguo Xintai" [China Needs a Great Power Mentality], *Huanqiu Shibao* [Global Times], September 12, 2002, p. 4; and Ye Zicheng and Li Ying, "Zhongguo Suoyi Bixu Jian Daguo Waijiao Xintai" [China Therefore Continues to Establish a Great Power Foreign Policy Mentality], *Huanqiu Shibao*, July 20, 2001. For a surprisingly frank Chinese assessment of China's "weak state mentality," see Wu Jianmin, "A Long Way to Go Before China Abandons Weak Nation Mentality," *Zhongguo Qingnian Bao* [China Youth Daily], March 21, 2006, as translated by the Open Source Center (OSC), formerly known as the Foreign Broadcast Information Service (FBIS).

These insecurities are reflected in many ways in official Chinese policy and are important to understanding how Chinese leaders perceive their own intentions. Chinese leaders publicly state that "China will never seek hegemony and never go in for expansion" and that China's cultural tradition is one of "advocating peace" (*chongshang heping* 崇尚和平), "emphasizing defense" (*zhongshi fangyu* 重视防御), and "creating unity" (*tuanjie tongyi* 团结统一).[10] Chinese leaders argue that China does not inherently threaten other nations but rather faces threats to its own security from both peripheral states and major powers with regional interests, all of which have exploited China in the past. The Chinese claim that they do not seek to seize, invade, or conquer the territories of other countries. They often argue that past uses of force and territorial disputes have been limited, punitive, and the result of external provocations. These arguments are a common theme in Communist party histories about past military interventions (e.g., Korea, India, and Vietnam) that claim that China conducted "defensive" military operations provoked by aggressive foreign adversaries. (Many of these accounts are disputed by Western historians.)

China's defensive security outlook manifests in policies that place a high priority on maximizing security around China's periphery, especially as it relates to border defense and territorial integrity. Chinese leaders are especially fearful of the use of force and other coercive measures (i.e., embargos or sanctions) by foreign powers to force China into making unwanted decisions, especially during a military crisis. Chinese writings about nuclear weapons doctrine, for example, are largely focused on possessing a sufficient nuclear weapons capability to avoid being blackmailed by a nuclear-armed adversary, as distinct from possessing a large and diverse nuclear arsenal intended for discreet military purposes, such as nuclear warfighting.[11]

---

[10] The initial phrase is from Jiang Zemin's work report to the 16th Party Congress, November 2002; also see Pang Xingchen, ed., *Zui Gao Juece: 1989 Zhihou Gongheguo Da Fanglue* [Highest Decisions: Important State Strategies After 1989], Beijing, China: Zhongyang Dangli Chubanshe, 2004, pp. 783–806.

[11] Swaine and Tellis, 2000, pp. 1–20; and Michael D. Swaine, "China: Exploiting a Strategic Opening," in Ashley J. Tellis and Michael Wills, eds., *Strategic Asia 2004–2005*, Seattle, Wash.: National Bureau of Asian Research, 2004, pp. 67–101. On Chinese motivations to

An important evolution in Chinese thinking has been a growing Chinese appreciation of the "security dilemma" in China's foreign affairs. Chinese officials and scholars, beginning in the mid-1990s, started to appreciate that certain Chinese actions (taken to protect China's security interests) were perceived as threatening to countries around China's periphery; Chinese policymakers began to understand that their "defensive" actions were motivating reactions from other countries that augmented instability and security competition in East Asia.[12] This Chinese recognition prompted a greater emphasis on reassurance as a feature of Chinese diplomacy, a theme that will be addressed in greater detail below.

Long-Term Diplomatic Priorities

China's three historical lenses are further reflected in three long-term and enduring diplomatic priorities: *sovereignty and territorial integrity, economic development*, and *international respect and status*. Whereas the historical lenses are somewhat abstract, these priorities are more concrete and have explicitly motivated China's foreign and security policy since the founding of the People's Republic of China in 1949. They are not just post-1978 phenomena. The policy manifestations of these three priorities and the leadership's relative emphasis on them have varied over the last 25 years—and will continue to do so. Whereas Mao's foreign policy stressed sovereignty, territorial integrity, and status (among other revolutionary ideas), in the reform era Chinese leaders have clearly

---

develop nuclear weapons, see John Lewis and Xue Litai, *China Builds the Bomb*, Stanford, Calif.: Stanford University Press, 1988.

[12] On this point about the security dilemma in Chinese policy, see Zhang Yunling and Tang Shiping, "China's Regional Strategy," in Shambaugh, 2006, p. 49. The Zhang and Tang chapter claims that Deng Xiaoping, at Lee Kuan Yew's urging, came to understand the security dilemma as early as the late 1970s as China was just opening to the international community. If this is the case, Chinese external behavior and policymaking toward Southeast Asia in the 1980s and early part of the 1990s did not seem to reflect this until the mid-1990s. Goldstein, 2005, and Michael Glosny, "Heading Toward a Win-Win Future? Recent Developments in China's Policy Toward Southeast Asia," *Asian Security*, Vol. 2, No. 1, 2006, pp. 24–57.

and consistently placed the priority on national economic development in China's foreign relations.[13]

Sovereignty and Territorial Integrity

Protecting China's sovereignty and territorial integrity are core Chinese national interests and are evident in foreign policies that seek to secure China's borders, promote reunification with Taiwan, limit foreign threats to Chinese territory (including maritime territorial claims), and minimize external interference in Chinese development and politics.[14] China shares land borders with 14 countries and its coastline is about 14,500 kilometers long. China has had numerous territorial conflicts with a majority of its neighboring nations over the past six decades, regarding both border and maritime areas. Addressing these territorial disputes and preventing foreign incursions into China has been a central preoccupation of Chinese diplomacy. China's successful efforts in the 1980s to negotiate the return of Hong Kong and Macao are regularly and frequently touted as major foreign policy successes of Deng's foreign policy approach. Of course, ensuring the mainland's eventual unification with Taiwan is a long-standing element of China's effort to protect its sovereignty and territorial integrity.

More recently, China perceives that it faces internal threats to its territorial integrity from "separatist groups," such as Muslim Uighurs in Xinjiang Province, and the Dalai Lama. China's recent emphasis on counterterrorism in its foreign policy is a manifestation of this desire to prevent such groups from linking up with al Qaeda or other highly capable terrorists groups. There is little, if any, debate in China about

---

[13] Wang Yizhou, "Forming a State Security Concept at the Turn of the Century," *Liaowang*, September 13, 1999a, pp. 23–24, as translated by OSC; and Wang Yizhou, "Chinese Diplomacy Oriented Toward the 21st Century: Pursuing and Balancing Three Needs," *Zhanlue yu Guanli* [Strategy and Management], December 1999b, as translated by OSC.

[14] M. Taylor Fravel, "Regime Insecurity and International Cooperation: Explaining China's Compromises in Territorial Disputes," *International Security*, Vol. 30, No. 2, November 2005, pp. 46–83; and Allen Carlson, *Unifying China, Integrating with the World: Securing Chinese Sovereignty in the Reform Era*, Stanford, Calif.: Stanford University Press, 2005, pp. 49–91.

the primacy of sovereignty and territorial integrity in Chinese foreign policy.[15]

Economic Development

Economic development as a foreign policy priority is principally a reform-era phenomenon. It refers to China's 30-year-long effort to ensure a stable external environment to improve the living standards of Chinese people and to build up China's "comprehensive national power" to achieve China's revival as a great power. Deng Xiaoping's 1992 aphorism "only development has real meaning" (*fazhan caishi ying daoli* 发展才是硬道理) remains a pervasive influence on China's foreign policies. In the words of China's Premier Wen Jiabao, "Development is the last word; it is not only the basis for resolving all internal problems but is also the basis for boosting our diplomatic power. The basis of competition between states lies in power."[16] Wang Yizhou, a well known international relations scholar at the Chinese Academy of Social Sciences, detailed the logic of the development–foreign policy linkage,

> The main threat to China's national security is not an invasion or war conducted by external enemy forces, but the question of whether China is able to maintain its own steady, orderly, and healthy development. . . . Political development, civilization development, social development, and value development are all components of the concept of development. Under the precondition of centering on economic development, China, through the above-mentioned all-dimensional development, will be able to greatly raise its international status and influence in the new century, and will be able to carry out its diplomacy on the basis of a more solid foundation of power. Therefore, going all-out to

---

[15] Huang Renwei, "On the Internal and External Environments for a Rising China," *SASS Papers,* No. 9, Shanghai Academy of Social Sciences, Shanghai, China: Shanghai Academy of Social Sciences Press, 2003, p. 98.

[16] Wen Jiabao, "A Number of Issues Regarding the Historic Tasks in the Initial Stage of Socialism and China's Foreign Policy," *Xinhua,* February 26, 2007, as translated by OSC.

ensure China's development is required by both domestic affairs and foreign affairs.[17]

During the first two and a half decades of reform and development (until about 2002), China's policies were principally focused on achieving *wenbao* (温饱), or the level of economic development at which all Chinese people are fed and clothed. Jiang Zemin, during the 16th Party Congress in November 2002, declared that China had achieved that level; he then set a new developmental goal by calling for China to "build a well-off society in an all around way" (*quanmian jianshe xiaokang shehui* 全面建设小康社会) within the next two decades. Although the precise meaning of Jiang's phrase is debatable, it generally means that China seeks to become a stable and prosperous middle power with a sizable middle class by about 2020.

China's continued economic development is also crucial to maintaining the CCP's grip on power. The party's ability to continue to raise the living standards of Chinese society serves as the fundamental basis for the CCP's continued legitimacy as the ruling party. As the ideological basis of the party has eroded, it has been replaced with an economic logic that demands that Chinese leaders provide greater economic opportunities for the Chinese people to stay in power.

International Status

Chinese policymakers and scholars have long viewed China's status as a respected major power as a core element of their nation's international behavior. Since the founding of the PRC in 1949, CCP leaders have traditionally linked China's status to such attributes as its permanent seat on the United Nations (U.N.) Security Council, its possession of nuclear weapons, its large population and landmass, and its historic legacy as a major power in Asia. China's perception of its international status changed after Mao and after the reform era began, especially since the fall of the Soviet Union and the Tiananmen incident, but Chinese leaders have always stuck to—indeed, clung to—these attri-

---

[17] Wang Yizhou, 1999b.

butes as indicators that China is a major power.[18] Although it is unclear how Chinese leaders measured variation in their status over time, maximizing status has consistently been a major objective in foreign policy decisionmaking.[19]

Also, China's emphasis on status is linked to its sensitivity to both its image and reputation in international politics, which are distinct concepts for China.[20] China cares about its image because it wants to be accepted as a member of the international community and does not like being ostracized or otherwise isolated, especially in international institutions. China pays attention to its reputation because of the material benefits that it believes can stem from a positive one, in terms of access to trade, aid, technology, and investment. China's intensive diplomacy after the Tiananmen incident in 1989 to rebuild its international image and reputation is an example of the value China puts on these factors in its foreign policy, for both symbolic and material reasons. A more recent manifestation of this long-term priority has been a government effort, beginning in the 1990s, to establish China's status as a "responsible major power" (*fuzeren de daguo* 负责任的大国).[21]

---

[18] Fairbank, 1968, pp. 1–19; Yong Deng, "Better Than Power: International Status in Chinese Foreign Policy," in Yong Deng and Fei-Ling Wang, eds., *China Rising: Power and Motivation in Chinese Foreign Policy*, New York: Rowman & Littlefield, 2005, pp. 51–72; Wang Hongying, "National Image Building and Chinese Foreign Policy," *China: An International Journal*, Vol. 1, No. 1, March 2003, pp. 46–72; and Alastair Iain Johnston, *Social States: China in International Institutions, 1980–2000*, Princeton, N.J.: Princeton University Press, 2008. For an interesting assessment of the status component of Chinese conceptions of "comprehensive national power," see Michael Pillsbury, *China Debates the Future Security Environment*, Washington, D.C.: National Defense University Press, 2000, pp. 203–258.

[19] This argument is made most strongly in Yong Deng, *China's Struggle for Status: The Realignment of International Relations*, Cambridge, UK: Cambridge University Press, 2008.

[20] Johnston, 2008; Johnston importantly notes in Chapter 3 that image and reputation are distinct concepts. Reputation is instrumental and pursued because of expectations of possible material gains from acting in a socially approved way, as perceived by other states. By contrast, image is an end in itself and is pursued out of a desire to be perceived by other states as exhibiting socially approved traits and characteristics.

[21] Alastair Iain Johnston, "International Structures and Chinese Foreign Policy" in Samuel S. Kim, ed., *China and the World*, 4th ed., Boulder, Colo.: Westview Press, 1998b, pp. 55–90; for a more recent work, see "Daguo de Fuze yu Daguo de Xintai," 2005.

China's emphasis on status—a nonmaterial attribute of states—is curious given China's traditional preoccupation with the relative position of major powers in the international system and the jockeying for power among them.[22] This is so because many Chinese strategists see status as critical to China's position among the major power centers and to ensuring Chinese accrual of both power and influence. Chinese policymakers and scholars argue that efforts to improve China's international status are important because other nations are already expressing concerns about China's growing influence in global politics. In other words, improving China's image and reputation (and the policies entailed therein) will help China to ameliorate external concerns of "the China threat" and, thus, will help avoid obstacles to becoming a strong, wealthy, and influential member of the international community.[23]

China's strivings for international respect and status manifest in a variety of policies and actions intended to reflect China's support for international rules, norms, and institutions. Chinese policymakers and scholars regularly talk about China playing a more active and constructive role in international organizations—such as in the U.N. Security Council, the World Trade Organization, and various regional security organizations—to demonstrate that China is a force for stability and economic development. Chinese analysts regularly appeal to the goal of acting as a responsible major power to explain China's activism in multilateral institutions and on nontraditional security issues. Such actions, according to Chinese Ambassador Wang Yi, boost China's international status and serve as a "touchstone for China's effort to join the ranks of the first-class powers in the world."[24]

---

[22] Thomas Christensen, "Chinese Realpolitik: Reading Beijing's World-View," *Foreign Affairs*, September/October 1996; for a more extensive treatment, see Alastair Iain Johnston, *Cultural Realism: Strategic Culture and Grand Strategy in Chinese History*, Princeton, N.J.: Princeton University Press, 1998a.

[23] "Wang Yi Tan Zhongguo de Guoji Diwei he Waijiao Zhengce" [Wang Yi Talks About China's International Position and Foreign Policy], September 4, 2004; Huang Renwei, 2003; Wang Hongying, 2003, pp. 46–72.

[24] On questions of international status, see "Wang Yi Tan Zhongguo de Guoji Diwei he Waijiao Zhengce," 2004; Wang Yizhou, 1999b.

CHAPTER THREE

Current Perceptions of the International Security Environment

Chinese assessments of their external security environment are the empirical basis on which China's top policymakers determine China's foreign policy. These assessments play an integral role in debates about which objectives and policies to pursue, and as these perceptions change so can China's behavior.[1] Chinese policymakers and analysts highlight several dimensions of their current security environment. Six predominant perceptions are examined in this chapter.[2]

---

[1]   For an interesting argument about how China evaluates its external environment, see Tang Shiping, "A Systematic Theory of the Security Environment," *Journal of Strategic Studies*, Vol. 27, No. 1, March 2004, pp. 1–34; and Tang Shiping, "From Offensive to Defensive Realism: A Social Evolutionary Interpretation of China's Security Strategy," in Robert S. Ross and Zhu Feng, eds., *China's Ascent: Power, Security, and the Future of International Politics*, Ithaca, New York: Cornell University Press, 2008, pp. 141–162.

[2]   This chapter draws on numerous Chinese assessments of the international security environment, including Zhang Youwen and Huang Renwei, eds., *Zhongguo Guoji Diwei Baogao 2008* [China's International Status Report 2008], Beijing, China: Renmin Chubanshe, 2008; Zhang Youwen and Huang Renwei, eds., *Zhongguo Guoji Diwei Baogao 2007* [China's International Status Report 2007], Beijing, China: Renmin Chubanshe, 2007; Zhang Youwen and Huang Renwei, eds., *Zhongguo Guoji Diwei Baogao 2005* [China's International Status Report 2005], Beijing, China: Renmin Chubanshe, 2005; Zhang Youwen and Huang Renwei, eds., *Zhongguo Guoji Diwei Baogao 2004* [China's International Status Report 2004], Beijing, China: Renmin Chubanshe, 2004; *Guoji Zhanlue yu Anquan Xingshi Pinggu 2004–2005* [Strategic and Security Review 2004–2005], China Institute for Contemporary International Relations, Beijing, China: Shishi Chubanshe, 2005; *Guoji Zhanlue yu Anquan Xingshi Pinggu 2003–2004* [Strategic and Security Review 2003–2004], China Institute for Contemporary International Relations, Beijing, China: Shishi Chubanshe, 2004; and *Guoji Zhanlue yu Anquan Xingshi Pinggu 2001–2002* [Strategic and Security

But, first, two overarching beliefs shade China's view of its current security environment. One is a widely held belief that China's future is inextricably (and increasingly) linked to the international community. Chinese leaders understand that China's current growth model combined with the acceleration of globalization have deeply connected China to the international community. China's success in accomplishing national revitalization depends on close and continuing interaction with global and regional powers, markets, and institutions. In the words of China's 2008 national defense white paper, "the future and destiny of China have been increasingly closely connected with the international community. China cannot develop in isolation from the rest of the world, nor can the world enjoy prosperity and stability without China."[3] Even in the wake of the global financial crisis in fall 2008 and the resulting rapid declines in Chinese growth, Hu Jintao affirmed during the December 2008 Central Economic Work Conference that the direction of global economic integration for China was correct and should continue.[4]

The second belief relates to the pervasive uncertainty among Chinese policymakers and scholars about the range and severity of threats to China. For some, China is the most secure it has been in the last 200 years and its global influence and status are both growing. For others, the security threats facing China are diverse and increasing, challenging China's ability to complete the task of national revival as a great power. The tensions between these two views are reflected in mainstream Chinese security assessments (such as the biennial defense white papers). But these debates are only somewhat reflected in

---

Review 2001–2002], China Institute for Contemporary International Relations, Beijing, China: Shishi Chubanshe, 2002.

Official assessments include *China's National Defense in 2008*, Beijing, China: State Council Information Office, January 2009; *China's National Defense in 2006*, Beijing, China: State Council Information Office, December 2006; *China's National Defense in 2004*, Beijing, China: State Council Information Office, December 2004; and *China's National Defense in 2002*, Beijing, China: State Council Information Office, October 2002.

[3]   *China's National Defense in 2008*, 2009.

[4]   Che Yuming and Zhou Yingfeng, "China's Central Economic Conference Will Focus on 'Ensuring Economic Growth,'" *Xinhua*, December 8, 2008, as translated by OSC.

Chinese policies. The leadership's emphasis on consensus decisionmaking and promoting unified thinking within the CCP has mitigated the effect of such debates on actual policymaking.[5] Ultimately, the relative balance between external threats and opportunities in Chinese assessments (both public and internal ones) will serve as an important indicator of future Chinese perceptions.

The Chinese government's current position is that, on balance, China faces a *favorable* external security environment for continued growth and development. As addressed in detail below, Chinese leaders believe that the current environment, for a variety of reasons, offers a strategic window of opportunity that should last about 20 years and should allow China to continue to grow its comprehensive national power and to build a "moderately well-off society." Chinese policymakers seek to maximize this window and, if feasible, to extend it for as long as possible.

Major Power Conflict

A primary and consistent feature of Chinese assessments of their external environment is a belief in the low probability of war among major powers, which would distract China from national development. As the 2008 national defense white paper stated, "factors conducive to maintaining peace and containing war are on the rise . . . thereby keeping low the risk of worldwide, all-out and large-scale wars for a relatively long period of time."[6] This does not mean that Chinese strategists believe that conflict between China and the United States over Taiwan is not possible (indeed, the Chinese military is intensely focused on preparing for such a contingency); rather, it means that the broad contours of major power relations have changed since the height of the

---

[5] These differences in viewpoints do not neatly bifurcate between the foreign ministry and the military but rather cut across government agencies, the military, and those in the analytical community. They are readily apparent in the assessments mentioned in this chapter's second footnote.

[6] *China's National Defense in 2008*, 2009.

Cold War, lessening the imminence of armed conflicts among major powers.

This important conclusion, in its initial incarnation, was articulated by Deng Xiaoping in the mid-1980s and was in direct opposition to Mao's assessment of the likelihood of "early war, major war and nuclear war" (*zao da, da da, he zhanzheng* 早打, 大打, 核战争). Deng's conclusion, in overturning Mao's pessimism, established the theoretical foundation for his pursuit of a more internationalist foreign policy and one that would assist economic development. Deng's seminal conclusion subsequently allowed the leadership's articulation in 1985 of the phrase "peace and development are the main trends of the times" (*heping yu fazhan shi dangjin shidai de zhuti* 和平与发展是当今时代的主体). This core conclusion and Deng's repeated references to it in the 1980s and 1990s set the foundation for China's reform-era foreign policy; and this phrase persists today in China's foreign policy discourse.[7]

Following a rapid and acute downturn in U.S.-China relations in the late 1990s (sparked by the accidental bombing of the Chinese embassy in Belgrade, among other events), there was a major and important internal Chinese debate about the continued relevance of "peace and development" as an accurate characterization of China's external security environment. After much internal discussion, Chinese leaders concluded that this core assumption had not changed.[8] As a result of this strategic conclusion, Jiang Zemin declared in 2002,

---

[7]   For a detailed and insightful overview of Deng's official thinking on foreign affairs, see Gong Li, "Deng Xiaoping Dui Mei Zhengce Sixiang yu Zhong-Mei Guanxi" [Deng Xiaoping's Thoughts on U.S. Policy and Sino-U.S. Relations], *Guoji Wenti Yanjiu* [China International Studies], No. 6, 2004, pp. 13–17. Also see Ren Xiao, *The International Relations Theoretical Discourse in China: A Preliminary Analysis*, Sigur Center Asia Papers, No. 9, Washington, D.C.: Elliot School of International Affairs at George Washington University, 2000; and Zhang Wankun Franklin, *China's Foreign Relations Strategies Under Mao and Deng: A Systematic Comparative Analysis*, Public and Social Administration Working Paper Series, Hong Kong: City University of Hong Kong, 1998.

[8]   For a primer on "peace and development," see David Finkelstein, *China Reconsiders Its National Security: The Great Peace and Development Debate of 1999*, Alexandria, Va.: The CNA Corporation, December 2000. On China's need for and perceived value in conducting such theoretical assessments, see Ren Xiao, 2000.

during the CCP's 16th Party Congress, that the next 20 years represented a "period of strategic opportunity" (*zhanlue jiyuqi* 战略机遇期) for China's growth and development. Jiang's characterization, that Hu Jintao has since affirmed, remains a core theoretical conclusion that justifies and validates the continuation of reform-era foreign policies focused on promoting China's stability, economic development, and, in broadest terms, accumulation of comprehensive national power.[9] In the words of now retired Ambassador Shen Guofang in a June 2007 speech,

> The first 20 years of the present century are a vital strategic opportunity that China must firmly seize and put to good use. These two decades have strategic significance for building a well-off society in an all-round way. It is by revolving around this goal that China plans its foreign policy, general strategy, and diplomatic activities. The purpose of all diplomatic work is to accomplish this goal.[10]

The low probability of war among major powers is balanced by persistent Chinese concerns about multiple and growing threats to Chinese, Asian, and global stability. The 2008 national defense white paper provides a comprehensive Chinese assessment of such concerns:

> World peace and development are faced with multiple difficulties and challenges. Struggles for strategic resources, strategic locations and strategic dominance have intensified. Meanwhile, hegemonism and power politics still exist, regional turmoil keeps spilling over, hot-spot issues are increasing, and local conflicts and wars keep emerging. The impact of the financial crisis trig-

---

[9] Jiang Zemin, "Build a Well-off Society in an All-Round Way and Create a New Situation in Building Socialism with Chinese Characteristics," report at the 16th National Congress of the Communist Party of China, November 8, 2002.

[10] Shen Guofang, "Zhongguo Xin Waijiao de Linian yu Shijian" [The Concept and Practice of China's New Diplomacy], *Shijie Zhishi* [World Affairs], No. 13, 2007, p. 43. The article is based on a speech: "The Theory of Harmonious World and China's New Diplomacy," Chinese International Affairs Forum 2007, the Institute of International Relations, Renmin University, Beijing, June 2007.

gered by the U.S. subprime mortgage crisis is snowballing. In the aspect of world economic development, issues such as energy and food are becoming more serious, highlighting deep-seated contradictions. Economic risks are manifesting a more interconnected, systematic and global nature. Issues such as terrorism, environmental disasters, climate change, serious epidemics, transnational crime and pirates are becoming increasingly prominent.[11]

Chinese strategists, pointing to past tensions in U.S.–European Union relations and U.S.-Russian relations throughout the 2000s, argue that the conflicts and contradictions among major powers have been growing and that these conflicts are a source of global instability. Many Chinese analysts attribute this largely to U.S. "unilateralist" policies. China's defense white papers, including in the most recent 2008 version, continue to refer to "hegemonism and power politics" as destabilizing forces in international security affairs; this phrase is a common Chinese reference to U.S. foreign policies and practices.[12] Qian Qichen, China's former vice premier and long-time foreign policy doyen, succinctly summarized—in a uniquely candid and revealing private speech—elite Community party views on the current state of great power relations:

> The United States wants to engage in unilateralism but can not dominate the world. . . . For a very long time to come in the future, relations among the major powers will continue to be marked by cooperation and competition, mutual exchanges and mutual restraint, as well as competition and compromise. In particular, the trend toward cooperation will be greater than the trend toward conflict. The major powers will continue to maintain a kind of stable mutual relationship.[13]

---

[11] *China's National Defense in 2008,* 2009.

[12] *China's National Defense in 2006,* 2006.

[13] Qian Qichen, "Xinshiji de Guoji Guanxi" [International Relations in the New Century], *Xuexi Shibao* [Study Times], October 18, 2004; this speech, which was highly critical of U.S. foreign policy, was given at the Central Party School and was not intended to be public. It was accidentally printed in *China Daily* in 2004.

Another notable Chinese concern, highlighted in China's last three defense white papers, is the growing militarization of international politics as a source of regional and global instability. The 2008 national defense white paper offered one of the starkest assessments in the past several years: "The influence of military security factors on international relations is mounting. Driven by competition in overall national strength and the development of science and technology, international military competition is becoming increasingly intense. . . . All countries are attaching more importance to supporting diplomatic struggles with military means. As a result, arms races in some regions are heating up, posing grave challenges to the international arms control and nonproliferation regime."[14]

For China, these trends in major power relations are directly affecting Chinese assessments about security and stability in Asia—the region of highest strategic importance to China. Although "the Asia-Pacific security situation is stable on the whole" as a result of growing economic interdependence and the influence of multilateral organizations, Chinese policymakers remain deeply concerned about the U.S. role: "The U.S. has increased its strategic attention to and input in the Asia-Pacific region, further consolidating its military alliances, adjusting its military deployment and enhancing its military capabilities."[15] A related Chinese concern is that limited, local conflicts are more likely to emerge on China's periphery as a result of the rise of religious, ethnic, resource, and territorial disputes.

---

[14] The 2004 white paper noted "the increasing impact of the military factor on the international situation and national security" as well as the "growing salience of the role of military capabilities in safeguarding national security"; the inclusion of both phrases was a shift from previous assessments. The 2006 white paper stated, "A revolution in military affairs is developing in depth worldwide. Military competition based on informationization is intensifying." *China's National Defense in 2004*, 2004; *China's National Defense in 2006*, 2006; and *China's National Defense in 2008*, 2009.

[15] *China's National Defense in 2008*, 2009.

Globalization and Multipolarity

Chinese views on the effects of globalization and the development of multipolarity on interstate relations are central to their perceptions of their external security environment. Their conclusions about these two trends serve as an important barometer of Chinese views on their economic power, the degree of global interdependence, and the degree of China's strategic time and space for continued development.

Globalization

Chinese policymakers and scholars argue that globalization has redefined interstate economic and political interactions since the end of the Cold War, resulting in both opportunities for and constraints on China. On balance, they see globalization as offering more opportunities than challenges. Globalization has increased the importance of economic power, enhanced interdependence among nations, and heightened the opportunities for mutually beneficial economic cooperation. Chinese policymakers talk about the value of economic diplomacy and possessing "soft power" in a globalized world. They see all these trends as redounding to China's benefit by allowing it to expand its influence. Ambassador Shen Guofang summarized Chinese views on the positive implications of globalization.

> Basically speaking, the great historical trend epitomized by globalization and the resultant institutional change bodes well for China's peaceful development and has created for China even more strategic space and maneuvering room.
>
> On the one hand, against the backdrop of globalization, interdependency among the various economic entities has deepened without interruption. All countries now attach more importance to the strengthening of economic diplomacy. The trends toward the diversification of interests among the various nations and peoples, toward the emergence of multiple political poles, and toward cultural pluralism are gaining strength all the time.
>
> On the other hand, the repercussions of globalization have been reshaping world politics and regional politics and fashioning new

national behavior. They also have challenged all nations in the world to build a harmonious world. Institutionalizing new diplomatic thinking in the age of globalization has become a new issue closely watched by every nation.[16]

At the same time, Chinese analysts note the costs and dangers of globalization: Globalization has exacerbated economic and social inequities that have disproportionately benefited developed countries at the expense of developing nations, including China. This has contributed to growing "North-South" tensions and the emergence of "economic neo-colonialism" in which developing nations are subordinated to and dependent on Western economic and technological superiority. For China, these trends are not a net negative development. The inequalities and North-South tensions create space for China to play a bridging role between those benefiting most from globalization and those being disadvantaged because China can speak with and for both collection of states. For many Chinese, this role provides China with the credibility to expand its political and economic influence in the developing world.[17]

Multipolarity

Following the end of the Cold War, most Chinese analysts predicted a quick evolution from a bipolar system to one initially dominated by U.S. power and, eventually, to the emergence of a multipolar system. In the 1990s, such a multipolar configuration among major powers evolved far slower than China expected and much to its dismay. Chinese policymakers were surprised and concerned about the U.S. ability to maintain its position of unipolar dominance. Many Chinese analysts initially described the post–Cold War "international pattern" (*guoji geju* 国际格局) of the early 1990s as "one superpower and many powers" (*yi chao duo qiang* 一超多强) but with a strong trend toward eventual multipolarity. Yet, by the late 1990s, given the continued and

---

[16] Shen Guofang, 2007.

[17] *Guoji Zhanlue yu Anquan Xingshi Pinggu 2003–2004*, 2004, pp. 124–143, 198–200, 240–254. Also see Shen Guofang, 2007, pp. 42–43.

unexpected predominance of U.S. economic and military power, a common Chinese modification of the latter characterization was, "the superpower is more powerful while many powers are less so" (*yi chao geng chao duo qiang bu qiang* 一超更超,多强不强).[18] The slow development of multipolarity—and specifically the U.S. ability to maintain its position of global predominance and its perceived preference for unilateral use of military force to advance its interests—has been a long-standing source of concern for many Chinese policymakers and strategists.

This perception is now changing and rapidly so. In the last five years, many Chinese assessments claim that the pendulum of global order has decidedly swung back in favor of multipolarity. This is now an official CCP determination, a significant development relevant to China's policy formulation and execution. Hu Jintao's October 2007 report to the 17th Party Congress was the most optimistic assessment to date; it stated "the *progress* toward a multipolar world is *irreversible*" (emphasis added). This was a much more definite view than Jiang Zemin's 2002 report to the 16th Party Congress, which characterized "the *trend*" toward multipolarity as "developing amid twists and turns" (emphasis added).[19] (Jiang's report to the 15th Party Congress in 1997 modestly claimed, "The world structure is moving towards multipolarization.")[20]

Chinese policymakers and scholars now commonly argue that multipolarity is accelerating as U.S. influence is diminishing in relative terms. Chinese assessments about multipolarity point to the global

---

[18] Interviews with Chinese analysts and scholars, Beijing and Shanghai, June 2005; regarding the first phrase, also see Phillip Saunders, "China's America Watchers," *China Quarterly*, Vol. 161, March 2000, pp. 41–65.

[19] Hu Jintao, "Hold High the Great Banner of Socialism with Chinese Characteristics and Strive for New Victories in Building a Moderately Prosperous Society in an All Around Way," report to the 17th National Congress of the Communist Party of China, October 15, 2007; Jiang Zemin, 2002.

[20] Jiang Zemin, "Hold High the Great Banner of Deng Xiaoping Theory for an All-round Advancement of the Cause of Building Socialism with Chinese Characteristics to the 21st Century," report to the 15th National Congress of the Communist Party of China, September 12, 1997.

financial crisis and the relative decline of the U.S. economy, on the one hand, and international resentment and alienation fostered by the U.S. intervention in Iraq and the U.S. conduct of the global war on terrorism, on the other. Chinese policymakers and analysts argue that the latter activities undermined U.S. economic power, military strength, and international legitimacy. A senior Chinese diplomat stated, "The uni-polar hegemonistic strategy of the United States has met setback after setback and its foreign strategy has pulled back."[21] Many Chinese analysts and scholars now estimate that a truly multipolar system may emerge in the next 20 to 30 years.

Another aspect of Chinese thinking about the acceleration of multipolarity is the strength of emerging powers, such as India, Brazil, Mexico, and China, and related organizations such as the G-20. "The rise of newly emerging powers has accelerated as has the rise of new regional organizations. Their voice on the international stage has grown stronger."[22] Although Chinese strategists realize that the emergence of a multipolar system remains a medium-term proposition, they see emerging powers and related organizations as accelerating this trend. China's 2008 national defense white paper affirmed this view:

> Economic globalization and world multi-polarization are gaining momentum. The progress toward industrialization and informationization throughout the globe is accelerating and economic cooperation is in full swing, leading to increasing economic interdependence, inter-connectivity and interactivity among countries. The rise and decline of international strategic forces is quickening, major powers are stepping up their efforts to cooperate with each other and draw on each other's strengths. They continue to compete with and hold each other in check, and groups of new emerging developing powers are arising. Therefore, a profound readjustment is brewing in the international system.[23]

---

[21] Shen Guofang, 2007, p. 42.

[22] Shen Guofang, 2007, p. 42.

[23] *China's National Defense in 2008*, 2009.

U.S. Power and Great Power Relations

A third, defining Chinese perception relates to the distribution of power among major powers in the current international system. For a nation like China, which is known for its historic disposition toward *Realpolitik* thinking, this calculation has a profound effect on its decision-makers. Chinese analysts commonly discuss such assessments in terms of the degree of unipolarity versus multipolarity in the international system. As noted above, despite past frustration, Chinese policymakers see current trends as distinctly favoring the emergence of a more multipolar system as new powers rise and the U.S. faces relative and gradual decline. Chinese analyses of great power relations heavily focus on U.S. power, the U.S. role in global politics, and U.S.-China relations.

The current U.S. position of relative predominance in international affairs, which the Chinese refer to as "hegemony," is a source of substantial concern and enduring dissatisfaction for Chinese policymakers. The U.S. position raises a number of concerns of varying degrees for Chinese policymakers.[24] Most generally, many Chinese fear that the United States seeks to constrain China's development of its economic, diplomatic, and military capabilities, particularly as it affects China's position in East Asia. This is a pervasive belief among policymakers, scholars, military officers, and the general public. The 2008 national defense white paper stated, "At the same time, the U.S. has increased its strategic attention to and input in the Asia-Pacific region, further consolidating its military alliances, adjusting its military deployment and enhancing its military capabilities. . . ." and that China faces "strategic maneuvers and containment from the outside."[25]

---

[24] The various concerns are detailed in Pang Xingchen, 2004, pp. 807–813; Yong Dong, "Hegemon on the Offensive: Chinese Perspectives on U.S. Global Strategy," *Political Science Quarterly,* Vol. 116, No. 3, 2001, pp. 343–365; Jia Qingguo, "Learning to Live with the Hegemon: Evolution of China's Policy Toward the U.S. Since the End of the Cold War," *Journal of Contemporary China,* Vol. 14, No. 44, August 2005a, pp. 395–407; Samantha Blum, "Chinese Views of U.S. Hegemony," *Journal of Contemporary China,* Vol. 12, No. 35, 2003, pp. 239–264; Wang Jisi, "China's Search for Stability with America," *Foreign Affairs,* Vol. 84, No. 5, September/October 2005, pp. 39–48.

[25] *China's National Defense in 2008,* 2009.

These general Chinese concerns about U.S. strategic intentions are particularly acute because of the Taiwan question. U.S. and Chinese sharp differences over Taiwan's status are China's most intense concern because it is a core national interest and the one most likely to precipitate armed conflict. Militaries in the United States and China are preparing for such a conflict, which accentuates the extent to which each side views the other as a potential adversary. Most Chinese see U.S. policy on Taiwan, in particular U.S. arms sales to the island, as seeking to prevent reunification and, thus, as part of a broader U.S. effort to prevent China's rise for fear that China will eventually eclipse the United States. Thus, Chinese opposition to U.S. policymaking on the Taiwan question is an important, but not singular, driver of the Chinese view that a mainstream U.S. strategic goal is to hinder and constrain China's rise.

Looking beyond the Taiwan issue, many Chinese believe that Washington sees itself as morally superior to Beijing, does not accept the legitimacy of the Chinese Communist Party, and thus seeks to bring about China's democratization. Many Chinese believe that the United States, because of an American sense of exceptionalism and superiority, seeks to ensure its long-term dominance in international affairs, as reflected in a perceived preference for unilateral actions and coercive diplomacy.

China's most acute concerns about U.S. intentions are seldom *directly* articulated in official statements, but these themes persist in the writings of scholars and analysts—and across a broad range of issues beyond military ones.[26] Many Chinese interpret U.S. policies and public debates about China—such as regarding the revaluation of the *renminbi*, reform of the Chinese economy, the bilateral trade deficit, China's role in East Asia, or modernization of the People's Liberation Army (PLA)—as indicative of U.S. efforts to weaken China and undermine its rise. Even a mainstream and centrist Chinese interna-

---

[26] Pang Xingchen, 2004; Huang Renwei, "Guoji Tixi de Gaibian yu Zhongguo Heping Fazhan Daolu" [Transformation of International System and China's Road to Peaceful Development], in Liu Jie, ed., *Guoji Tixi yu Zhongguo de Ruanliliang* [The International System and China's Soft Power], Shanghai, China: Sheshi Chubanshe, 2006; Yong Dong, 2001; Blum, 2003.

tional relations scholar, Huang Renwei, characterized U.S. policy this way:

> The United States has been trying to "regulate" and confine China's international behavior with the international rules and regulations that have been set under its dominance, with a view to slowing down China's development as well as to guarding against and doing away with the latent threat of China's challenge to US hegemony. . . .
>
> The United States has been attempting to raise the "democracy criteria" that bar China from access to the international system, and to infiltrate China with Western values, with a view to transforming China from a country of "different nature and different category" into one of the "same nature and same category." At the same time, by encroaching upon national sovereignty through the international system, the US and Western force is exerting greater and greater influence on China's internal evolution process.[27]

As a result, many Chinese strategists characterize U.S. policy as *both* engagement and containment (with the relative priority on each shifting over time) and as viewing China as both an enemy and a friend. This has become a mainstream conclusion among policymakers and scholars in China.[28]

Despite these concerns, Chinese policymakers and foreign policy analysts also now emphasize Washington's growing reliance on Beijing to manage global economic and security challenges. This perception, which began in the early part of this decade, has become even more pronounced following the global financial crisis, the damage to the U.S. economy, and the formation of the G-20 mechanism in which China sees itself as playing a leading role. Huang Renwei nicely summarized this Chinese view:

---

[27] Huang Renwei, 2006.

[28] Pang Xingchen, 2004.

On the one hand, the United States is trying by every means available to use the West-dominated international system to control the "alien" socialist China, confine China's international maneuvering room while incorporating China into this system, and prevent the rapidly rising China from challenging US hegemony. There are long-term and fundamental strategic differences between China and the United States on the development direction of transformation of the international system and their respective position in the force structure.

On the other hand, China is playing an increasingly important, constructive role in safeguarding the stability of the international system, which has made the United States realize that China is not like the Soviet Union in the Cold War, nor is it a destructive force confronting the existing international system. Given the increasingly high price for maintaining its hegemony, the United States cannot but consider cooperating with China so that China can share the cost for preserving the international system.[29]

Chinese concerns about U.S. predominance and possible containment strategies are matched by the recognition that the United States remains central to China's ultimate goal of national revitalization. Many in China realize, reluctantly so given the perception of relative U.S. decline, that China's developmental goals cannot be successful without stable relations with the United States; at a minimum, many in China see that adversarial relations with the United States could derail China's current trajectory. The complexity of Chinese perceptions of the United States and U.S.-China relations was articulated by Chinese scholar Wang Jisi:

> In recent years, the U.S. image in China has become increasingly diffuse. Several images of the United States now coexist in China: a paper tiger that was defeated by China and is weakening itself through hubris and over-extension; the only hegemonic power that threatens world peace and stability; an opponent that violates China's territorial integrity and denies it national reunifica-

---

[29] Huang Renwei, 2006.

tion; an economic engine that drives the world economy and, to an increasing extent, the Chinese economy; an admirable society boasting the world's most advanced scientific, technological and educational institutions; a model of modernization from which China can learn; and an ideologically driven power that wants to shape China's political destiny.[30]

Despite these somewhat contradictory views of the United States, many in China continue to refer to the U.S.-China relationship as the "key of the keys" (*zhong zhong zhi zhong* 重中之中), an internal CCP formulation adopted in the 1990s under Jiang Zemin to underscore U.S. centrality to Chinese foreign policy.[31] Under Hu Jintao, the degree to which this policy line remains prominent is unclear. Since 2002, Hu Jintao has executed subtle shifts in U.S.-China relations and Chinese foreign policy. Hu has paid as much, if not more, attention to China's relations with its Asian neighbors. He has injected a more practical and less emotional tone to China's relations with the United States in which China seems more willing to tolerate bilateral tensions and withstand U.S. demands but equally willing to expand substantive cooperation in existing and new areas of mutual interest.

Mainstream Chinese strategists argue that, on balance, China's most important bilateral relationship remains with the United States but in a world characterized by more diffuse types of power and a greater number of important relationships, including with states, groups of states, and institutions. This calculation about U.S.-China relations stems from three views.[32] First, the United States is still a key source of trade, investment, and technology for China's economic development. The United States remains China's largest trading partner, for example, and China is the largest holder of U.S. government debt and is also the fastest growing export market for the United States. The degree of

---

[30] Wang Jisi, "Reflecting on China," *American Interest*, Summer 2006.

[31] This official CCP line as well as other key foreign policy phrases are listed in Pang Xingchen, 2004, p. 783.

[32] Huang Renwei, 2006; Jia Qingguo, 2005a; and Wang Jisi, 2005.

China's interdependence with the U.S. economy is high and not likely to change significantly in the next two decades.

Second, the United States provides key international "public goods" to Asia in the form of regional security and stability and freedom of navigation from which China benefits. There is a tacit recognition in China that U.S. alliances, security commitments, and forward deployments have significantly contributed to the regional stability in Asia that facilitated Chinese economic reform and development over the past 30 years.[33] This view has lessened in recent years as China has become more concerned about U.S. efforts to expand its alliance with Japan and its security cooperation with India.[34]

Third, avoiding conflict and overt geopolitical competition with the United States is critical to China's effort to ensure a stable and peaceful security environment; major strategic competition or outright military conflict with the United States—more than with any other nation—would significantly disrupt China's security environment. Under severe conditions, it could lead China to shift national resources from economic development to military modernization—an outcome not desired by China's leaders. Chinese scholars write about the need for "space" and "time" for China's rise, and stable relations with the United States is critical to both. To be sure, Chinese analysts also recognize that although a stable, if not amicable, relationship with the United States is a necessary condition for its rise, it is by no means a sufficient one.[35]

As an indication that China seeks to balance its myriad interests in relations with the United States, some Chinese strategists have argued that China can accept a hegemonic power while opposing its hegemonic behavior. In other words, China can live in a world with a unipolar power as long as doing so does not directly undermine Chi-

---

[33] Wang Jisi, 2005; and Jia Qingguo, 2005a.

[34] On this point, see Wu Xinbo, "The End of the Silver Lining: A Chinese View of the U.S.-Japanese Alliance," *Washington Quarterly,* Vol. 29, No. 1, Winter 2005/06, pp. 119–130. To be sure, some in China have never viewed U.S. alliances in the region as anything but a threat to Chinese security.

[35] Huang Renwei, 2006.

nese interests. This distinction may allow Chinese policymakers and analysts to balance the need for stable U.S.-China relations against their concerns about U.S. predominance and Washington's "unilateral" use of its power. Whether such a formulation is widely accepted among China's top leaders remains unclear.[36]

Beginning in the 2004–2005 time frame, China's most acute concerns about U.S. power and the implications for China have lessened because Chinese analysts believe that U.S. policies have alienated many states, undermined U.S. influence, and accelerated its relative decline. Mainstream Chinese analyses about the U.S. global position are replete with references to being tied down in the Middle East, for example. Huang Renwei put it this way:

> So, the United States is trapped in a vicious cycle when it challenges the international system. The strategic assets that it is trying to promote in the existing international system are offsetting the strategic liabilities that it is bearing. This will undermine the system, with the liabilities more and more quickly exceeding the assets, which will shake the foundation of the hegemonic position of the empire. This is a very peculiar and important phenomenon in the contemporary international system, and it offers China an important strategic opportunity to join and merge into the international system.[37]

Nontraditional Security Challenges

Within the last five years and especially after the terrorist attacks of September 11, Chinese officials and analysts have begun to highlight the threats to China's interests posed by nontraditional security challenges, including terrorism, the proliferation of weapons of mass destruction (WMD), narcotics and human trafficking, environmental degrada-

---

[36] Wang Jisi, "Meiguo Baquan de Luoji" [The Logic of American Hegemony], *Meiguo Yanjiu* [American Studies], Vol. 17, No. 3, Fall 2003, pp. 28–40. Also see Wang Jisi, 2005; and Jia Qingguo, 2005a.

[37] Huang Renwei, 2006.

tion, the spread of infectious diseases, and natural disasters. Chinese leaders, policymakers, and analysts view these emerging threats as ones that can, and have, directly and acutely affected China's external security environment. Ambassador Shen Guofang argued,

> Non-traditional security threats have become more striking. A variety of new issues, global and transnational, have developed continuously. We cannot be optimistic about the international security situation, what with the surge in energy prices, global warming, the ecological crisis, the gap between the rich and the poor, cross-national crime, and frequent outbreaks of major epidemics.[38]

A decade ago, few Chinese leaders would have shared such concerns, and today they are universally accepted. This shift is largely a function of China's own experiences in managing its responses to such crises as 9/11, the SARS outbreak in 2003, continuing problems with Avian influenza, the accelerating HIV/AIDS crisis in China, and regional nuclear proliferation. The Chinese foreign ministry now refers to nontraditional security issues as having "unprecedented complexity and destruction and . . . [posing] a direct threat to world peace and security."[39] Hu Jintao's speech at the July 2006 G-8 meeting in Russia was devoted to these themes, indicating their priority in national policy, and he outlined numerous proposals to address such challenges. This was the first time that China's top leader had addressed nontraditional challenges in such detail.[40]

There is also an instrumental logic to China's sudden focus, early this decade, on nontraditional security challenges. On one level, following 9/11, Beijing's new emphasis on counterterrorism and counterpro-

---

[38] Shen Guofang, 2007, p. 42.

[39] *China's Foreign Affairs: 2004 Edition*, English edition, Beijing, China: World Affairs Press, 2004, p. 6.

[40] China attended a dialogue meeting between G-8 nations and developing countries in St. Petersburg. This speech was given in that context because China is not a G-8 member state. "Written Statement Made by Hu Jintao at Dialogue Meeting Between Leaders of G-8 and Developing Nations," *Xinhua*, July 17, 2006, as translated by OSC.

liferation served as a basis for stabilizing and broadening U.S.-China relations. Chinese policymakers viewed 9/11 and the resulting shift in U.S. national security priorities as a unique opportunity to put the bilateral relationship on more stable and long-term footing. Chinese leaders believed that this shift in U.S. priorities after 9/11 took China out of the crosshairs of U.S. national security planning. Indeed, Chinese policymakers and analysts now regularly highlight U.S. "reliance" on Chinese cooperation to address common, nontraditional security challenges.[41]

On a second level, China has focused heavily on nontraditional security challenges in its interactions with its East Asian neighbors, especially in regional forums, to expand China's influence. China has used bilateral and multilateral discussions of nontraditional security challenges as a basis for broadening the scope of its political and military engagement with Asian countries; Beijing has also expanded diplomatic and material cooperation in managing responses to such problems as the outbreaks of infectious diseases. In addition, China's bilateral and multilateral dialogues on nontraditional challenges are central to its effort to appear benign and cooperative to countries on its periphery. Such discussions also draw an implicit contrast with U.S. regional security dialogues and operational cooperation with Southeast Asian nations, which in recent years have focused heavily on counterterrorism cooperation and joint military operations. In focusing on nontraditional challenges, China seeks to reinforce shared "Asian" conceptions of national security in which the latter concept is not just military security but encompasses attention to Southeast Asian nations' priority on domestic stability, economic development, and consensus-based solutions to bilateral disagreements.

---

[41] This argument is nicely detailed in Swaine, 2004, pp. 67–101.

Energy Insecurity[42]

China's acute concern about energy supplies is a relatively new but important factor shaping its international behavior, especially its relationships with key supplier countries in Central Asia, the Middle East, and Africa. China's need for imported oil and gas became a pressing issue in the early part of this decade when China's economic growth and energy demand growth "re-coupled," unlike during the 1980 to 2000 period when China's gross domestic product (GDP) grew much faster than its energy needs. In 2001, China's economy began to grow faster than projected and the energy intensity of economic activity grew faster than the GDP. This recoupling led to a surge in energy demand, for both industrial activity as well as transportation. Even though China had become a net importer of oil in 1993, it was not well prepared for the nation's accelerating growth and growing energy intensity. This situation resulted in shortages in oil, coal, and electricity and prolonged power shortages in many provinces. This demand surge and the corresponding shortages thrust energy security onto China's foreign policy agenda, as Chinese companies made a mad dash to secure access to energy supplies.[43]

In China, energy security is defined in terms of two issues: price volatility and security of delivery. China feels vulnerable on both fronts, and such perceptions are shaping its diplomacy. China's intense policy focus on energy security (which initially had a frenzied quality to it) stems most specifically from its rapidly growing demand for crude oil and a corresponding increase in its reliance on imported crude oil; the latter grew from 1.6 million barrels per day (b/d) in 2001 to 4.1 million b/d in 2007. These increases reached consumption levels that some Chinese had projected for their country in 2020. China became the

---

[42] This section draws from the following sources: Zhang Youwen and Huang Renwei, eds., *China's International Status Report 2004*, 2004, pp. 249–271; *Guoji Zhanlue yu Anquan Xingshi Pinggu 2003–2004*, 2004, pp. 201–221; and *Guoji Zhanlue yu Anquan Xingshi Pinggu 2004–2005*, 2005, pp. 45–62.

[43] Erica Downs, "China's Energy Rise," unpublished manuscript, March 27, 2009; Erica Downs, *China*, the Brookings Foreign Policy Studies Energy Security Series, Washington, D.C.: The Brookings Institution, December 2006b.

world's second-largest consumer of oil (after the United States) in 2003 and the world's third-largest importer of oil (after the United States and Japan) in 2004.[44] In 2008, China imported about 45 percent of its total national oil demand, with 76 percent of China's crude oil imports coming from the Middle East and Africa (with about 45 percent from the Middle East alone).[45] These numbers need to be kept in context: crude oil imports provide for about 10 percent of China's total energy needs.

At least three geopolitical considerations drive Chinese concerns about security of delivery.[46] First, the Middle East (the region of China's greatest dependence on crude oil imports) is perceived as unstable, where the risks of supply disruptions are high. (Africa is not seen as being as volatile.) Chinese analysts became especially concerned about reliance on Middle East oil after the U.S. war in Iraq in 2003, which some in China viewed as heavily motivated by U.S. desires to control Iraq's oil assets and thus to increase U.S. leverage over global oil markets. One prominent Chinese analysis concluded, "There is no doubt that U.S. control over the world's oil resource was significantly strengthened in the wake of the success of [the] Iraq War."[47] Along these lines,

---

[44] Yet, these numbers need to be viewed in a global context. The total increase in U.S. demand in 2005 was more than the total Chinese oil consumption that year. Also, according to the International Energy Agency, in 2005 China used 6.6 million b/d of oil, which constitutes about one-third of U.S. oil consumption of 20.8 million b/d; and China imported 3.0 million b/d, which was about 25 percent of the U.S. level of 13.5 million b/d.

[45] Tian Chunrong, "2006 Nian Zhongguo Shiyou Jinchukou Gaikuang Fenxi" [Analysis of China Oil Imports and Exports in 2006], *Guoji Shiyou Jingji* [International Oil Economics], No. 3, 2007, pp. 16–17.

[46] The following sources cover this entire section unless otherwise indicated: *Guoji Zhanlue yu Anquan Xingshi Pinggu 2001–2002*, Chapter Five, 2002; *Guoji Zhanlue yu Anquan Xingshi Pinggu 2003–2004*, Chapter Ten, 2004; *Guoji Zhanlue yu Anquan Xingshi Pinggu 2004–2005*, Chapter Two, 2005; and Zhang Youwen and Huang Renwei, 2004, pp. 249–271.

[47] For example, one analysis argues that the U.S. war in Iraq was a strategy of killing three birds with one stone: "First, [the] US could secure the oil supplies for itself. Second, it could prevent the combination of Islam extremist forces and the 'oil weapon' that might be used to jeopardize [the] US economy. Third, the control over Iraq's oil supply will contribute to [the] accomplishment of US' global strategy." Zhang Youwen and Huang Renwei, 2004, pp. 249–271.

Chinese analysts assess that the extensive U.S. military presence in the Middle East accentuates China's vulnerability to future supply cutoffs enforced by the United States. Second, importing oil from the Middle East and other regions requires long-distance ocean transportation for which China can provide little independent protection. The Strait of Malacca, in particular, is one critical access point for most of China's seaborne oil imports and an access point that the Chinese navy is not capable of policing. Some Chinese policymakers have reportedly termed this vulnerability China's "Malacca Dilemma," although the origin and veracity of this particular phrase remains unclear.[48] A third perceived Chinese vulnerability is that it relies on overseas tanker companies to ship about 90 percent of its oil imports. These three concerns are motivating China's efforts, via diplomacy, to gain access to energy resources that are closer to China, available for pipeline or ground transport, and thus not as subject to possible disruption.

China's Rise in International Affairs[49]

A new and pervasive element of China's perception of its current security environment is the "rise of China" in global affairs. This idea is becoming more than just a perception shaping policymaking; it is also an overarching theme and focus of China's global diplomacy. China's confidence in its accomplishments and its global influence is palpable in the comments of policymakers and analysts. Many Chinese argue that as the world becomes more multipolar and U.S. power declines in relative terms, China is becoming a more influential international actor. In the words of former Vice Premier Qian Qichen in an internal speech:

> It can be said that the 21st century cannot be the "American century." It is not that the Americans do not want it but that it is

---

[48] Ian Storey, "China's 'Malacca Dilemma,'" *China Brief,* The Jamestown Foundation, Vol. 6, Issue 8, April 12, 2006.

[49] This section draws heavily from the arguments in Zhang Youwen and Huang Renwei, 2004, especially the introduction and Chapter One; also see Huang Renwei, 2003.

not possible. This has been proven by the Iraq issue. The United States wants to engage in unilateralism but it cannot dominate the world. . . . Speaking about international relations in the new century, one has to talk about China. China is the most vibrant force in the world today. The rapid growth of our country has led to widespread attention in the international community.[50]

China's confidence is based, in part, on a recognition of the growing reliance by many of China's neighbors on trade and investment with it. Chinese analysts talk about China as a "large world market," a "huge commercial ship," or a "giant businessman" that plays a central role in the world economy. And by dint of its large and globalized economy, the Chinese believe they are generating extensive political influence in Asia and beyond. China's 2008 national defense white paper put it this way: "The achievements made in China's modernization drive have drawn worldwide attention."[51] A foreign ministry assessment concluded: "China has been able to release its huge economic potential against the backdrop of economic globalization and the change in the international system."[52]

Beyond its perceived economic power, Chinese policymakers and analysts also highlight China's activism in multilateral organizations and its role in managing regional security problems, such as the North Korean nuclear crisis, as a further indication of China's accumulating geopolitical influence. This very assessment was starkly stated, for the first time, in the 2008 national defense white paper: "China is playing an active and constructive role in multilateral affairs, thus notably elevating its international position and influence." A prominent Chinese analysis cited China's regional activism as contributing to "the coming of a new kind of geopolitics in Asia."[53] Chinese scholar Huang Renwei put it in even broader terms: "As a major driver of the current transformation of the international system, China is playing an increasingly

---

[50] Qian Qichen, 2004.

[51] *China's National Defense in 2008*, 2009.

[52] Shen Guofang, 2007, p. 42.

[53] Yang Jiechi, 2008, p. 91.

important and influential role. In fact, China has become a main partic-
ipant in and builder of the international system in transformation."[54]

Building on these successes, Chinese analysts and policymakers
now regularly discuss using China's new global position to shape the
rules and norms of major international organizations in ways consistent with Chinese interests.[55] Ambassador Shen Guofang summarized
many of these arguments in a June 2007 speech:

> China's rapidly growing economy, its gradually increasing politi-
> cal and diplomatic influence, and the striking rise in its inter-
> national status are all influencing the international structure in
> far-reaching ways. . . . China's own unique strengths and influ-
> ence demand that it play an important role in international
> affairs. . . .
>
> China should enhance its ability to determine the agenda and its
> ability to make use of the rules by playing a substantive role in all
> kinds of consultations and the writing of international rules. It
> should show even more initiative in participating in international
> affairs and in building the multilateral system.[56]

Chinese analysts argue that China's effort to "rise" while not pro-
voking global resentment is working: China has effectively reduced
Asian fears of China's rising economic and military power. Chinese
analyses highlight the appeal of China's cooperative approach to foreign affairs based on the strategy of integrating into the current system
as opposed to trying to overthrow it. Such analyses also regularly highlight the appeal of Chinese concepts such as "common interest" and
the "new security concept," which stress China's focus on economic
interdependence, regional integration, and multilateral security cooperation. As a result, many Chinese analyses argue that China's "hard
power" and "soft power" in international relations are growing, and its
nascent "soft power" stands in stark contrast to international resent-

---

[54] Huang Renwei, 2006.

[55] Wen Jiabao, 2007.

[56] Shen Guofang, 2007, p. 42.

ment toward the United States stemming from U.S. policies on Iraq and counterterrorism.[57]

Chinese analyses continue to point out that the process of rising through domestic economic development and global integration is not without its costs and risks. Chinese policymakers are well aware of the problems experienced by past rising powers, and they specifically seek to avoid the conflict-provoking approaches of Imperial Japan, Germany in the 1930s, and the Soviet Union in the 20th century. These concerns are reflected in the leadership's ultimate choice of its diplomatic slogan of "peaceful development" over its predecessor "peaceful rise"; the latter formulation could be interpreted as presumptuous to some and confrontational to others.[58]

Last, Chinese analysts are aware that China's pursuit of domestic development through international trade and foreign investment has fostered vulnerability to maritime threats because of the heavy concentration of China's economic assets along its eastern and southern coastlines. Additional vulnerabilities stem from China's reliance on external demand (from the United States and the European Union) for growth, its reliance on access to global sea lanes for trade, and its growing need for unfettered access to investment, technology, and natural resources from foreign sources to modernize its economy. Thus, although Chinese analysts are aware of the benefits associated with China's growing international status and global economic integration, they also recognize the inherent risks and vulnerabilities of their position.

---

[57] Huang Renwei, 2006, 2003; Zhang Youwen and Huang Renwei, eds., *Zhongguo Guoji Diwei Baogao 2005*, 2005; and Wen Jiabao, 2003.

[58] On this debate in China, see Glaser and Medeiros, 2007.

CHAPTER FOUR

China's Foreign Policy Objectives

The lenses through which China looks at the world, its long-term diplomatic priorities, and its perceptions of its current security environment collectively manifest themselves in five foreign policy *objectives*. They are fostering economic development, reassurance, countering constraints, diversifying access to natural resources, and reducing Taiwan's international space. These five differ from China's long-term diplomatic priorities because they are more specific and reflect current perceptions; thus, they could more easily change in response to internal or external stimuli.

These objectives constitute the core of China's current international behavior. In most cases, they reflect China's responses to its security environment and its effort to shape that environment in a way that fosters China's development, sovereignty, and international status. The government has articulated some, but not all, of the objectives in its speeches and publications; others are analytical extrapolations from Chinese writings and government actions. Importantly, the degree to which China emphasizes any one of these objectives in its foreign policy differs, depending on the nation and region and over time; these variations will be addressed in the analysis of China's foreign policy actions in Chapters Five and Six.

Understanding Official Policy

An analysis of China's current objectives begins with an understanding of the formal, government-articulated strategic guidelines, or *tifa* (提法), that guide Chinese foreign policy. These phrases constitute the conceptual edifice of the CCP's diplomacy. It is important to understand these concepts because they reveal how China's leaders define and articulate their goals and how they communicate with one another.

When assessing the meaning and value of such party guidelines for "foreign affairs work" (*waijiao gongzuo* 外交工作), two caveats are in order. First, the meanings of these phrases change over time as the guidelines themselves become conceptually developed and distinct from previous *tifa*. Within the CCP, such guidelines are often initially articulated without much meaning (and often do not appear very distinct from previous ones articulated by past party leaders); they become developed over time based on actual practice and circumstance. Some just die the slow death of nonuse but are seldom rejected outright (so as not to insult a former party leader).

Second, the application of such guidelines is subject to a classic party dictum of "adhering to principles while being flexible," which in practice seems to give Chinese policymakers the political license to occasionally take actions contrary to these guidelines, while claiming fidelity to the party's dictates. These practices are common in Leninist political systems. Despite such flexibility in interpretation, these guidelines have had and continue to have a real effect on foreign policy, as both a constraint and an enabler.

At least three concepts constitute the foundation of the CCP's current foreign policy.

All-Around Diplomacy

Chinese policymakers describe their increasingly active and robust diplomacy using the expression "all-around diplomacy" (*quanfangwei waijiao* 全方位外交). On face value, this principle sounds rather broad and explains little, but in a Chinese context, it possesses specific and new (or newly emphasized) dimensions of statecraft. All-around diplomacy is meant to contrast China's current approach with past CCP guiding principles—such as "leaning to one side"—which had a more ideological nature.[1] This phrase reinforces (to foreign as well as Chinese audiences) the notion that Chinese foreign policy will continue to focus on protecting China's national interests (i.e., sovereignty, development, and respect) and not on ideological goals, as was often the case in past years. All-around diplomacy is also meant to emphasize the comprehensive nature of Chinese foreign policy: It will include all nations, developed and developing, and will include multiple regions, such as Africa, the Middle East, Latin America, and Europe as well as Asia. Chinese foreign policy will embrace all modes of international interactions (bilateral, multilateral, and regional), and such interactions will encompass economics, politics, military, science and technology, culture, education, and tourism. In the words of reports from the high-level 2006 Central Conference on Foreign Affairs Work, "China has created a pattern of opening to the outside world *in all directions, at all levels, and in broad areas*. . . . [emphasis added]"[2] Thus, all-around diplomacy is meant to signal the degree to which the Chinese leaders support a highly internationalist and nonideological foreign policy.

---

[1] For example, in the 1950s, China pursued a policy of "leaning to one side" (*yi bian dao*) with the Soviet Union; in the 1960s, China adopted the principle of "fighting against both United States and Soviet Union" (*liang ge quan tou da ren*); in the 1970s, the key principle was "one line of diplomacy" (*yi tiao xian*), which was cooperating with the United States to contain the Soviet Union; and in the 1980s, China gradually began to move away from such ideologically oriented foreign policies with first its "independent foreign policy of peace" (*duli zizhu heping waijiao zhengce*). Zhang Wankun Franklin, *China's Foreign Relations Strategies under Mao and Deng: A Systematic Comparative Analysis*, Public and Social Administration Working Paper Series, Hong Kong: City University Hong Kong, 1998.

To be sure, Western research on Chinese foreign policy during the Cold War has also demonstrated that, despite the rhetorically ideological orientation of Chinese foreign policy in the 1950s, 1960s, and 1970s, national interest calculations had a driving influence on Chinese decisions as well. In other words, China's foreign policy was not necessarily as ideological as it sounded. On this point, see Peter Van Ness, *Revolution and Chinese Foreign Policy: Peking's Support for Wars of National Liberation*, Berkeley, Calif.: University of California Press, 1970.

[2] "Central Foreign Affairs Meeting Held in Beijing; Hu Jintao, Wen Jiabao Deliver Important Speeches; Wu Bangguo, Jia Qinglin, Zeng Qinghong, Huang Ju, Wu Huanzheng, Li Changchun, Luo Gan Attend Meeting," *Xinhua*, August 23, 2006, as translated by OSC; and "Adhere to Peaceful Development Road, Push Forward Building of Harmonious World," *People's Daily*, editorial, August 24, 2006, as translated by OSC.

Peace and Development

As noted in Chapter Three, since the mid-1980s Chinese leaders have affirmed the relevance of "peace and development as the main trend of the times" as the basis for China's reform-era foreign policy. In recent years, this seminal phrase has assumed two new forms. Chinese leaders now talk about the trinity of "peace, development, and *cooperation*" as the "basic principles" (*jiben yuanze* 基本原则) of China's diplomacy. The addition of "cooperation" is a Hu Jintao innovation, which is meant to underscore China's commitment to multilateral organizations. Chinese leaders have also placed a growing emphasis on the theme of "economic development" in China's multilateral and bilateral diplomacy. The importance of "development" as a guiding principle is evident in China's foreign economic relations, its changing foreign aid practices, its proliferating bilateral economic and financial dialogues, and its contributions to U.N. activities. In addition, in 2004, the concept of "peaceful development" became a prominent member of China's foreign policy orthodoxy. This phrase is meant to reflect China's effort to avoid the mistakes of past rising powers by reassuring other states about the means and direction of China's activism in international politics. With this idea, China is conveying that it will be mindful of other nations' interests as it ascends in the international system, and it will not use military competition as a means to realize national revitalization.[3]

Harmonious World

In 2005, Hu Jintao began calling for the building of "a harmonious world" (*hexie shijie* 和谐世界) in international affairs. This principle is an external manifestation of his domestic policy of building a "harmonious society" (*hexie shehui* 和谐社会). The meaning of "harmonious world," as with "harmonious society," is still taking shape and gaining clarity. Because it is a distinctly Hu Jintao idea, it may become the key principle in China's diplomacy until China's fifth generation of leaders ascends to power in 2012. Although initially articulated earlier, Hu's

---

[3] The classic articulation of this slogan can be found in *China's Peaceful Rise: Speeches of Zheng Bijian 1997–2005*, Washington, D.C.: Brookings Institution Press, 2005.

vision for a harmonious world was further developed at a key Central Foreign Affairs Work Conference in August 2006.[4] For Hu, a harmonious world is one in which states act in ways that respect each other's national sovereignty, tolerate diversity (in national political systems and values), and promote national development by equitably spreading economic benefits. Although these ideas are all long-standing principles in Chinese diplomacy, they reflect Hu Jintao's effort to define a distinctive approach to foreign policy.[5]

Hu's conception of a harmonious world has two dimensions, and time will tell whether or how they manifest in actual policy. First, a harmonious worldview suggests that China's leaders are moving away from their traditionally reactive and combative view of foreign affairs as a "struggle" (*douzheng* 斗争) against any number of external forces (e.g., hegemony and power politics). This shift was a specific theme of the 2006 Foreign Affairs Work Conference. There are a growing number of indications that this shift is taking effect, at least in official rhetoric. Hu Jintao's work report to the 17th Party Congress, for the first time, did not call for establishing a "new international political and economic order," a phrase that Deng started using in these reports as far back as 1988, and it had achieved near-canonical status in China's foreign affairs lexicon. Instead Hu's 2007 report used a phrase that was less evocative of a challenge to the current international system: China will "work to make the international order fairer and more equitable."[6] In addition, Chinese media reports now seldom use the phrase "opposing hegemonism and maintaining world peace" as a "task" (*renwu* 任务) in foreign affairs work; rather, the new formulation is "maintaining world peace and advancing common development."[7] Chinese officials

---

4   Bonnie Glaser, "Ensuring the 'Go Abroad' Policy Serves China's Domestic Priorities," *China Brief,* The Jamestown Foundation, Vol. 7, No. 5, March 8, 2007.

5   "Adhere to Peaceful Development Road, Push Forward Building of Harmonious World," 2006. This editorial was published following the Central Foreign Affairs Conference in Beijing on August 21–23, 2006.

6   The author is indebted to Michael Glosny for this important point.

7   "Central Foreign Affairs Meeting Held in Beijing," 2006; and "Adhere to Peaceful Development Road, Push Forward Building of Harmonious World," 2006. The changes in this

have also been downplaying their advocacy of "multipolarity," because some Chinese realize it is viewed as an implicit effort to constrain and balance U.S. power. In its place, Chinese government statements now more commonly call for greater "multilateralism" in interstate relations, which, as noted above, is a key theme in Hu Jintao's diplomacy.[8]

A second dimension of Hu's harmonious world concept is the emphasis on how intimately tied China has become with the international community. Hu seeks to foster greater awareness throughout the Chinese system about using the intense linkages between domestic and international affairs as a way to promote better policy coordination across the Chinese bureaucracy. Hu reportedly attributes many of the problems plaguing China's diplomacy to the lack of such coordination. According to media reports about the 2006 Central Foreign Affairs Work Conference, a key phrase in the conference's final report was "internal, external, two great situations" (*guonei guowai, liangge daju* 国内国外，两个大局).[9] In other words, China can promote a harmonious world only if domestic actors in China (e.g., corporations with overseas activities) are aware of China's foreign policy equities and if, conversely, China's foreign policy directly and substantially assists domestic economic development.

Core Diplomatic Objectives

Economic Development

A persistent and consistent economic logic drives China's foreign policy and foreign relations. This logic has two dimensions, one traditional and the other more recent. First, as Chinese leaders have often stated over the past 30 years, China seeks to maintain a favorable international environment conducive to continued domestic reform, devel-

---

language can be assessed by comparing such documents as the annual national defense white papers.

[8]   Interviews with Chinese officials and scholars, Beijing and Shanghai, 2005, 2008.

[9]   Interviews with Chinese officials and scholars, June and November 2006; "Central Foreign Affairs Meeting Held in Beijing," 2006; and Glaser, 2007.

opment, and modernization. This goal was set out by Deng and has been the core foreign policy objective during the entire reform era.[10] This slogan is not merely propaganda; it has real meaning behind it. Chinese diplomacy seeks to minimize threats on its peripheries (e.g., Russia, East Asia, Southeast Asia, and Central Asia) that would cause China to divert national resources away from economic reform and the leadership's management of China's developmental challenges. Insofar as maintaining robust growth and balanced development are central to the CCP's continued legitimacy, Chinese foreign policies seek to stabilize China's regional security environment and address emerging threats (e.g., territorial disputes and transnational challenges) to ensure that the leadership can continue to focus on economic development and growing China's comprehensive national power.

China's interpretation of this overarching goal has changed over time, as China's perceptions of its security environment and its conception of its national interest have evolved. China's pursuit of economic development now requires it to pay attention to transnational issues, such as environmental and health crises, which have complicated China's relations with its neighbors. Most concretely, counterterrorism has a strong domestic component because of Chinese concerns about Muslim separatists in Xinjiang and Central Asia.

A second and increasingly salient manifestation of the domestic economic logic to China's diplomacy is its use of foreign policy to expand access to trade, aid, investment, resources, and technology and, specifically, to forge and maintain bilateral political relationships that will ensure continued access to these critical inputs to economic growth. There are several new external manifestations of China's long-standing priority on domestic growth and development. In short, acting locally for China now requires that it think globally. In this regard, Chinese leaders have newly designated "economic diplomacy" as a high priority for Chinese foreign policy. As China's economy grows and globalization accelerates, diplomacy is no longer exclusively about protecting Chinese sovereignty, regional security, and international status but features a greater emphasis on the specific contributions of

---

[10] Yang Jiechi, 2008.

China's diplomacy to domestic development. In the words of Ambassador Wu Jianmin, "Fifty years ago, an ambassador would be laughed at if he talked about economics. Fifty years later, if an ambassador does not know about economics, he will become a laughing stock."[11]

Reassurance

In the mid-1990s, Chinese leaders and analysts began to recognize that specific Chinese policies, such as pursuit of its disputed territorial claims in the South China Sea and missile tests around Taiwan in 1995–1996, had prompted concerns among its Asian neighbors about Beijing's intentions, which appeared to many as potentially aggressive and threatening. Chinese policymakers again noticed in the early 2000s that China's rapidly growing economy and expanding military capabilities were prompting varying degrees of concern from other Asian powers and the broader international community. This gradual recognition led to the adoption of a regional strategy that sought to reassure Asian states that China would not only not undermine their economic or security interests but would contribute to them. In short, China wanted to represent an opportunity, not a threat.[12]

China subsequently implemented several specific policies to address these diverse anxieties. It has sought to foster an image as a benign regional actor and as a "responsible major power" by demonstrating the economic and cultural benefits of engagement with China. This effort motivated, in part, China's activism within multilateral economic and security organizations in Asia—ones from which it had long been aloof. Specific aspects of this new reassurance strategy are detailed in Chapter Six of this monograph; many of China's regional reassur-

---

[11] Chen Hui, "China's Diplomacy Is Moving Toward All Spectrum—Interview with Professor Wu Jianmin, Director of the Foreign Affairs Institute, and Deputy Secretary General cum Spokesperson of the CPPCC," *Zhongguo Jingji Daobao* [China Economics Daily], July 16, 2005, as translated by OSC.

[12] Zhang Yunling and Tang Shiping, 2006, pp. 48–70; Tang Shiping, "Projecting China's Foreign Policy: Projecting Factors and Scenarios," in Jae Ho Chung, ed., *Charting China's Future*, Lanham, Md.: Rowman & Littlefield, 2006, pp. 129–145; Jia Qingguo, "Peaceful Development: China's Policy of Reassurance," *Australian Journal of International Affairs*, Vol. 59, No. 4, December 2005b, pp. 493–507; and Goldstein, 2005, pp. 102–176.

ance efforts are reflected in its regional policy line known as "great peripheral diplomacy" (*da zhoubian waijiao* 大周边外交).[13] China's articulation of the "peaceful rise"/"peaceful development" strategy in 2003–2004 is the most public manifestation of China's awareness of security dilemma dynamics and the need to address regional anxieties through reassurance.[14]

Chinese policymakers did this because they feared that such concerns would motivate China's Asian neighbors to constrain China in the region or, collectively, to balance Chinese power. China's recognition of its role in such security dilemma dynamics in Asia and the degree to which Chinese actions affect others' perceptions was an important step in the evolution of Chinese strategists' thinking. This realization stands in contrast to years of simplistically rejecting the security concerns of China's neighbors by reciting mantras about China being "a peace-loving nation" that pursued equality, mutual benefit, and win-win cooperation.[15]

Countering Constraints

A third Chinese objective can be characterized as countercontainment or counter*constrainment*.[16] It involves Chinese strategies and policies that seek to reduce other nations' ability or willingness to constrain

---

[13] Jia Qingguo, 2005b; and Cui Tiankai, "Regional Integration in Asia and China's Policy," speech delivered at Hong Kong University, Hong Kong, February 4, 2005.

[14] Zheng Bijian, "China's 'Peaceful Rise' to Great-Power Status," *Foreign Affairs*, Vol. 85, No. 5, September/October 2005, pp. 18–24.

[15] Zhang Yunling and Tang Shiping, 2006; Jia Qingguo, 2005b; and Goldstein, 2005, pp. 102–176.

[16] Given the fact that few Chinese policymakers or analysts openly write about such a competitive aspect of China's diplomacy, there are not many published sources to reference for this section. Such writings more often remain internal government documents. The arguments in this section, thus, are drawn from numerous conversations with Chinese analysts and scholars in Beijing, Shanghai, and Washington, D.C., in 2005, 2006, and 2008.

That said, Chinese writings about U.S.-China relations hint at such arguments by noting that the U.S. policy toward China is one of both engagement and containment, taking China as "an enemy and a friend" (*yidi yiyou*). These analyses stop short of specifying Chinese responses to such an approach. For an authoritative view on U.S.-China relations, see Pang Xingchen, 2004, pp. 807–813.

China's influence and freedom of action in global affairs. As argued in Chapter Three, Chinese policymakers, analysts, and the general public perceive many U.S. policies as designed to hinder or prevent China's emergence as a great power. The most intense concerns about U.S. containment efforts stem from perceptions of U.S. foreign and defense policies (though these concerns also extend to U.S. economic policies as well). Many Chinese argue that the United States is using its alliances in Asia and its regional military deployments to contain Chinese power. These deep concerns are most evident in Chinese commentaries about changes to the U.S.-Japan alliance, U.S. military interactions with Taiwan, the emerging U.S.-India strategic relationship, U.S. military deployments in Central Asia, and the U.S. military's force enhancements in the Western Pacific.

In the words of a mainstream Chinese assessment, "The United States has never given up its efforts to establish a 'small-sized NATO' [North Atlantic Treaty Organization] [in Asia] and has been trying its best to build a strategic balance of power in Asia using Japan and other regional powers to pin down and to use against China. At the same time, the United States has asked China to enhance military transparency so that it can see a clearer picture of China's strategic intention and capability."[17] Chinese policymakers and analysts have expressed similar concerns during U.S.-China negotiations over trade and financial issues, in which some Chinese see high-profile U.S. policies, such as pushing for appreciation of the renminbi and liberalization of its financial sector, as trying to limit China's growth.[18]

Few Chinese policymakers publicly articulate such worries about U.S. intentions as official policy because that would be seen as confronting the United States. Rather, these Chinese concerns are reflected

---

[17] Huang Renwei, 2006; and, more generally, Pang Xingchen, 2004, pp. 807–813.

[18] This theme is common in most Chinese analyses of U.S.-China economic issues. Interviews in Beijing and Shanghai, June 2008.

in statements calling for more "multipolarity," building "democracy in international relations," and the construction of a "harmonious world." China's advocacy of these phrases constitutes their implicit opposition to the U.S. unipolar position and U.S. unilateral policies, which many Chinese see as focused on regime change and coercive actions not sanctioned by international law or international institutions.[19]

China's responses to these concerns are readily apparent in its international behavior. Its diplomacy worldwide—but especially in Asia—seeks to forge political relationships that collectively create an environment in which the United States cannot use its diplomacy or military cooperation to constrain China's freedom of action and especially cannot work with other Asian states to balance or otherwise constrain China. Most specifically, Chinese foreign policy seeks to build bilateral diplomatic relationships in which regional policymakers are sensitive to China's views on key regional and global problems, specifically including the Taiwan issue. Huang Renwei described it this way:

> Entering the international system and participating in its transformation, China will be able to greatly broaden its effective strategic room of maneuver in terms of time and space. Hence, the hegemon will not be able to implement its strategy of containing China. Economic diplomacy and multilateral diplomacy will become the breakthrough and the supporting points for China's foreign policy, [and] Asian regional cooperation mechanisms offer China an important arena for practice in innovating international order. . . .
>
> Considering the relationship between China and the international system, we can reach a basic view: promoting common interests with other late-coming big powers is not only a requirement to be fulfilled in order to prevent the United States from roping in

---

[19] A prominent exception to this was a 2004 speech by former Foreign Minster Qian Qichen at China's Party School that was not supposed to be made public. Qian explicitly detailed Chinese concerns about the U.S. role in the world and the threats it presents to a "fair and just international order" (Qian Qichen, 2004).

other big powers and establishing a strategic alliance containing China, but also a requirement to be fulfilled in order to ensure stable transformation of the international system.[20]

To be sure, countercontainment is not the primary objective in Chinese global diplomacy or in Asia. If it were, Chinese diplomacy would likely be far more confrontational with the United States and its regional allies; for example, China would actively try to pull and prod U.S. allies away from the United States by proffering China as an alternative security partner. Rather, Chinese diplomacy has focused on economic opportunism and expanding its multilateral cooperation. In particular, it has been seeking to create new and expand existing multilateral organizations in which the United States has a limited role but also as a way to develop a regional order in East Asia in which U.S. influence is diluted. And China seeks to do this gradually so as not to appear to directly oppose the United States or its allies. Thus, counter-containment is a distinct Chinese objective, but it does not manifest itself in a confrontational set of policies that emphasize defense coop-eration and zero-sum interactions. This objective may receive greater expression in the future if U.S.-China relations become more competi-tive, if China's regional influence grows, and if Beijing sees itself as less dependent on stable relations with Washington.

A critical dimension of China's strategy of countercontainment/counterconstrainment is avoiding confrontation with the United States, as that would ultimately defeat the purpose of the effort. China does not want to appear as if it actively seeks to undermine U.S. power and influ-ence in Asia or to eventually push the United States from the region. Such steps could precipitate outright rivalry with the United States and some of its allies, potentially derailing China's effort to maintain a stable periphery. In fact, many Chinese strategists openly acknowledge now that U.S. military presence and security commitments in Asia contribute to regional stability, and China (and the region) could suffer

---

[20] Huang Renwei, 2006.

if such arrangements dissolved.[21] Yet, Chinese policymakers and analysts have long-standing concerns about the U.S. military posture in
Asia, and these concerns have become more acute of late because of the
expanding scope of U.S.-Japan and U.S.-Australia alliances, trilateral
coordination among the three allies, and growing U.S. security cooperation with India and Singapore.

Therefore, Chinese foreign policy on this question faces a major
dilemma. On the one hand, China seeks the time and space for its
national rejuvenation; to do so, it believes that it needs to negate other
nations' abilities to constrain its foreign policy pursuits and related economic objectives. On the other hand, Beijing needs to execute such a
counterconstrainment policy in a way that avoids generating the very
antagonism that could most directly derail its objectives. This is a deli-
cate balancing act and a central challenge for Chinese foreign policy
in the region and in its relations with the United States. Several factors
may determine how China manages this balancing act: the relative
stability of U.S.-China relations, Chinese perceptions of U.S. goals in
Asia, U.S. perceptions of China's regional diplomacy, and the extent of
regional accommodation or alienation to China.

Expanding and Diversifying Access to Natural Resources

A relatively new objective for Chinese foreign policy is expanding and
diversifying access to natural resources, especially hydrocarbon energy
resources.[22] Beginning early in this decade, not only did China's GDP
growth accelerate (from 8 percent in 2002 to 12 percent in 2007)
but the resource intensity of GDP growth increased as well (measured in terms of the amount of resource inputs used for each dollar
of GDP output). This trend required that China go abroad in search
of resources to fuel continued growth, and not just oil and natural gas.
China substantially increased its imports of iron ore, crude oil, natural

---

[21] Wang Jisi, "China's Changing Role in Asia," in Kokubun Ryosei and Wang Jisi, eds., *The
Rise of China and a Changing East Asian Order*, Tokyo, Japan: Japan Center for International
Exchange, 2004; Wu Xinbo, 2005/06; and Wang Jisi, 2005.

[22] "Guoji Nengyuan Anquan Xingshi yu Zhongguo Nengyuan Waijiao," in *Guoji Zhanlue
yu Anquan Xingshi Pinggu 2004–2005*, 2005, pp. 45–62; and Downs, 2006b.

gas, copper, wood, cement, soy, and manganese. The degree of resource intensity involved in Chinese growth may decline somewhat because of a pending slowdown in GDP growth (perhaps down to 6–8 percent in 2009), efficiency gains, and shifts in China's growth model. But these changes will be gradual and will be most focused on demand for hydrocarbon resources and heavily polluting industries, such as steel and cement production. According to projections by Deutsche Bank, China's demand for most of these resources is expected to grow significantly in the next 15 years. Between 2006 and 2020, China's import demand for iron ore is projected to increase by 380 percent, soy by 80 percent, coal by 7,400 percent, copper by 600 percent, manganese by 30 percent, and wood by 330 percent.[23] As a result, the desire to expand access to these strategic resources now drives much of China's diplomacy in such resource-rich regions as Africa, the Middle East, and Latin America.

Resource security, for China, encompasses diversifying both suppliers as well as supply routes. As noted in the previous chapter, there is both a demand and supply logic behind this objective. On the demand side, China's need for secure and consistent access to imported resources is expanding, even during this period of relative global slowdown. On the supply side, Chinese policymakers have deep concerns about China's regional dependencies, especially its reliance on the Middle East for about 45 percent of its crude oil imports.[24]

China's acute anxieties are manifesting in diplomacy, at all levels and using multiple tools, which seeks to build new and to expand existing political relationships to ensure consistent access to energy supplies and natural resources. China's rapid expansion of relations with Saudi Arabia and other Gulf states (e.g., Oman and the United Arab Emirates) in the last five years is one such example. China also protects key

---

[23] The Deutsche Bank report on China's resource demand is referenced in Chris Alden and Andy Rothman, *China and Africa: Special Report*, CLSA Asia-Pacific Markets, September 2008, p. 4.

[24] Downs, 2006b; Yitzhak Shichor, "Blocking the Hormuz Strait: China's Energy Dilemma," *China Brief*, The Jamestown Foundation, Vol. 8, No. 18, September 23, 2008; Erica Downs, "The Chinese Energy Security Debate," *China Quarterly*, No. 177, March 2004, pp. 21–41; and Zhang Youwen and Huang Renwei, 2007, pp. 99–106.

bilateral relationships to ensure continued access to resources on preferential terms. These goals are reflected in China's effort to upgrade relations with sub-Saharan African nations and includes shielding important suppliers from international pressure on human rights questions, notably Sudan, Zimbabwe, and Uzbekistan. China has also sought to improve bilateral relations with nations along key ocean and land supply routes, such as Malaysia, Singapore, and Indonesia (along the Straits of Malacca, Lombok, and Sunda) and Kazakhstan in Central Asia. It seeks to minimize the possibility of disruption, including foreign interdiction.[25]

Reducing Taiwan's International Space

A final, but by no means insignificant or new, foreign policy objective for China is reducing Taiwan's international space and limiting other nations' ability to confer status or legitimacy on Taiwan. This strategy is a long-standing one for China and is part and parcel of its incessant effort to prevent Taiwan's independence and, ultimately, to bring about reunification. China's desire to eliminate Taiwan's international space is evident in both its multilateral and bilateral diplomacy; this has been the case for decades. This strategy motivates some of China's interactions in major multilateral organizations, such as the United Nations and the World Health Organization, to deny Taiwan a level of participation that could carry with it the hint of legitimacy.

Bilaterally, China takes steps to prod nations away from recognizing Taiwan and toward Beijing. Taiwan currently has diplomatic relations with 23 nations, spread out among Latin America (12), Africa (4), the South Pacific/Oceania (6), and the Vatican.[26] China's efforts

---

[25] Downs, 2006b, p. 31; and Gabriel B. Collins and William S. Murray, "No Oil for the Lamps of China?" *Naval War College Review*, Vol. 61, No. 2, Spring 2008, pp. 79–95.

[26] This list of nations includes Belize (1989), Burkina Faso (1994), Dominican Republic (1957), El Salvador (1961), Gambia (1995), Guatemala (1960), Haiti (1956), Vatican City, The Holy See (1942), Honduras (1965), Kiribati (2003), Marshall Islands (1998), Nauru (1980–2002, 2005), Nicaragua (1990), Palau (1999), Panama (1954), Paraguay (1957), Saint Kitts–Nevis (1983), Saint Vincent and the Grenadines (1981), São Tomé and Príncipe (1997), Swaziland (1968), Solomon Islands (1983), and Tuvalu (1979). These data are from the Web site of the Ministry of Foreign Affairs, Republic of China (Taiwan).

have resulted in a competition, often referred to as "dollar diplomacy," in which China uses large aid packages and other financial incentives (such as construction of a sport stadium in the Dominican Republic) to persuade nations to switch their diplomatic recognition from Taipei to Beijing, and vice versa. This effort has accelerated in this decade, as China's financial resources have expanded and Beijing's concerns about Taiwan's international activities have grown. Press reports in 2008 revealed that Costa Rica agreed to switch its recognition to China in June 2007 after Beijing pledged, in a secret deal, to provide $130 million in aid and agreed to buy $300 million in Costa Rican government bonds, drawing on its sizable foreign exchange reserves.[27] China has targeted several other Latin American and African nations to prod them to change their diplomatic ties, and successes on this score are accumulating. Since 2003, Costa Rica, Chad, Grenada, Malawi, Liberia, the Dominican Republic, and Senegal have all switched to diplomatic recognition of China. A few countries in Latin America, such as Paraguay and Panama, are thought to have seriously considered such a shift. But China and Taiwan agreed in the second half of 2008 to freeze this diplomatic competition to create an environment favorable to cross-Strait confidence-building following the March 2008 election of Ma Ying-jeou as president of Taiwan.

---

[27] Graham Bowley, "Cash Helped China Win Costa Rica's Recognition," *New York Times*, September 12, 2008.

CHAPTER FIVE

China's Expanding Diplomatic Toolkit

One of the most notable features of China's international behavior in the past decade has been the number of newly utilized and enhanced tools of statecraft that it has put into operation in pursuit of its objectives. This monograph identifies five categories of tools: economic diplomacy, leadership diplomacy, multilateral diplomacy, strategic partnerships, and military diplomacy. In many instances, the application of these tools is overlapping and mutually supportive; the distinctions among these five types of statecraft are drawn for ease of analysis.

Economic Diplomacy

Economic diplomacy (*jingji waijiao* 经济外交) has become a central theme in China's foreign policy under Hu Jintao. Economic diplomacy has come to mean using trade, investment, and, increasingly, finance policies to support China's diplomatic goals and also using classic diplomacy to advance China's economic development, such as by ensuring access to foreign markets. Both aspects of economic diplomacy are somewhat novel for China, which has traditionally viewed diplomacy and economic affairs as separate and distinct. Wen Jiabao highlighted this concept's importance in a seminal August 2004 State Council meeting that was regarded as a milestone event anointing the concept. The idea was further developed during a December 2004 foreign ministry "Seminar on Diplomacy and the Economy." During the latter meeting, Assistant Foreign Minister Lu Guozeng explained the contribution of economically oriented diplomacy to national development. He stated:

> New developments in the international and domestic situations are imposing higher and higher requirements on our work in various fields. We have to further implement the concept of scientific development, coordinate domestic development and opening up to the outside world, firmly grasp the opportunities for development and strive to build a better-off society. . . . With the development and change in the situation, the implications and functions of diplomacy are also changing. It is gradually expanding from political and security areas to economic and cultural fields. While ensuring national sovereignty and security, diplomacy has to shoulder heavier and heavier tasks in safeguarding national economic interests and promoting domestic development.[1]

Multiple Tools

China's economic diplomacy has several dimensions. One of the most prominent ones has been China's initiation, negotiation, or conclusion of free trade agreements (FTAs). As of 2009, China has concluded FTAs with Chile, Hong Kong, Macao, Pakistan, Singapore, Peru, and New Zealand and is in negotiation with a few others, notably Australia and the Gulf Cooperation Council (GCC).[2] China's largest FTA, with the ten members of the Association of Southeast Asian Nations (ASEAN), is set to enter into force in 2010, though some "early harvest" tariff liberalization measures were adopted in 2004 (Table 5.1).

China's use of FTAs contributes to three Chinese foreign policy objectives: (1) expand China's access to markets, investment, and technology, (2) gain access to strategic resources, and (3) reassure other nations that China's growth will not undermine their economic

---

[1] Lu Guozeng, Assistant Foreign Minister, "Vigorously Strengthen Economic Diplomacy to Serve the Building of a Better-off Society in an All Around Manner," address to the Seminar on Diplomacy and Economy, December 18, 2004.

[2] "Zhongguo Ziyou Maoyi Qu Fuwu Wang" [China Free Trade Area Service Web site], Ministry of Commerce, PRC, undated.

Table 5.1
China's Free Trade Agreements

Country	Status of Agreements/Negotiations
ASEAN	China and ASEAN signed a goods agreement in November 2004 and began tariff reductions on about 90 percent of the goods in July 2005. An agreement covering trade in services took effect in July 2007 and covers construction, environmental protection, tourism, transportation, and education. Talks on investment and expanding services are ongoing with the expectation of a full FTA by 2010.
Australia	Negotiations were initiated in May 2005 and are still ongoing. Australia wants to negotiate a comprehensive agreement, whereas China wants to negotiate sequential agreements, beginning with goods trade.
Chile	China and Chile signed a trade in goods agreement in November 2005, with the goal of eliminating tariffs on 97 percent of goods by 2015. A services trade agreement was signed in April 2008. Negotiations on an investment agreement are ongoing.
Costa Rica	A joint feasibility study was completed in July 2008.
Gulf Cooperation Council	In April 2005, China and the GCC agreed to begin negotiations on an agreement of goods and then on services trade. Negotiations began in 2006 and are ongoing.
Hong Kong (Special Administrative Region)	The China–Hong Kong Closer Economic Partnership Arrangement (CEPA) was concluded in June 2003. This is a comprehensive FTA, now covering all goods from Hong Kong and 27 services sectors.
Iceland	Research on FTA feasibility started in March 2006 and negotiations on a comprehensive FTA began in April 2007. No agreement has been reached yet.
India	In 2005, a bilateral task force was formed to conduct a feasibility study on an FTA. The study was completed in 2008 but no decision has been made on initiating negotiations.
Macau (Special Administrative Region)	A CEPA was concluded in October 2003 and entered into force in January 2004. All of Macau's products are eligible for tariff-free access to China, and companies in 26 services sectors have preferential treatment on the mainland.
New Zealand	Bilateral negotiations were initiated in December 2004. An agreement was signed in April 2008 and entered into force in October 2008. The agreement liberalizes trade in goods and services, and the changes are progressive over time.
Norway	Norway launched an FTA feasibility study in July 2007 and it is ongoing.

Table 5.1—continued

Country	Status of Agreements/Negotiations
Pakistan	China and Pakistan signed an agreement on goods and investment in November 2006, with the goal of 85–90 percent tariff liberalization by 2011. An agreement on services trade was signed in February 2009.
Peru	Negotiations on a merchandise trade agreement were completed in November 2008, and the agreement was signed in April 2009.
Singapore	Negotiations began in October 2006 and an agreement on merchandise and services trade was signed in October 2008; it went into force on January 1, 2009. The provisions of the China-ASEAN agreement on investment will be incorporated into this FTA.
South Africa	Negotiations began in 2006, and China accepted voluntary limits on textile exports in 2006. Media reports indicate that negotiations are on hold.
Southern African Customs Union	Negotiations began in June 2004 but little progress has been made, to date. Swaziland's ties with Taiwan are a major barrier to progress.
South Korea	Research on an FTA began in 2004 and a bilateral feasibility study group meeting occurred in July 2007. As of spring 2009, South Korea had not agreed to initiate negotiations, despite Beijing's pressing Seoul to do so.

SOURCES: Various media reports; People's Republic of China, Ministry of Commerce, "Zhongguo Ziyou Maoyi Qu Fuwu Wang," undated.

NOTE: Southern African Customs Union nations include Botswana, Lesotho, Namibia, South Africa, and Swaziland.

interests. More tactically, China has successfully used FTAs to gain commitments from several countries to provide China with market-economy status (MES), a legal determination under World Trade Organization (WTO) rules. For some nations, such as Australia, China required MES as a condition for simply beginning negotiations on an FTA. As of early 2009, nearly 80 countries had recognized China as a market economy under WTO rules. Notable exceptions include the United States, Japan, and the European Union (EU). MES is important for China as a mark of status for the success of its economic reforms and also because it reduces the potential penalties that states could impose on China in anti-dumping and countervailing duty cases under WTO rules.

China's economic diplomacy has several finance dimensions as well. In early 2006, China initiated "finance dialogues" (*jinrong duihua* 金融对话) with several countries to go beyond bilateral exchanges on classic trade and investment issues. This new channel is specifically between finance ministries and central banks, and it covers macroeconomic policymaking, national finance and tax policies, and exchange rate practices. To date, China has established such dialogues with the United States, the United Kingdom (UK), Germany, Brazil, India, Russia, and Japan.[3] With a select group of major global economies, China initiated high-level economic dialogues, including with the United States, Japan, the UK, and the EU.

In late 2008 and early 2009, China further developed its financial diplomacy by rapidly concluding currency swap agreements totaling 650 billion renminbi (RMB) ($95 billion) with six nations; the aim of these agreements is to improve these nations' access to renminbi as a way to facilitate trade transactions during the global recession and the shortage of U.S. dollars. According to the Web site of the People's Bank of China, "Central banks use currency swaps to address the short-term liquidity problem and cope with the current crisis more efficiently and safeguard stability of the financial system." As of April 2009, China has signed agreements with Argentina (70 billion RMB), Hong Kong Monetary Authority (200 billion RMB), Malaysia (80 billion RMB), Belarus (20 billion RMB), South Korea (180 billion RMB), and Indonesia (100 billion RMB).[4]

Moreover, China continues to expand its outward direct investment (ODI), with a cumulative total stock of $117.9 billion globally in 2007.[5] The substantial and rapid growth in ODI is partly a result of a

---

[3] Sun Lei, "China Plans Financial Diplomacy, Seeks Right to Have Say in Economic and Trade Matters," *21 Shiji Jingji Baodao* [21st Century World Economic Journal], April 26, 2006, as translated by OSC.

[4] Belinda Cao and Judy Chen, "China Will Expand Currency Swap Accords to Help Trade," *Bloomberg News,* March 31, 2009.

[5] The data in this section are from *2007 Nian Zhongguo Dui Wai Zhijie Touzi Tongji Gongbao* [2007 Statistical Bulletin of China's Outward Foreign Direct Investment], Beijing,

state-directed policy that was adopted in the late 1990s and reinforced in 2003. It is called the "go out" strategy (*zou chu qu* 走出去), and it calls for Chinese companies to move into global markets to grow their revenue, to learn to be globally competitive, and, if possible, to acquire international brands. Chinese companies, mainly state-owned enterprises, have invested in foreign transportation, infrastructure, and telecommunications projects. In some cases, these projects are undertaken to allow other Chinese companies to gain preferential access to energy and other strategic resources; some of these investments have even been made on a loss-making basis to gain access to these nations' resources. This approach has been used in Africa and Latin America. China also touts its growing ODI as a sign of China's contribution to the economic development of other nations, as a further means of reassuring other nations and increasing China's influence[6] (Figure 5.1).

Foreign aid is a fourth major aspect of China's economic diplomacy. China's foreign aid includes both development and humanitarian assistance, with the latter as a new practice. China's development aid takes the form of grants, loans, and technical assistance, which is similar to official development assistance (ODA) as defined by the Organisation for Economic Cooperation and Development (OECD). Using the OECD standard, China's development aid is a "relatively small source of global aid," according to a Congressional Research Service report.[7] However in evaluating Chinese foreign aid, it is also important to include China's state-sponsored or subsidized overseas investment; this is often provided through the China Development Bank or the China Export-Import Bank, which are not part of China's

---

China: Ministry of Commerce of the People's Republic of China, September 27, 2008.

[6] China's cumulative ODI in 2004 was $37 billion. "China Makes More Overseas Investment in 2005 Mainly in Asia," *People's Daily Online*, February 11, 2006, as translated by OSC.

[7] Thomas Lum, Hannah Fischer, Julissa Gomez-Granger, and Anne Leland, *China Foreign Aid Activities in Africa, Latin America and Southeast Asia*, Congressional Research Service, Washington, D.C.: Library of Congress, February 2009, p. i.

Figure 5.1
China's Annual Outward Direct Investment, 1990–2007

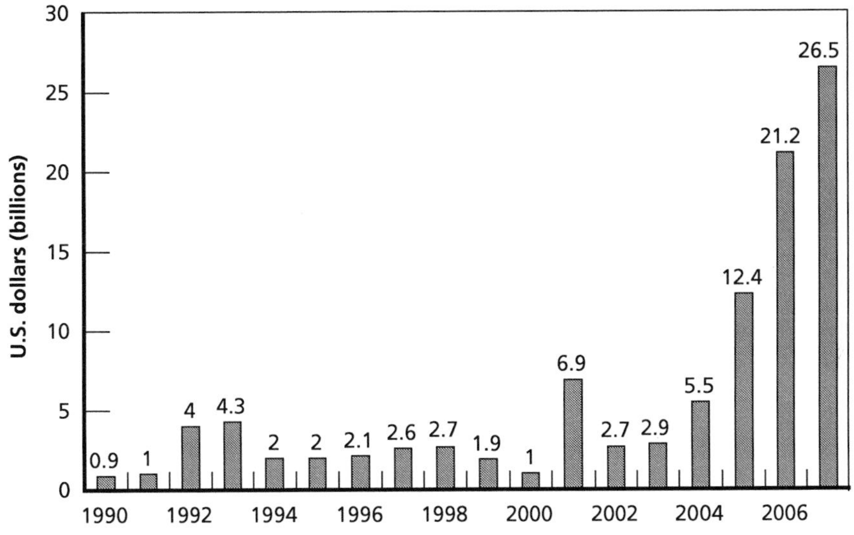

SOURCE: Ministry of Commerce of the People's Republic of China.

RAND *MG850-5.1*

nascent foreign aid bureaucracy. When this latter category of funds is factored in, China "becomes a major source of foreign aid."[8]

It remains unclear how the State Council organizes and directs China's foreign aid bureaucracy, which appears to be fragmented and uncoordinated. The government does not define foreign aid or publish comprehensive statistics, making calculations difficult and inconsistent. China's Ministry of Commerce, which is officially in charge of the foreign aid budget, started publishing aggregate statistics on foreign aid only in 2002.[9] The official Ministry of Commerce figure for external assistance in 2002 was $602.77 million; in 2003, it was $630.36

---

[8]   Lum et al., 2009, p. i.

[9]   Michael A. Glosney, *Meeting the Development Challenge in the 21st Century: American and Chinese Perspectives on Foreign Aid*, China Policy Series, Policy Brief 21, New York: National Committee on United States–China Relations, August 2006b.

million; in 2004, it was $731 million[10]; in 2005, it was $922 million; and in 2006, it was $1.1 billion.[11] According to CRS data, these statistics significantly undercount Chinese foreign assistance by not including, for example, subsidized financing for overseas investment projects. "PRC foreign assistance and government-supported economic projects in Africa, Latin America, and Southeast Asia grew from less than $1 billion in 2002 to $27.5 billion in 2006 and $25 billion in 2007."[12]

China's provision of foreign aid has grown particularly fast since 2004 as Beijing has sought to use its assistance to build and sustain political relations with its Asian neighbors and especially with African nations. In 2004, China pledged to provide $400 million to help finance, using preferential loans, the development of the first phase of a new railroad line in the Philippines. China has pledged to forgive the loan debts of poor countries in Southeast Asia (such as Cambodia and Laos); in 2005 and 2006, Hu Jintao promised to forgive more than $10 billion in past loans to African nations. Notably, during the November 2006 China-Africa Cooperation Forum (CACF) in Beijing, the Chinese government announced a large eight-part, multiyear development aid package for all African nations. The package included a doubling, by 2009, of China's 2006 level of aid to Africa; $5 billion in concessional financing to African companies; major loan forgiveness for

---

[10] These data are from Phillip C. Saunders, *China's Global Activism: Strategy, Drivers and Tools*, Institute for National Strategic Studies, Occasional Paper 4, Washington, D.C.: National Defense University Press, June 2006, p. 14; also see *2006 China Statistical Yearbook*, Beijing, China: China Statistics Press, 2006; *2007 China Statistical Yearbook*, Beijing, China: China Statistics Press, 2007.

The data from the statistical yearbooks were originally in Chinese yuan. The 2005 number was converted to dollars using the rate of 1.0 U.S. dollar = 8.1 yuan (December 15, 2005), and the 2006 number was converted to U.S. dollars using the rate of 1.0 U.S. dollar = 7.8 yuan (December 15, 2006). Exchange rates were provided by the International Monetary Fund.

[11] *2006 China Statistical Yearbook*, 2006; and *2007 China Statistical Yearbook*, 2007.

[12] Lum et al., 2009, p. i.

heavily indebted poor countries; and extensive technical assistance.[13] In June 2007, China agreed to forgive almost $10 million in Iraqi debt accumulated by the previous government—both government-to-government debt and that of Chinese state enterprises. Interestingly, a year later, Iraq concluded its first major oil deal with a foreign nation since 2003, with a Chinese state-owned firm, for technical assistance in developing oil fields; the deal was reportedly worth $3 billion.[14]

Although China's foreign aid has traditionally focused on development assistance (often with corresponding market access for Chinese firms), provision of humanitarian aid is a new and growing dimension of its foreign aid portfolio. In response to the tsunami disaster in Southeast Asia in 2004–2005, the Chinese government donated $83 million in assistance, which was the largest amount of humanitarian assistance China had ever provided at that time. The Chinese government publicly reported in early 2006 that in 2005 it had offered (but not necessarily distributed) a record amount of humanitarian aid:

---

[13] According to *Xinhua*, the eight specific steps included the following: (1) double its 2006 assistance to Africa by 2009; (2) provide $3 billion (U.S. dollars) of preferential loans and $2 billion of preferential buyers' credits to Africa in the next three years; (3) set up a China-Africa development fund, which will reach $5 billion, to encourage Chinese companies to invest in Africa and provide support to countries there; (4) build a conference center for the African Union to support African countries in their efforts to strengthen themselves through unity and support the process of African integration; (5) cancel debt in the form of all the interest-free government loans that matured at the end of 2005 and were owed by the heavily indebted poor countries and the least-developed countries in Africa that have diplomatic relations with China; (6) further open up China's market to Africa by increasing, from 190 to over 440, the number of export items to China receiving zero-tariff treatment from the least-developed countries in Africa having diplomatic ties with China; (7) establish three to five trade and economic cooperation zones in Africa in the next three years; (8) over the next three years, train 15,000 African professionals; send 100 senior agricultural experts to Africa; set up ten special agricultural technology demonstration centers in Africa; build 30 hospitals in Africa and provide RMB 300 million of grant for building 30 malaria-prevention and treatment centers to fight malaria in Africa; dispatch 300 youth volunteers to Africa; build 100 rural schools in Africa; and increase the number of Chinese government scholarships to African students from the current 2,000 per year to 4,000 per year. "Backgrounder: Eight Steps China Will Take to Boost China-Africa Strategic Partnership," *Xinhua*, January 30, 2007.

[14] Erica Goode and Riyadh Mohammed, "Iraq Signs Oil Deal with China Worth up to $3 Billion," *New York Times*, August 28, 2008.

almost one billion RMB ($123.45 million) in disaster relief to three large projects (e.g., Indian Ocean Tsunami relief, Pakistan earthquake relief, and Hurricane Katrina relief) as well as a smaller amount of aid to North Korea, Vietnam, Romania, Iran, Guinea-Bissau, and Ecuador. Chinese officials have stated that the government has established an "emergency response mechanism" to enable quick dispersal of disaster relief aid in the future.[15]

An Alternative Development Model?

China's economic diplomacy immediately raises concerns about whether it is promoting its experience of rapid and sustained economic growth as an alternative to Western models of development, a competition of ideas commonly referred to as the "Beijing Consensus" versus the "Washington Consensus." Although China clearly sees value in using a variety of economic and financial policies to promote Chinese interests, it is far less clear that it has a distinct development model, that others could replicate it, and that China is promoting itself as an alternative to U.S. or Western approaches.

China's economic policies over the last 30 years are not unique compared with other Asian countries, and China's policies have been fairly consistent with the Washington Consensus. China's hybrid "socialist-market economy" is similar (but not identical) to the post–World War II experiences of Japan, Singapore, South Korea, and Taiwan in using state ownership and state direction to promote industrial development, to build a large export sector, and to open up to foreign investment. Indeed, South Korea and Taiwan were one-party governments for the first several decades of their economic development.

China's approach has also been consistent with key attributes of the Washington Consensus; China has emphasized low fiscal deficits, gradual structural reforms, privatization, trade promotion, infrastructure development, workforce training, and innovation.[16] China ben-

---

[15] Cary Huang, "Record $1 Billion Yuan in International Aid Granted by Beijing in 2005," *South China Morning Post*, January 19, 2006; this media report is based on a Beijing press conference by then–Assistant Minister of Commerce Chen Jian.

[16] To be sure, there are some important differences between China's approach and the classic formulation of the Washington Consensus. The speed and scope of China's market-based

efited from a unique set of attributes that few economies share, such as the huge productivity gains associated with the transition from a largely agrarian to an industrial economy; a massive, low-cost workforce that has become increasingly well-skilled (but is still relatively low-cost); a huge and appealing domestic market; and an entrepreneurial tradition that emphasizes business competition.

For these and other reasons, Chinese leaders seldom proclaim that China represents a unique development model that others should follow, preferring to highlight China's unique conditions. Chinese leaders are happy to share China's experiences with developing nations (including both successes and failures) and to highlight the weaknesses of Western ideas.[17] But they also stop short of stating that China's success can and should be replicated by developing nations. This diplomatic approach is motivated, in part, by China's effort to appear cooperative and as not imposing its ideas on others. Some Chinese are concerned that promoting a Beijing Consensus would directly confront the United States and other Western powers, undermining its reassurance strategy. It is instructive that the idea of a Beijing Consensus was developed by a Western journalist, not by Chinese policymakers.[18] None of China's top leaders—the president, premier, or foreign minister—have promoted this idea, preferring instead to emphasize China's uniqueness.

To the extent that China is seen as promoting such a model, it is because many developing nations admire China's economic successes and profess support for a "China model." For example, many African nations during the 2006 China-Africa Cooperation Forum in Beijing noted their desire to replicate China's experiences, even though few have taken any steps resembling Chinese policies. Some developing

---

reforms have been far more gradual and partial than that proscribed under the "shock therapy" approach of the Washington Consensus. The state sector is smaller but remains sizable in China, even 30 years after the reform program began. For example, China's banking sector remains largely state-owned and most lending is state-directed.

[17] China's criticism of the responses of the United States, the World Bank, and the International Monetary Fund to the Asian Financial Crisis in 1997–1998 is a prominent example of its willingness to point out the failures of Western economic policymaking.

[18] Joshua Ramos Cooper, *The Beijing Consensus: Notes on the New Physics of Chinese Power*, London, UK: Foreign Policy Centre, 2004.

nations, such as Brazil and Venezuela, have sought partners in opposing some Western economic policies and have looked to China for support; they try to draw China into an effort to oppose these policies and practices, even though China supports many of them. China is most interested in increasing its global economic clout through trade and finance interactions (as described above) and by expanding its role in international financial institutions.

Leadership Diplomacy

China's top party and state leaders now frequently travel abroad in direct pursuit of China's diplomatic objectives. Some in China have termed this new trend "leadership diplomacy" (*lingdao waijiao* 领导外交). Although leaders of all countries conduct such activities, for China the number and frequency of leadership visits have significantly increased since the beginning of the reform period and especially under Hu Jintao. Before 1978, foreign trips were relatively few and evidenced no unique pattern. China's third generation of leaders, led by Jiang Zemin, increased the number of such trips. As demonstrated in Figure 5.2, China's top leaders (defined as the president, the premier, the head of the National People's Congress (NPC), or the chairman of the Chinese People's Political Consultative Conference) have significantly ramped up their foreign travels since 1992, growing from 122 between 1981 and 1991 to 424 in the 1992–2006 period.

As seen in Figure 5.3, the regional distribution of leaders' visits from 1949 to 2006 highlights, in broad terms, China's long-standing diplomatic priorities: Asia has been the primary focus for decades (with 250 visits), followed by Europe (196), Africa (92), Latin America (50), Oceania (26), and North America (19). The final figure of only 19 trips to North America should not be so surprising given the freeze in U.S.-China relations during the Cold War. According to a study by Chinese scholars Zhang Qingmin and Liu Bing, between 1949 and 1991 senior Chinese leaders visited North America only seven times; this compares with

Figure 5.2
Chinese Leaders' Trips Abroad, 1949–2006

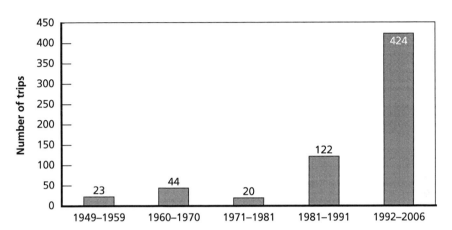

SOURCE: Zhang Qingmin and Liu Bing, "Shounao Chufang yu Zhongguo Waijiao"
[Leader's Trips Abroad and Chinese Diplomacy], *Guoji Zhengzhi Yanjiu* [International
Politics Quarterly], No. 106, April 2008, p. 3.
RAND *MG850-5.2*

98 trips to Asia, 54 to Europe, and 31 to Africa.[19] During the 1992–2006
period, senior leader visits increased most substantially to Asia, Europe,
and Latin America (Figure 5.4).

In the last ten years, China's top leaders have regularly used trips
to advance high-priority diplomatic objectives.[20] Several Politburo officials traveled to North Korea between 2003 and 2008 as part of China's effort to manage the North Korean nuclear crisis and the negotiations within the Six Party Process. Premier Wen Jiabao's frequent
travels abroad have been at the forefront of China's efforts to improve
its relations with East Asian and South Asian nations. Notably, Wen
Jiabao traveled to Thailand in 2003 in the wake of the SARS crisis in
China to reassure China's neighbors that it was taking serious steps

---

[19] These data are from Zhang Qingmin and Liu Bing, 2008, p. 3.

[20] Scott L. Kastner and Phillip C. Saunders, "Testing Chinese Diplomatic Priorities: The
Correlates of Leadership Travel Abroad Under Jiang Zemin and Hu Jintao," unpublished
presentation at the American Political Science Association annual meeting, Boston, Mass.,
August 30, 2008.

Figure 5.3
Regional Distribution of Chinese Leaders' Visits, 1949–2006

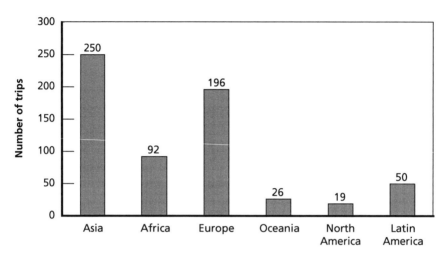

SOURCE: Zhang Qingmin and Liu Bing, 2008, p. 7.
RAND MG850-5.3

Figure 5.4
Period Breakdown of Chinese Leaders' Regional Visits, 1949–2006

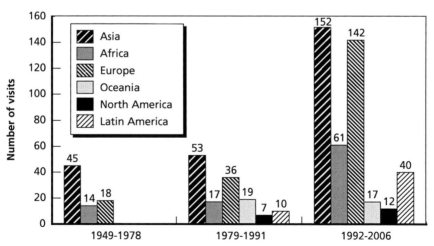

SOURCE: Zhang Qingmin and Liu Bing, 2008, p. 8.
RAND MG850-5.4

to curb the spread of the disease. Since then, Wen has become the senior Chinese representative to the annual week of meetings of the ASEAN+3 (ASEAN plus China, Japan, and South Korea) and the East Asia Summit. Wen hosted the ASEAN-China 15th anniversary conference in Nanning, China, in 2007, as a way to underscore the importance to China of its ties to ASEAN states and vice versa. Wen has also been at the forefront of China's effort to embrace India; he traveled to India for a major bilateral summit in April 2005 that resulted in the establishment of a strategic partnership with India—a first for these longtime rivals. Perhaps most significantly, Premier Wen visited Japan in April 2007 in a seminal visit that "thawed the ice" in Sino-Japanese relations and injected some stability into that rocky relationship.

Beyond Asia, Wen Jiabao has been at the center of China's effort to manage its response to the global financial crisis that began in 2008. Wen was China's representative to the World Economic Forum in Davos, Switzerland, in early 2009. With the intention of reassuring the international community, he publicly stated that China expected an 8 percent growth rate in 2009, defying most international projections. Attendance at Davos was followed by visits to capitals of the major EU states, including Berlin, Brussels (EU headquarters), Madrid, and London.[21] In 2006, Wen Jiabao took a week-long, seven-nation tour of Africa, which helped prepare for China's hosting of the high-level China-Africa summit meeting in November 2006, which included 48 African nations. Wu Bangguo, the chairman of the NPC and the second-highest official in the party, has often traveled abroad to establish dialogues with the elected parliaments in other nations with the goal of boosting the legitimacy of China's parliament in the eyes of Chinese citizens and other countries' populations.

President Hu Jintao's major trips abroad since assuming power in 2002 have been a central part of China's effort to expand its presence and influence in the developing world (mainly Africa, the Middle East, Central Asia, and Latin America) and specifically to improve China's access to strategic minerals and energy resources. Hu's four trips to

---

[21] Andrew Edgecliffe-Johnson, Gillian Tett, John Thornhill, and Catherine Belton, "Wen and Putin Criticise Western Leaders at Davos," *Financial Times*, January 29, 2009.

Africa (in 2002, 2006, 2007, and 2009) and two to Latin America (in 2004 and 2008) have directly expanded China's economic interactions with these regions.[22] Hu Jintao has visited Africa four times since 2002, visiting over 18 African nations in total, which is an unprecedented regional focus for a Chinese president. In early 2009, Hu traveled to the four, nonresource-rich African nations of Senegal, Mali, Tanzania, and Mauritius to try to underscore that China's Africa diplomacy was not just focused on gaining access to natural resources. This four-nation trip followed a longer 12-day tour in 2007 of seven African countries, including visits to such controversial destinations as Sudan and Zimbabwe.

Furthermore, Hu Jintao is actively involved in managing China's relations with former Soviet states. He has visited Russia almost annually since 2002, and he attends the annual summits of the Shanghai Cooperation Organization. In 2007 and 2008, he made state visits to Kyrgyzstan, Kazakhstan, Tajikistan, and Turkmenistan.

China also deploys the president for strategic purposes when it seeks to upgrade its commitment to a nation, to a group of countries, or to an international issue. In 2003, Hu Jintao attended, for the first and only time (to date), the China-EU summit when a "strategic partnership" was formed; this was during a period when Beijing sought to leverage tensions in trans-Atlantic relations to advance China-EU cooperation on international issues. In May 2008, Hu Jintao made a state visit to Japan to fully normalize China-Japan relations; this was the first trip to Japan for China's top leader since Jiang Zemin's 1998 visit, which many in both countries viewed as a failure because Jiang lectured the Japanese about historical issues. Hu Jintao is China's representative to the annual meetings of the G-8, even though China is not a full member of that group. Hu attended the G-20 summit in Washington in November 2008 and in London in April 2009.

Hu and Wen's presumed successors have jumped on the leadership diplomacy bandwagon. Vice President Xi Jinping, who many believe will succeed Hu Jintao, has similarly focused his foreign trips on improving China's ties with developing nations. During his first

---

[22] For useful data on the Chinese leader's travels abroad, see Saunders, 2006, pp. 21–22.

foreign trip as vice president, in 2008, he visited North Korea, Mongolia, and three Middle Eastern nations (Saudi Arabia, Yemen, and Qatar). Later that year, he visited five Latin American nations (Mexico, Jamaica, Colombia, Venezuela, and Brazil) and Malta. In February 2009, Xi again visited Venezuela, China's eighth largest supplier of imported crude oil (in 2007). Vice Premier Li Keqiang, during his first overseas trip in his current position, visited Kuwait and Indonesia in December 2008.

Another dimension of China's leadership diplomacy has been the designation and use of "special envoys" (*teshi daibiao* 特使代表) to handle particularly problematic issues in Chinese foreign policy. Since 1993, China has designated several new special envoys and deployed them all over the world. China's first special envoy was assigned to the North Korean nuclear issue, and China currently has designated envoys to address issues in Africa/Sudan, the Middle East, and, in 2009, to Afghanistan/Pakistan. As depicted in Figure 5.5, the number of foreign visits of special envoys increased substantially in 2006 and 2007, suggesting Chinese leaders' growing interest in this new diplomatic tool.

Multilateral Diplomacy

A new, important, and deftly used diplomatic tool for China is its participation in multilateral organizations (Tables 5.2 and 5.3). China clearly sees such organizations as venues in which to advance its vision of fostering a multipolar world, greater "democracy in international relations," and building a harmonious world. The 2008 national defense white paper was uniquely clear on this point, "China is playing an active and constructive role in multilateral affairs, thus notably elevating its international position and influence."[23] More instrumentally, China uses multilateral organizations as mechanisms for reassurance, gaining access to key economic inputs, limiting U.S. influence in certain regions,

---

23 *China's National Defense in 2008*, 2009.

Figure 5.5
Frequency of Special Envoys' Foreign Travels, 1993–2007

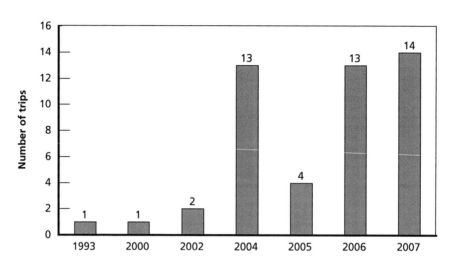

SOURCE: Li Zhifei, "Lengzhan Hou de Zhongguo Teshi Waijiao" [China's Special Envoy Diplomacy During the Post–Cold War Era], *Guoji Guanxi Xueyuan Xuebao*, No. 3, 2008, May 2008, p. 26.
NOTE: Foreign visits are counted as a single trip abroad.
RAND *MG850-5.5*

and expanding China's regional influence in general. In fact, China has played a central role in creating a variety of new multilateral forums in regions all over the world. This process has given Chinese leaders a unique stake in the vitality of these mechanisms.

China's embrace of multilateral organizations has been most pronounced and most effective in East Asia.[24] Since the early 1990s, China has become actively involved in the Asia Pacific Economic Cooperation (APEC) (1991), the ASEAN Regional Forum (ARF) (1994), ASEAN+1 (ASEAN plus China) (1996), ASEAN+3 (1997), and the East Asia Summit (EAS) (2005). Such participation has been instrumental in China's effort to burnish its image, grow economic cooperation, and

---

[24] China's use of and activities in such global multilateral organizations as the United Nations will be addressed below.

Table 5.2
China's Membership in Regional Organizations

Regional Organization	Level of Participation	Start Date	Members
		East Asia	
ASEAN	Dialogue partner	July 1996	ASEAN, China; this arrangement is also known as ASEAN+1
ASEAN+3	Member	December 1997	ASEAN, China, Japan, and South Korea
ARF	Member	July 1994	23 countries consisting of the ten ASEAN nations (Brunei, Burma, Cambodia, Indonesia, Laos, Malaysia, the Philippines, Singapore, Thailand, and Vietnam), 11 "Dialogue Partners" (Australia, Canada, China, EU, India, Japan, New Zealand, North Korea, Russia, South Korea, the United States), Mongolia, and Papua New Guinea
APEC	Member	November 1991	Australia, Brunei Darussalam, Canada, Chile, Hong Kong, Indonesia, Japan, Malaysia, Mexico, New Zealand, Papua New Guinea, People's Republic of China, Peru, the Philippines, Russia, Singapore, South Korea, Chinese Taipei, Thailand, the United States, and Vietnam
EAS (East Asia Summit)	Founding member	December 2005	Ten ASEAN nations and Australia, China, India, Japan, New Zealand, Russia, and South Korea
ACD	Founding member	June 2002	Bahrain, Bangladesh, Bhutan, Brunei Darussalam, Cambodia, China, India, Indonesia, Iran, Japan, Kazakhstan, Kuwait, Lao, Malaysia, Mongolia, Myanmar, Oman, Pakistan, Philippines, Qatar, Russia, Saudi Arabia, Singapore, South Korea, Sri Lanka, Tajikistan, Thailand, the United Arab Emirates, Uzbekistan, and Vietnam
		South Asia	
SAARC	Observer	November 2005	Afghanistan, Bangladesh, Bhutan, India, Maldives, Nepal, Pakistan, and Sri Lanka

Table 5.2—continued

Regional Organization	Level of Participation	Start Date	Members
Central Asia			
SCO	Founding member	June 2001	Kazakhstan, Kyrgyzstan, China, Russia, Tajikistan, and Uzbekistan
Latin America			
OAS	Observer	May 2004	35 independent nations of the Americas
Africa			
CACF	Founding member	October 2000	45 African countries
Middle East			
GCC	Cooperative partner, FTA agreement under negotiation	July 2004	Bahrain, Kuwait, Oman, Qatar, Saudi Arabia, and the United Arab Emirates
CACF	Founding member	September 2004	China and 22 countries of the Arab League

expand its regional influence. In 2003, China was key to the creation and maintenance of the Six-Party process for negotiating North Korea's denuclearization. In 2002, China was a founding member of the Asian Cooperation Dialogue (ACD), which fosters dialogue among separate regional organizations, such as ASEAN, the South Asian Association for Regional Cooperation (SAARC), and the Gulf Cooperation Council.

China has been working to expand regional nongovernment interactions as well. In 2001, a group of Chinese nationals and overseas Chinese business leaders established the Boao Forum for Asia (BFA), a nongovernmental, nonprofit international organization based on Hainan Island in China and modeled after the World Economic Forum in Davos. As with the Davos meeting, BFA draws together senior Asian officials, business leaders, and scholars. The BFA was the venue, in

Table 5.3
Regional Organizations Established by China

Regional Organization	Start Date	Ministerial/Summit Meetings	Members
SCO	April 1996 (Shanghai Five), June 2001 (SCO)	Nine summit meetings as of June 2009; many other minister-level meetings	Kazakhstan, Kyrgyzstan, China, Russia, Tajikistan, and Uzbekistan
CACF	October 2000	The first two minister-level conferences in October 2000 and December 2003; the third ministerial and first summit-level meeting in November 2006 in Beijing; the fourth ministerial will occur in Egypt in late 2009	45 African countries
CACF	September 2004	Two ministerial conferences in September 2004 and May 2006	22 countries of the Arab League
BFA	February 2001	Nine annual conferences held	Membership is not designated by nationality as a nongovernment forum

2003, for the launching of China's new foreign policy strategy of "peaceful rise/peaceful development."

Beyond East Asia, China initiated the formation, in 1996, of the Shanghai Five, which included China, Russia, Kazakhstan, Kyrgyzstan, and Tajikistan; this forum subsequently became the more formal Shanghai Cooperation Organization (SCO) in 2001 with the addition of Uzbekistan. Since 2005, China has been an official observer of SAARC, along with the United States.[25] (In exchange, China supported India's participation in the SCO as an observer.)

Beyond Asia, in 2000 China formed the China-Africa Cooperation Forum; it has held three ministerial meetings to date, including

---

[25] Both China and the United States joined as observers in 2005. Other SAARC observers include Japan, South Korea, and the European Union. During the 2007 meeting, Iran requested observer status, which had not been granted as of fall 2008.

hosting a major 48-nation summit in Beijing in late 2006. In 2004, China created the China-Arab Cooperation Forum that has held two ministerial meetings to date. China joined many of the major regional forums in Latin America. It become a full member of the Inter-American Development Bank (IADB) in 2008 and is an observer in the Organization of American States (OAS). It has established dialogues with the Rio Group, the Mercosur common market group, the Caribbean Community, and the Latin American Conference.[26]

Strategic Partnerships

China has developed a diplomatic mechanism to expand its international influence—the establishment of "strategic partnerships" (*zhanlue huoban guanxi* 战略伙伴关系) with both individual states and groupings of states. Table 5.4 summarizes these partnerships.

For China, *strategic partnership* has a different meaning from the Western connotation of the term.[27] They are not treated as quasi-military alliances, which involve extensive security and military cooperation, as implied by the term "strategic." Rather, in the Chinese foreign policy lexicon, a partnership is strategic for two reasons: (1) It is comprehensive, including all aspects of bilateral relations (e.g., economic, cultural, political, and security), and (2) both countries agree to make a long-term commitment to bilateral relations, in which bilateral problems are evaluated in that context and, importantly, occasional tensions do not derail them. Establishing these partnerships allows China to raise the level of its interactions

---

[26]   David Shambaugh, "China's New Foray into Latin America," *YaleGlobal Online*, November 17, 2008.

[27]   For an introduction to Chinese thinking about strategic partnerships, see Ye Jiang, "Luelun Gaige Kaifang Yilai Zhongguo Quanfangwei Waijiao de Daguo Waijiao Zhong de Daguo Zhanlue Tiaozheng" [A General Discussion of the Strategic Adjustment of the Big Power Strategy in China's Omni-Dimensional Diplomacy Since the Reform and Opening Period], *Mao Zedong Deng Xiaoping Lilun Yanjiu* [Mao Zedong, Deng Xiaoping Theory Research], No. 8, August 2008, pp. 38–44.

Table 5.4
China's Strategic Partnerships

Country	Formulation	Date/Venue	Joint Military Exercises	Recognize China as a "Market Economy"
		Major Powers/Developed Countries		
Russia	Strategic Cooperative Partnership/Treaty on Good Neighborliness, Friendship and Cooperation	1996/2001 Jiang Zemin–Boris Yeltsin summit	Peace Mission 2005; Peace Mission 2007	September 2004
France	Comprehensive Strategic Partnership	1997	Joint maritime search-and-rescue exercise (2004, 2007)	
Italy	Comprehensive Strategic Partnership	2004 Wen Jiabao visit		
UK	Comprehensive Strategic Partnership	2004 Wen Jiabao visit	Joint maritime search-and-rescue exercise (2004)	
Canada	Strategic Partnership	2005 Hu Jintao visit		
Portugal	All Around Strategic Partnership	2005 Wen Jiabao visit		
Spain	Comprehensive Strategic Partnership	2005 Hu Jintao visit		
Germany	Comprehensive Strategic Partnership/Strategic Partnership in Global Responsibility	2006 Chancellor Angela Merkel visits China		
South Korea	Strategic Cooperative Partnership	2008 President Lee Myung-bak's first visit to China		November 2005

Table 5.4—continued

Country	Formulation	Date/Venue	Joint Military Exercises	Recognize China as a "Market Economy"
		Developing Countries		
Brazil	Long-term and Stable Strategic Partnership	1996 Jiang Zemin visit		November 2004
Mexico	Comprehensive Strategic Partnership	2003		November 2004
Argentina	Comprehensive Strategic Partnership	2005 Hu Jintao visit		December 2004
Venezuela	Comprehensive Strategic Partnership	2005 Hu Jintao visit		
India	Strategic and Cooperative Partnership for Peace and Prosperity	2005 Wen Jiabao visit	Joint maritime search-and-rescue exercise (2003, 2005); Joint counterterrorism exercise (2007, 2008)	
Kazakhstan	Comprehensive Strategic Partnership	2005 Hu Jintao visit	Joint counterterrorism exercise with SCO states (2003)	September 2004
Indonesia	Comprehensive Strategic Partnership	2005 Hu Jintao visit		
South Africa	Strategic Partnership	2004 Zeng Qinghong visit; expanded in June 2006		June 2004
Nigeria	Strategic Partnership	2005 President Obasanjo visit to China		December 2004
Algeria	Strategic Partnership	2004 Hu Jintao visit to Algeria		November 2006

Table 5.4—continued

Country	Formulation	Date/Venue	Joint Military Exercises	Recognize China as a "Market Economy"
Vietnam	Strategic and Comprehensive Cooperative Partnership	2008 General Secretary of the Communist Party Nong Duc Manh visit to China	Joint maritime patrols of the Tonkin Gulf (2007)	September 2004
Multilateral Organization/Region				
Africa	Strategic Partnership for Sustainable Development in the 21st Century	2000 First China-Africa Cooperation Forum in Beijing		Benin, Democratic Republic of the Congo, Djibouti, Nigeria, Togo South Africa, and Suriname
EU	Comprehensive Strategic Partnership	2003 During 6th China-EU summit		None
ASEAN	Strategic Partnership for Peace and Prosperity	2003 During 9th ASEAN+1 meeting in Bali, Indonesia		All ten ASEAN countries recognized China's market economy status in September 2004

SOURCES: Multiple English news reports based on searches in Lexis-Nexis news database and Chinese media sources.

NOTE: The Chinese search terms were "zhanlue" (strategic) and "huoban" (partner) or "guanxi" (relations).

with partner countries (or groupings) and also allows China to set the scope, content, and pace of engagement. This logic explains the eclectic variety of states, groupings of states, and multilateral organizations with which China has established such strategic partnerships.[28]

These strategic partnerships have broad and varied content. China stresses several themes, including opportunities for joint economic development resulting from trade and investment; coordination in international affairs, which means adopting common foreign policy positions, such as at the U.N.; cooperation on nontraditional security issues; enhancing the influence of multilateral organizations; the mutual endorsement of U.N. principles and the rule of law in international relations; and promoting China's concepts of "democracy and equality in international relations."[29]

China has more specific goals in pursuing these partnerships as well. It uses them as mechanisms to expand economic opportunities (especially to gain preferential access to nations' markets, investment, and natural resources), to stabilize and shape China's regional security environment, to reduce external constraints on China, and to bolster its international reputation as a responsible major power. Importantly, Beijing uses these diplomatic structures to generate bargaining leverage in its bilateral interactions. Such partnerships allow China to define the standards of cooperation that partners are expected to meet; this increases China's ability to manipulate its interlocutors to accept Chinese goals.

In recent years, China has also initiated "strategic dialogues" with many of these nations; this is a further indication of its effort to deepen political relationships to further generate influence and leverage. These dialogues usually occur at the level of deputy foreign minister or vice foreign minister, and the topics cover a wide range of security issues including arms control, WMD nonproliferation, nontraditional secu-

---

[28] Interviews with Chinese officials and scholars, Beijing and Shanghai, 2005, 2006, and 2008.

[29] These themes are based on the author's reading of several final documents and official statements issued after the formation of these partnerships and after official bilateral meetings with China's strategic partners.

rity challenges, and long-standing territorial disputes. China first established such a channel with Russia in 1996 following a summit meeting, but it was not given the name of "strategic dialogue" until years later. A similar pattern emerged with France in the late 1990s. In 2005, China's convening of such strategic dialogues took off. In that year alone, Beijing held inaugural sessions with the United States, India, the UK, Japan, and the EU. In 2006, during a summit meeting in Beijing, China and Germany also pledged to initiate an annual strategic dialogue.

To varying degrees, China has used its strategic partnerships with major powers, such as with Russia, France, and the EU, to broaden its economic relationships, to foster the development of other power centers in global politics, and to seek support for its vision of a multipolar global order. These major power partnerships do not amount to building an anti-U.S. coalition to balance against U.S. power. However, these partnerships allow China greater options and help it to foster an environment that could be used to constrain U.S. unilateral actions, especially if that power is directed at Chinese interests.[30] There is no overtly anti-U.S. element in such Chinese diplomacy, but China's discomfort with perceived U.S. unilateralism is one of the drivers of its strategic partnerships. These themes and motivations were readily apparent in the 2003 EU-China Joint Statement, which founded that strategic partnership during a period of trans-Atlantic tension, as well as in the Russia-China Joint Communiqué and the SCO's summit statement in July 2005.

China's strategic partnerships with these major powers are bounded by two considerations that limit their potential to be potent mechanisms for balancing U.S. power. First, China's interests with all of these major powers, especially Russia and India, both converge and diverge—on different issues and to different degrees. There is no single, dominant political or strategic logic to any of these strategic partnerships that could serve as the basis for collectively and consistently coun-

---

[30] Prominent Chinese examples of such U.S. behavior include the U.S. use of force in Kosovo and Iraq, NATO expansion, the Proliferation Security Initiative, and the U.S. withdrawal from the Anti-Ballistic Missile Treaty.

tervailing U.S. power. Indeed, most of China's strategic partners are not interested in creating a *de facto* coalition to balance U.S. power, with the possible exception of Russia. These nations have numerous interests in positive relations with the United States. Also, although there are many cooperative dimensions to China's strategic partnerships, they are also fraught with tensions on both economic and security questions. For example, Russia and China may have common interests related to constraining U.S. influence globally and in Central Asia, but they diverge on economic issues and security questions revolving around access to Central Asian energy supplies and Chinese influence in Russia's Far East.[31] Also, for China, Russia has shown itself to be an unreliable partner in the past. China's unwillingness in summer 2008 to endorse the Russian position on the independence of the Georgian enclaves exemplifies the limits of the Sino-Russian strategic partnership.

A second major consideration is that, historically, China has not favored or relied on alliances (or even strong bilateral partnerships) in its diplomacy. China's historic disposition in favor of independence and against relying on alliances calls into question the extent to which it can or will rely on them now. Although China has formed alliances in the past (e.g., the China–Soviet Union alliance of the 1950s), it was never entirely comfortable with them. Beijing prefers, instead, greater autonomy to maximize its leverage and maneuverability.[32] This enduring predisposition is evident in the intensifying concerns among Chinese elites about the economic and security vulnerabilities that have resulted from China's global interdependence and the globalization of

---

[31] On the latter issues, see Paul Goble, "Only Interests Are Permanent: Russian-Chinese Relations as a Challenge to American Foreign Policy," testimony before the U.S.-China Economic and Security Review Commission on "China's Growing Global Influence: Objectives and Strategies," July 21, 2005.

[32] Fairbank, 1968; Garver, 1993, pp. 2–30; Andrew J. Nathan and Robert S. Ross, *Great Wall and Empty Fortress*, New York: W. W. Norton and Co., 1997; Harry Harding, "China's Cooperative Behavior," in Thomas W. Robinson and David Shambaugh, eds., *Chinese Foreign Policy: Theory and Practice*, Oxford, UK: Clarendon Press, 1994, pp. 375–400; and David Shambaugh, "Patterns of Interaction in Sino-American Relations," in Thomas W. Robinson and David Shambaugh, *Chinese Foreign Policy: Theory and Practice*, Oxford, UK: Clarendon Press, 1994, pp. 197–223.

national security challenges.[33] China's historical predispositions were further confirmed in 2001 when Russia shifted away from its emerging anti-U.S. cooperation with China and turned back toward greater rapprochement with the United States, even before 9/11. Specifically, Russia abandoned China in their joint opposition to U.S. missile defense policies.

These events, thus, suggest a third possible constraint on the scope of China's strategic partnerships: Most major powers have more interests at stake in their relations with the United States than with China. Some states may not be willing to jeopardize their ties with the United States to coordinate with China in an effort, implicit or explicit, to constrain the United States.

Military Diplomacy[34]

Military diplomacy has assumed a greater role in China's international behavior. A key turning point came in 2004 when China indicated in its national defense white paper that it had elevated the value of military diplomacy "to the strategic level" in national statecraft.[35] Following this important determination, PLA actions have since reflected a greater use of bilateral and multilateral military-to-military interactions to broaden its political relations with neighbors in East, Central, and South Asia, as well as Africa and Latin America. China is clearly using its military diplomacy to reassure Asian nations, to demystify the PLA, to expand China's influence with militaries, to gain experience

---

[33] Yong Deng and Thomas G. Moore, "China Views Globalization: Toward a New Great-Power Politics?" *Washington Quarterly*, Vol. 27, No. 3, Summer 2004, pp. 117–136.

[34] This section draws on the data provided in several past Chinese defense white papers, including *China's National Defense in 2002*, 2002; *China's National Defense in 2004*, 2004; *China's National Defense in 2006*, 2006; and *China's National Defense in 2008*, 2009; also see Kenneth W. Allen and Eric A. McVaden, *China's Foreign Military Relations*, Washington, D.C.: Henry L. Stimson Center, October 1999.

[35] For the first time in a national defense white paper, the 2004 white paper's section on "national defense policy" included a subsection on "military exchanges and cooperation."

and knowledge from more capable militaries, and to shape PLA counterparts' perceptions of China.

Although the content of these exchanges is still quite limited given the PLA's penchant for carefully guarding national defense information, the scope of China's military exchanges is growing. According to China's 2008 national defense white paper:

> China has established military ties with over 150 countries, and has military attaché offices in 109 countries. A total of 98 countries have military attach offices in China. In the past two years [2006–2008] senior PLA delegations have visited more than 40 countries, and defense ministers and chiefs of the general staff from more than 60 countries have visited China.
>
> . . . .
>
> In the past two years [2006–2008] it has sent over 900 military students to more than 30 countries. Twenty military educational institutions in China have established and maintained intercollegiate exchange relations with their counterparts in over 20 countries, including the United States, Russia, Japan and Pakistan. Meanwhile, some 4,000 military personnel from more than 130 countries have come to China to study at Chinese military educational institutions.[36]

This expanding breadth of China's military diplomacy is a further indication that China is using such exchanges to manage its security relations with other nations. These interactions could become more substantive over time, depending on China's goals and recipients' willingness to increase interactions with the PLA.

Moreover, China now conducts *annual* defense exchanges with all its Asian neighbors, select European and African countries, and major powers such as the United States and Russia; it even conducts intelligence exchanges within some of its defense consultations. Joint exercises have become a new component of China's defense diplomacy. From 2002 to 2008, the PLA conducted over 40 joint military exer-

---

[36] *China's National Defense in 2008*, 2009.

cises and joint training exercises with over 20 countries, which is a new and growing practice for the PLA.[37] China has also invited other countries to attend its military exercises and has observed major Western military exercises, such as U.S. Pacific Command's 2006 Valiant Shield exercise off Guam.[38]

As part of its military diplomacy, China continues to export conventional weapons to a regular collection of small countries in Asia (e.g., Burma, Cambodia, Pakistan, and Thailand), sub-Saharan Africa (e.g., Sudan and Zimbabwe), and the Middle East (e.g., Algeria, Egypt, and Iran). Globally, China's annual arms deliveries have remained at a limited level for the past decade, between $500 million to $1 billion per year. This ranks China as the fifth- or sixth-largest exporter to developing nations, and its share of the global market has remained between 3 and 5 percent (albeit with an uptick to almost 7 percent in 2007). U.S. and Russian arms exports dominate the global market (Figure 5.6).

Chinese arms exports are not a major source of political influence for China but rather reflect the buyers' lack of access to other suppliers or their lack of funds. The continued lack of appeal of China's inexpensive but often unreliable weapon systems reduces China's ability to use such deals to forge long-term strategic relations with countries that have access to more advanced systems on the global arms market. China's long-standing defense industrial relationship with Pakistan is a partial exception. China's weapons are most appealing to two categories of states: small, poor countries (mainly in Africa) who cannot afford more advanced systems, and countries such as

---

[37] The maritime exercises were usually search-and-rescue exercises. The 2005 China-Russia large-scale amphibious assault exercise on the Shandong Peninsula was an obvious exception. The land-based joint exercises, usually with Central Asian states, were often termed counter-terrorism exercises and varied in complexity. "2007 Zhongguo Junfang Junshi Yanxi Midu Pinfan Kancheng 'Junshi Nian'" [China's Military Exercises Frequent in 2007; It Could Be Called 'Military Exercise Year'], *Zhongguo Qingnian Bao* [China Youth Daily], December 28, 2007.

[38] In 2005, according to Chinese data, China invited 41 military observers from 24 countries to watch the "North Sword–2005" exercise organized by the Beijing Military Area Command.

Figure 5.6
Chinese Arms Exports to Developing Nations, 2000–2007

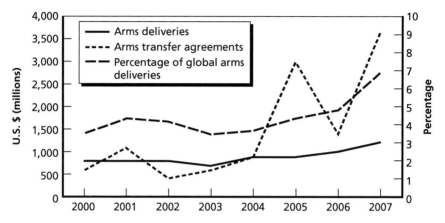

SOURCE: Richard F. Grimmett, *Conventional Arms Transfers to Developing Nations, 2000–2007*, Congressional Research Service, Washington, D.C.: Library of Congress, October 2008.

RAND *MG850-5.6*

Burma and Sudan whose access to the global arms market is restricted. As a result, China has sold to the same set of countries for the last decade, with the occasional one-off deals. The limited competitiveness of Chinese arms exports could change if, in the coming years, China develops next-generation systems and then decides to export the more advanced weapon systems that currently populate the PLA's arsenal. If this shift occurred, then arms sales could become a more significant part of China's security cooperation with other countries and a source of political influence.

CHAPTER SIX

China's Foreign Policy Actions

China has developed and deployed numerous effective policies to shape its external environment in pursuit of its top international objectives, as defined in Chapter Four. This is evident in the activism and the diversity of its statecraft: China has systematically expanded the scope and improved the quality of its bilateral relationships; it has demonstrated a pronounced embrace of multilateral organizations, in numerous regions and on several functional issues; its economic diplomacy is robust and multifaceted; and Beijing has better incorporated military diplomacy into its foreign policy quiver. This chapter examines the content and character of these policy actions as they are reflected in its diplomacy all over the world.

Policy Framework for Foreign Relations

China has expanded the depth, scope, and quality of its bilateral relationships in the last decade. This is part and parcel of China's ongoing effort both to leverage existing influence and to generate new influence. This has been a distinct trend in Chinese diplomacy and will likely remain so given China's long-standing preference for bilateral interactions, even in the context of a greater use of multilateralism.

China's bilateral relationships are guided by a principle that informs how Chinese leaders rank and value them. Chinese officials and scholars cite the following principle: "Major power relations are *critical (or key)*; relations with neighboring countries are *primary (or the priority)*; and relations with developing countries are the *foundation (or* base)" (*da guo shi guanjian, zhoubian shi shouyao, fazhanzhong guojia shi jichu* 大国是关键, 周边是首要, 发展中国家是基础). In recent years, a fourth element has been added to this principle: "Multilateral is the stage" (*duobian shi wutai* 多边是舞台). As an indication of the relevance of these ideas, Hu Jintao even referred to them in his report to the CCP's 17th Party Congress in October 2007.[1] Chinese officials and scholars refer to the entire four-part phrase as the "four big pillars" (*si da zhizhu* 四大支柱) of Chinese foreign policy.

The application of this principle to China's actual foreign policy behavior is not fixed, and Chinese scholars debate how much it should, can, and does guide actual policymaking.[2] Specifically, the implied relative prioritization between "major powers" and China's "neighbors" (*zhoubian guojia* 周边国家) vacillates over time and among leaders. Many Chinese analysts argue that China should focus most of its energies on neighboring nations to ensure a stable and secure regional security environment and that China should not become too preoccupied with major power relations and the perceived status associated with those relations. In fact, as of 2009, this view seems to dominate Chinese policymaking.[3] Others in China argue that such policies cannot come at the expense of China's relations with the United States, Russia, Japan, and Europe, which are central to ensuring a stable regional environment and to facilitating global stability and prosperity. In this sense,

---

[1]   Some official Chinese sources still refer to this phrase as a "guiding principle" (*zhidao fangzhen*) of China's foreign affairs work; Hu Jintao, 2007; Yang Jiechi, 2008; Shen Guofang, 2007; Ruan Zongze, "Zhongguo Waijiao Chuangzao Heping Jueqi Pingtai" [Chinese Foreign Affairs: Creating the Peaceful Rise Platform], *Liaowang Xinwen Zhoukan* [Liaowang Weekly], No. 50, December 15, 2003, pp. 14–16; and Cai Wu, online interview with Vice Minister of the CCP Central Committee's International Liason Department, "Jianchi Fengxing Heping Waijiao Zhengce Tigao Yingdui Guoji Jushi Nengli" [Persist in Pursuing a Peaceful Foreign Policy and Improving Our Ability to Respond to the International Situation], June 21, 2005.

[2]   For a novel and interesting criticism of some of these principles, see Wang Jisi, "Guanyu Gouzhu Zhongguo Guoji Zhanlue de Jidian Kanfa" [Some Thoughts on Building a Chinese International Strategy], *Guoji Zhengzhi Yanjiu* [International Politics Quarterly], No. 4, 2007, pp. 1–5.

[3]   Shen Guofang, 2007; and interviews with Chinese officials and scholars, Beijing and Shanghai, 2007.

stable and amicable relations with major powers are necessary, but not sufficient, for the success of China's rise, as unspecified as that goal remains among Chinese policymakers.[4]

The tension between these two priorities (e.g., major powers versus regional powers) involves a constant balancing act for China, and its handling of this tension will provide insights into the foreign policy preferences of its current and future leaders.[5] Some in China maintain that Jiang Zemin placed the priority on improving major power relations because of his personal preference for (and presumed status associated with) interacting with foreign leaders from major powers. By contrast, Chinese analysts argue that Hu Jintao appears to have taken a more balanced and pragmatic approach toward major power relations: He emphasized them when necessary while putting greater energy into regional diplomacy in Asia to stabilize China's periphery (which has seen numerous crises) and growing China's influence with developing nations.[6] China's relations with each of these three categories of states—major power, peripheral states, and developing nations—are analyzed below.

Relations with Major Powers[7]

Since the early 1990s, Chinese leaders have articulated three principles to guide China's relations with major powers: "non-alliance, non-confrontation, and not directed against any third party" (*bu jiemeng, bu duikang, bu zhendui di san fang* 不结盟, 不对抗, 不针对第三方).[8]

---

[4] Interviews with Chinese officials and scholars, Beijing and Shanghai, 2005 and 2006.

[5] This tension in Chinese foreign policy will be addressed in more detail in Chapter Seven.

[6] Interviews with Chinese officials and scholars, Beijing and Shanghai, 2005, 2008.

[7] In most mainstream Chinese analyses of international relations, the countries referred to as "major powers" are the United States, Russia, Japan, and the European Union. Some Chinese analyses treat Russia as a middle power, but it is most often referred to as a major power.

[8] Pang Xingchen, 2004, pp. 807–808; *Guoji Zhanlue yu Anquan Xingshi Pinggu 2004–2005*, 2005, pp. 114–133; and Zhang Youwen and Huang Renwei, 2004, pp. 123–155.

At a basic level, these principles indicate the leaders' general approach to managing relations with major powers. These principles are used within the Chinese bureaucracy to communicate leaders' goals, so they have value and relevance by dint of that function. It would be a mistake to dismiss these principles as entirely propagandistic. They are broadly consistent with China's interactions with other major powers, but they do not capture the complexity and subtleties in China's relations with the United States, Russia, and others.

Economic linkages play a strong and persistent role in China's relations with major powers, specifically with the United States, Japan, and the EU. For China, there is a consistent economic logic to these relationships, which is key to understanding China's policies toward these states. China has developed and grown ties with them to ensure access to their markets, investment, and technologies. The United States, EU, and Japan have been for the past 30 years and continue to be among China's top trading partners and sources of investment.

However, China's rhetoric about and actions toward major powers have only partially adhered to the three principles noted above. Although China has not formed any alliances, its efforts to constrain U.S. influence globally and to limit U.S. and Japanese perceived efforts to constrain China in Asia have become distinct, albeit not primary, features of its international behavior. China has not made overt rivalry with the United States or Japan a feature of its diplomacy but, as argued above, competition exists (with varying degrees of intensity).

United States

China's relations with the United States have a distinctly different dynamic from its relations with other great powers. Since normalization, China has, on balance, given U.S.-China relations pride of place in much of its foreign policy. Chinese policymakers have historically treated U.S.-China relations as Beijing's most important relationship—first, because the United States is seen as a critical source of trade, investment, and technology and, second, because it believes that if this relationship deteriorates, China's "period of strategic opportunity" to reach the next stage of national development would be disrupted.

The U.S.-China relationship is also unique for China among its ties with major powers because it is currently characterized by a great deal of cooperation and competition—on both economic and security issues. At specific times, both the cooperative and competitive elements of the relationship have been quite intense; Washington's and Beijing's mutual efforts to restrain North Korea's nuclear program have overlapped with growing disagreements about how to respond to Iran's nuclear program and how to resolve festering disagreements in bilateral economic relations.

The dueling cooperative and competitive dimensions of bilateral ties are structural features of U.S.-China relations. On the one hand, stable bilateral relations are important to both nations' economic and security interests; outright conflict would be costly for both. On the other hand, Beijing feels threatened by U.S. global predominance and some aspects of U.S. Asia policy (as discussed above); Washington is equally concerned about China's growing economic and military power, and U.S. leaders remain deeply uncertain about China's future intentions. The possibility of armed conflict over Taiwan is driving military planners and military modernization programs in both countries; this possibility, and the insecurity it generates, looms darkly as a major structural constraint on more cooperative bilateral relations. The latter force risks a militarization of the competitive dimensions of U.S.-China relations. As a reflection of these complexities, Chinese policymakers commonly use the principle of "seeking common ground while reserving differences" to characterize U.S.-China relations and to capture its complexities, albeit subtly.[9] No leaders on either side currently refer to bilateral relations as a "strategic partnership," largely at U.S. insistence; rather, U.S. and Chinese policymakers have referred to their relations using a bevy of adjectives, such as positive, constructive, cooperative, candid, and comprehensive.[10]

---

[9] Wang Jisi, 2004.

[10] Under the George W. Bush administration, U.S. officials referred to U.S.-China ties as "cooperative, constructive and candid." Official Chinese speeches use only the former two words, not "candid." The latter term was an American addition. Barack Obama's administration refers to U.S.-China ties as "positive, cooperative and comprehensive."

How does this situation influence Chinese policies toward the United States? It manifests in Chinese policies that seek to expand opportunities for cooperation (to prevent outright rivalry from developing) and to constrain the United States where possible. These two goals are partly reflected in the CCP's guiding principle for U.S.-China relations of "increase trust, reduce problems, strengthen cooperation, and avoid confrontation" (*zengjia xinren, jianshao mafan, jiaqiang hezuo, bu gao duikang* 增加信任，减少麻烦，加强合作，不搞对抗). This strategic guideline was initially articulated by Deng in the early 1990s, reiterated frequently by Jiang Zemin, and persists today, albeit commonly in the form of official references to "developing cooperation and avoiding confrontation" (*fazhan hezuo, bu gao duikang* 发展合作，不搞对抗). China's continued use of this and other official phrases will serve as a bellwether for the direction of its policies toward the United States.[11]

Chinese policymaking toward the United States in the 2000s reflects this dual approach. China used the events of 9/11 and the grand shift in U.S. national security priorities as an opportunity to put relations on a more solid foundation. Chinese policymakers signaled to the United States that China wants to avoid becoming a strategic competitor of the United States. Since then, China has sought to expand bilateral cooperation on several fronts. Regardless of the scope and content of Chinese cooperation on these and other security issues, which varies from thin to robust, Chinese policymakers and analysts regularly stress the high quality of U.S.-China cooperation on combating global terrorism and WMD proliferation, highlighting it as a new basis of stability in bilateral relations.[12]

As China's regional and global interests have diversified, practical cooperation with the United States on nontraditional security issues has grown. U.S. and Chinese agendas on WMD proliferation have generally converged in the last decade, and new areas of real coopera-

---

[11] On the origins of this phrase, see Gong Li, 2004; for more recent uses, see Chu Shulong, "U.S.-China Relations: Stability Overtaking All," *Huanqiu Shibao* [Global Times], April 19, 2006, as translated by OSC; this official line can also be found in Pang Xingchen, 2004.

[12] Wang Jisi, 2005; and Swaine, 2004.

tion have also opened on such issues as combating infectious diseases, narcotics and human trafficking, and organized crime. According to U.S. government assessments, China has been helpful on several global security issues, including North Korea's and Iran's nuclear programs; political and economic reconstruction in Iraq and Afghanistan; UNSC deliberations on Lebanon, Burma, and Sudan; and in generating international support for global health and energy security initiatives. Nevertheless, there is much more the United States seeks from China.[13]

There is a competitive dimension to China's U.S. policy as well: countering perceived U.S. efforts to limit China's capabilities and influence, in Asia and globally.[14] Beijing seeks to create the conditions under which U.S. policy cannot frustrate or hinder China's top foreign policy objectives in the near term and the ultimate goal of national rejuvenation as a great power. China also wants to be involved in all major decisions affecting its economic and security interests. On the one hand, this involves probing (mainly in Asia) for ways to reduce perceived U.S. containment and to constrain U.S. freedom of action in the region, especially with regard to U.S. efforts to secure regional assistance in prosecuting a military conflict over Taiwan. China seeks to create a regional environment that is highly sensitive to Chinese preferences and interests. On the other hand, China seeks to accomplish the above goal in ways that do not openly and brazenly appear to compete with U.S. goals or otherwise confront the United States. As an expression of China's effort to balance these competing goals, some

---

[13] These Chinese activities are detailed in John D. Negroponte, Deputy Secretary of State, "U.S.-China Relations in the Era of Globalization," opening statement before the Senate Foreign Relations Committee, May 15, 2008; and Thomas J. Christensen, Deputy Assistant Secretary of State for East Asian and Pacific Affairs, statement before the U.S.-China Economic and Security Review Commission on "Shaping China's Global Choices Through Diplomacy," March 18, 2008. See also Thomas J. Christensen, Deputy Assistant Secretary of State for East Asian and Pacific Affairs, testimony before the U.S.-China Economic and Security Review Commission on "China's Role in the World: Is China a Responsible Stakeholder?" August 3, 2006a.

[14] Given the sensitivity of this issue, few Chinese openly express such sentiments about U.S. policy and the dilemmas these views pose for China's U.S. policy. These arguments are based on interviews with Chinese officials and scholars, Beijing and Shanghai, 2005, 2006, and 2008. One useful source on this issue is Pang Xingchen, 2004.

Chinese strategists now argue that China can live with a hegemonic power but they oppose hegemonic behavior. This distinction allows Chinese policymakers and analysts to balance the need for stable U.S.-China relations against their concerns about U.S. predominance and Washington's perceived unilateral use of its power, which many Chinese fear could be directed at China in the future.[15]

These dueling Chinese goals have manifested in various efforts, at the regional and global levels, to reduce the U.S. ability to pressure China and to create greater space and leverage for China. In the late 1990s, Chinese diplomats approached various East Asian nations about pulling away from their alliances and security partnerships with the United States in an effort to remold regional security affairs. This effort was partly reflected in China's promulgation of its "new security concept," which, in its initial incarnation in 1997, offered an alternative vision to the U.S. alliance-based "hub-and-spoke" security system in Asia.[16] This attempt faltered because few U.S. allies and security partners accepted China's proposals, preferring the reliability of U.S. security commitments. More recent Chinese actions to secure its periphery are addressed in the section below on China's diplomacy in Asia; most of China's actions in East Asia are focused on reassuring regional nations, expanding the role of regional organizations and securing support for China's position on Taiwan. These efforts seek to create a regional security environment in which other states do not seek to balance China and pay more heed to its views.

Beyond Asia, China's efforts to constrain U.S. power are expressed in Chinese calls for more "democracy in international relations," which is a code phrase for opposition to perceived U.S. predominance. Since the mid-1990s, China has sought to expand its relationship with Russia

---

[15] Wang Jisi, 2003, 2005.

[16] For a complete description of the new security concept and China's intended use of it, see David M. Finkelstein, "Chinas 'New Concept of Security,'" in Stephen J. Flanagan and Michael E. Marti, eds., *The People's Liberation Army and China in Transition*, Washington, D.C.: National Defense University Press, 2003, pp. 197–201. Some of the more competitive dimensions of the new security concept are detailed in Carlyle A. Thayer, "China's International Security Cooperation Diplomacy and Southeast Asia," *Australian Defence Force Journal*, No. 127, 2007, pp. 16–32.

as a nascent counterbalance to U.S. power and to constrain the United States in such global forums as the U.N. Security Council. This effort was motivated in part by China's opposition to NATO expansion, broadening of the U.S.-Japan alliance, NATO military operations in Kosovo, and U.S. ballistic missile defense policies.

Last, China appears to be gradually reducing its dependence on the United States, economically and politically. This is a long-term trend and one that may be happening as much by default as by design. As China expands its global activities and its involvement in multilateral institutions, its sources of prosperity, security, and status are growing. Reducing political and economic reliance on the United States is reflected in China's embrace of the EU and Russia over the past decade; Beijing's growing relationships in Africa, Latin America, and the Middle East; and its activism within the U.N.[17] A consequence is that this trend will minimize the extent to which China believes it needs constantly stable bilateral relations with the United States to pursue its foreign policy objectives. Thus, China may be more willing to challenge the United States and resist U.S. pressure to change its behavior on controversial issues.

Russia

Beginning with Gorbachev's normalization of Sino-Soviet relations in 1989, China-Russia relations have since undergone a sea change. Beijing has made gradual and consistent efforts to upgrade relations, driven largely, but not exclusively, by mutual concerns about U.S. power and the U.S. democracy-promotion agenda. Both nations seek to constrain U.S. diplomatic and military power, to the extent possible. In 1994, China and Russia formed a "cooperative partnership," followed by a "strategic cooperative partnership" in 1996, and the signing of a full treaty on "Good Neighborliness, Friendship, and Cooperation" in 2001. These agreements led to a series of sustained high-level interac-

---

[17] To be sure, China's pursuit of these various foreign policy objectives has multiple motivations, such as gaining access to foreign markets and natural resources. Yet, China's efforts to broaden its global interdependence beyond heavy reliance on the United States and to augment its international influence appear to be increasingly prominent motivations for Beijing's foreign policymaking.

tions, which remain the "thickest" part of this bilateral relationship. Since 1996, Chinese and Russian leaders have held annual summit meetings. Hu Jintao's first trip abroad as China's head of state in 2003 was to Russia. China and Russia jointly created and then expanded the organization that became the SCO in 2001 (even though it has also become a venue for competition). In 2004, the border dispute was finally and completely resolved. In 2005, they conducted, for the first time, a large and sophisticated joint amphibious landing exercise in China's Shandong Province on its eastern coastline, and a second joint exercise (this time involving only land forces) was held in Russia in 2007. (A third is planned for late summer 2009.) Chinese strategists see these agreements, treaties, and related events as indicating a very institutionalized relationship to which Russia is committed.[18]

There are other important layers to this relationship as well. Russia has materially contributed to several of China's modernization needs. Beginning at the end of the Cold War, Russia served as China's principal supplier of sophisticated and much needed weapon systems (e.g., modern air defense systems, advanced fighters, multipurpose destroyers, submarines, and supersonic antiship cruise missiles), which filled critical gaps in the PLA's capabilities during a key stage in China's military modernization program. In 2007, Russia was China's fourth-largest supplier of crude oil imports, at 9 percent. Energy trade has become a new aspect of bilateral relations as China's need for imported oil has grown and Beijing has sought to diversify sources of supply, especially to non-seaborne delivery routes.

China's desire for coordination on common global and regional security challenges is the strongest and most enduring Chinese motivation for ties with Russia (even though energy cooperation has been

---

[18] For recent Chinese accounts of cooperation between China and Russia, see, "Zhong-E Guanxi Puxie Xin Pianzhang" [Writing New Chapters in China-Russia Relations], in Zhang Youwen and Huang Renwei, eds., *Zhongguo Guoji Diwei Baogao 2008*, Beijing, China: Renmin Chubanshe, 2008, pp. 214–218; "Zhong-E Zhanlue Xiezuo Huoban Guanxi de Xin Tisheng" [New Progress in China-Russian Strategic and Cooperative Relations], in Zhang Youwen and Huang Renwei, eds., *Zhongguo Guoji Diwei Baogao 2007*, Beijing, China: Renmin Chubanshe, 2007, pp. 255–264; and Pang Xingchen, 2004.

expanding).[19] Chinese analysts consistently view ties with Russia from the perspective of China's relative position among the major powers in the international system. For China, cooperation with Russia helps to promote greater multipolarity and multilateralism, lessening U.S. influence. Russian leaders share Chinese elites' discomfort with U.S. power and relative predominance, in particular with the U.S. perceived penchant for military alliances, regime change, democracy promotion, and unilateral diplomatic and military actions. According to an authoritative Chinese study:

> There is increasing consensus between the two countries on international issues. Both China and Russia oppose any form of hegemony and power politics, calling for maintaining world peace, and promoting development around the globe. Both countries are against a single-power world, with the belief that a multi-power world represents the trend of history. Both sides are of the view that holding onto Cold War mentality and making efforts to meddle with other nations' domestic politics constitute the cause at the root to instability around the world.[20]

Given these concerns, Chinese analysts and officials see relations with Russia as a way to reduce the U.S. ability to pressure China and Russia, constrain U.S. influence in general, and generate leverage for both in their interactions with Washington. A Chinese assessment put it this way:

> It is the wish of both sides to limit U.S. influence in some regions, to maintain stability in Central Asia, the Korean Peninsula and Japan adopting a policy of peace and non-armament. . . .

---

[19] Pang Xingchen, 2004; Zheng Yu, "Strategic Cooperation Between China and Russia," *China Strategy: China's Bilateral Relationships*, Vol. 3, Washington, D.C.: Center for Strategic and International Studies, July 2004, pp. 25–27; *Guoji Zhanlue yu Anquan Xingshi Pinggu 2004–2005*, 2005, pp. 114–133, 158–180; and Zhang Youwen and Huang Renwei, 2004, pp. 123–155.

[20] Pang Xingchen, 2004, p. 845; the bilateral document referred to in this quotation is the December 2002 China-Russia joint statement issued during Putin's state visit to China.

> China-Russia strategic collaborative partnership will play an important role in bringing stability to the volatile global situation and the formation of a multi-power pattern.
>
> The pressures that both countries are under have a considerable bearing on the development of China-Russia relations, e.g., the U.S. strategic bullying has served as a catalyst in the development of China-Russia relations.
>
> The situation that China and Russia find themselves in has convinced both sides to increase cooperation and support each other with the goal of consolidating their respective major power position on international stage.
>
> The more the U.S. is worried about the Sino-Russia relations, the more China and Russia should fortify their relations. By doing so, they can effectively stand up to the unilateral behavior and hegemony of the U.S.[21]

As a further reflection of this logic, the timing of major enhancements in China-Russia relations (i.e., forming a strategic partnership in late 1996 and signing a treaty in early 2001) coincided with periods of tensions in U.S.-China relations. Similarly, Chinese and Russian positions during key UNSC debates have become increasingly aligned in the latter part of the 2000s, as both seek to restrain U.S. initiatives. On North Korea nuclear issues at the U.N., China takes the lead, with Russia's support; and on Iran nuclear issues, Russia takes the lead with support from China. In 2006 and 2007, there was a near 100 percent similarity in Chinese and Russian votes in the UNSC, including vetoes.[22] As a reflection of their common concern about U.S. power, many Chinese also hope that Russia would be willing to support China in a conflict with the United States over Taiwan; Chinese

---

[21] Pang Xingchen, 2004, pp. 842–847.

[22] This latter claim is based on an analysis of Russian and Chinese voting patterns in the UNSC from 2004 to 2007. Also, interviews with U.S. diplomats at the U.S. Mission to the United Nations, New York, February 2007. For an excellent annual report on U.N. voting patterns, see U.S. Department of State, *Voting Practices at the United Nations,* various years.

analysts point to the 2005 joint amphibious exercise as an indication of growing military cooperation, which could be leveraged during a cross-Strait crisis.[23]

In Central Asia, Russia and China share the common goal of reducing U.S. military presence and democracy-promotion efforts. Both fear that the U.S. military will remain in Central Asia for years. One of their acute concerns relates to the "color revolutions" as an America-led effort to spread democracy. As a consequence, both countries supported the SCO's 2005 summit statement calling for a time line for U.S. withdrawal from Central Asia, with Russia and Uzbekistan leading that effort.

However, there is a competitive dimension to China-Russia relations in Central Asia as well. Russia fears that China's expanding trade and energy interactions in the region could, over time, allow China to become a dominant regional actor. Russia remains wary of the SCO as a Chinese vehicle to promote Beijing's security agenda and economic interests in the region, and China has similar concerns about Russian efforts to constrain Chinese behavior, in particular its access to energy resources. Within the SCO, China and Russia jockey for influence to prevent the other from dominating the organization; at the same time, most Central Asian states play China and Russia off one another to maximize the benefits to themselves. During the 2008 summit, none of the SCO states were willing to endorse Russia's position on the independence of South Ossetia and Abkhazia, which indicates the limits of Russian influence within the organization.[24]

There is a thinness to, and latent tensions in, Sino-Russian interactions. Unlike China's relationship with countries such as the United States, there is a low level of social and cultural contacts between Russians and Chinese, which has fed negative stereotypes on both sides (especially Russian fears of Chinese domination of Eastern Siberia). High-level diplomatic and military interactions are far more institutionalized than are people-to-people contacts. A glaring example of

---

[23] Interviews with Chinese scholars, Beijing, April 2007.

[24] David L. Stern, "Security Group Refuses to Back Russia's Actions," *New York Times*, August 28, 2008.

this is marginalization of the study of the Russian language in China. In 2007, about 40,000 Chinese college students and 80,000 middle school students were learning Russian. More than 200 million Chinese students are learning English.[25] Chinese analysts are aware of these limitations, and they are frank about this in their assessments: "Because of the differences of the two social systems, and differences on the ways of thinking and background of the reforms, China and Russia also run into some frictions and clashes."[26] These will hinder the development of closer, quasi-alliance policy coordination.

There are some important constraints on the relationship. Unlike China's relations with the other major powers, economic relations with Russia are limited, albeit growing. Russia has never been one of China's major trading partners or a major investor in the Chinese economy. In 2007, bilateral trade was at an all-time high of just $48 billion; this compares to $356 billion for the EU, $302 billion for the United States, and $236 billion for Japan in the same year.[27] Also, China's share of Russian global trade is consistently much larger than Russia's share of China's global trade. Economic relations, in terms of its dollar value, have been dominated by the arms trade for over a decade, but this is changing. China has started importing more crude oil and other resources from Russia and exporting more manufactured goods to it.

This pattern of bilateral trade is also a source of tension; Russia wants to export more value-added capital goods to China (e.g., equipment and machinery) and fears having its market flooded by imports of cheap Chinese consumer goods. As the global price of oil dropped in late 2008, bilateral trade numbers stopped rising as fast as in previous years. Also, China's purchase of major weapons platforms from Russia

---

[25] These figures are from Yu Bin, "China-Russia Relations: Between Crisis and Cooperation," *Comparative Connections*, Vol. 10, No. 4, April 2009.

[26] Pang Xingchen, 2004, p. 847.

[27] These data are based on Chinese statistics; Thomas Lum and Dick K. Nanto, *China's Trade with the United States and the World*, Congressional Research Service, Washington, D.C.: Library of Congress, January 4, 2007, p. 44; and *2007 Nian Yi Dao Shier Yue Zhongguo yu Ouzhou Guojia Maoyi Tongji Biao* [2007 January–December Statistics Chart for Trade Between China and European Countries], Ministry of Commerce of the People's Republic of China, January 24, 2008.

may be reaching its limit as the arms trade relationship fundamentally changes. In 2008, the estimated value of Russian arms sales to the PLA was about $1.4 billion, less than a third of the amount purchased in 2006; Russian sources suggest that it may stay at this lower level in the coming years (Figure 6.1). This change is occurring because China has filled the most critical gaps in its force structure. China increasingly wants military co-production and technology-sharing agreements with Russia (vice complete weapons platforms), so that it can further develop its already improving defense industry. It is unclear whether Russian firms will be willing to share their design and production technologies with China. Chinese copying of Russian defense equipment and technologies has been an acute concern among Russian defense enterprises, further constraining future cooperation. During the delayed meeting of the Joint Intergovernmental Commission on Military-

Figure 6.1
Russian Arms Exports to China, 1999–2008

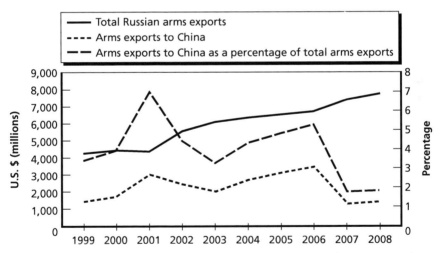

SOURCES: Data for 1999 to 2007 are from Stockholm International Peace Research Institute, SIPRI Arms Transfer Database, April 2009. Data for 2008 are estimates based on media reporting; Igor Chernyak, "Interview with Rosoboroneksport General Director Anatolly Isaykin," *Rossiyskaya Gazeta*, April 10, 2009, as translated by OSC.

RAND *MG850-6.1*

Technical Cooperation in December 2008, China and Russia signed an intellectual property protection agreement, but no new arms contracts were agreed upon. Future trends in Sino-Russian arms tradeinteractions will be a useful measure of the health of the broader political relationship.[28]

For China, a long-standing tension in bilateral relations is Russia's reliability. This has and will limit the depth of cooperation between Moscow and Beijing, especially as new disagreements creep into this relationship. In China's eyes, the history of its relations with the Soviet Union and Russia is replete with examples of the abandonment of China. In 2001, following 9/11, Putin turned toward the United States and in China's eyes "placed relations with China in the secondary position."[29] This occurred only a few months after the China-Russia treaty was signed. As part of Russia's shift, Putin dropped the Sino-Russian joint opposition to U.S. missile defense policies and, specifically, U.S. withdrawal from the Antiballistic Missile Treaty, leaving China in the highly uncomfortable position as the leading and highly vocal opponent. Russian realignment with Chinese interests occurred a few years later on such key issues as North Korea and Iran, as Moscow and Beijing sought to constrain what they perceived as U.S. preference for unilateral actions and disregard for international institutions.

Chinese concerns about Russian reliability and Russia's competitive impulses remain, however. China has faced numerous difficulties in getting Russia to develop an oil pipeline from Siberia to northeastern China. Following an initial bilateral agreement in 1995 about building a pipeline from Angarsk to Daqing, Russia began to waver in 2003 because of a bid from Japan for Russia to build an alternative pipeline from Siberia to Nakhodka. The so-called "An-Da pipeline" plan was shelved when its main advocate, Yukos CEO Mikhail Khodorkovsky, was imprisoned on corruption charges that were widely viewed as a move by political opponents in the Kremlin. As a result, the former project was replaced with the East Siberia-Pacific Ocean pipeline with

---

[28] Paul Holtom, "Russia and China's Defense Industrial Relationship and Arms Sales: Is the Party Over?" unpublished conference paper, April 2009.

[29] Pang Xingchen, 2004, p. 832.

a spur to China. The first phase of this project is complete (and runs from Irkutsk to Skovoridino, near the Chinese border) but the Russians have not started working on the spur from Skovoridino to China. Beijing's February 2009 $25 billion loan to Russia will likely accelerate work on this project; the loan is meant to help Russian state firms build the spur and develop reserves in Eastern Siberia, with completion of the spur to China expected in 2010 or 2011.[30]

In addition, Chinese officials and analysts are well aware of the "China-threat theory" within Russia, which Beijing believes reflects not only public and media views but those of some government officials as well. Russian concerns are based on China's growing economic and military power and Chinese migration into Russia's Far East. Although Chinese policymakers and analysts reject these arguments, they know that they reflect Russian elites' ambivalence toward China and Russian concerns that it is fostering the development of a future strategic rival. This, in turn, fuels Chinese anxieties about Russia's commitment to the treaty-enshrined Sino-Russian strategic partnership. The fact that Russia is willing to sell its most advanced weapon systems to India, but not to China, is not lost on Chinese leaders. Frictions and delays in the arms trade relationship in the latter part of this decade indicate both nations' growing concerns. As noted above, there is a competitive dimension to Chinese and Russian interactions in Central Asia and within the SCO; this may grow as China forges more energy deals with Central Asian states.[31]

Last, China's wariness about Russia's reliability is also the result of what the Chinese claim are differences in "diplomatic culture": Russia seeks to be a global superpower again and is willing to confront the United States, whereas China claims not to have such aspirations currently and prefers more subtle means of constraining the United States. Such Russian aspirations are closely watched by Chinese analysts and

---

[30] Zheng Yu, 2004; on the February 2009 loan, see David Winning, Shai Oster, and Alex Wilson, "China, Russia Strike $25 Billion Oil Pact," *Wall Street Journal*, February 18, 2009.

[31] Elizabeth Wishnick, *Russia, China, and the United States in Central Asia: Prospects for Great Power Competition and Cooperation in the Shadow of the Georgian Crisis*, Carlisle, Pa.: U.S. Army War College, February 2009.

are a key variable in their calculations of prospects for further cooperation on international security issues.[32]

Japan

Among China's relationships with major powers, that with Japan is
undergoing, perhaps, the most profound adjustment. For China, Sino-
Japanese relations have shifted *from* ties defined by stability, relative
amity, and growing economic cooperation in the 1980s and 1990s *to*
a relationship defined by even greater economic interaction, increasing levels of enmity, general instability, and competition for regional
leadership. Chinese policy toward Japan, since the middle part of this
decade, however, has begun to focus on creating a more stable bilateral
relationship, as has Japan's policy toward China. In China, this policy
evolution has been driven by concerns about the rapid deterioration in
Sino-Japanese ties, fears of runaway anti-Japanese sentiment among the
Chinese public, and corresponding concerns about anti-Chinese sentiments in Japan.

Historically, there has been a widely accepted economic logic to
China's Japan policy, and this logic largely defined Sino-Japanese relations for decades. During the 1950s, 1960s, and 1970s, Japan never cut
off all trade with China even though the two countries lacked formal
diplomatic relations, which were established in 1972. As China entered
its reform period, Japan became a critical source of trade, direct investment, and, perhaps most important, overseas development assistance
in the form of annual grants and subsidized loans. Japanese firms
were also important sources of manufacturing equipment, expertise,
and technology in sectors China viewed as central to its own industrial modernization, such as automobiles, shipbuilding, and consumer
electronics.

In the 1980s and 1990s, China's resentment of Japan's imperial
history and anti-Japanese nationalism did not function as a major
constraint on bilateral relations, and when these sentiments flared up,

---

[32] This is based on interviews with Chinese scholars, Beijing, 2007.

Chinese leaders managed them.[33] Although Chinese elites and the public expressed deep mistrust of Japanese intentions and acute fears of Japanese remilitarization, there was little security competition in bilateral relations. In the first two decades of China's reform period, both China and Japan had limited international goals and both were focused largely on fostering regional stability and economic development. Lingering territorial disputes and historical problems were managed within the framework of limited state ambitions and mutually beneficial economic cooperation.

In the late 1990s, Sino-Japanese relations started to become more tense, competitive, and volatile. Both nations began to define their external interests more broadly and both their militaries were modernizing, which altered threat perceptions in Beijing and Tokyo. Chinese leaders began talking about the rise of China in Asia, and China became far more active in regional security affairs. Also, Chinese foreign policy elites began to question the restraint value of the U.S.-Japan alliance as the Japanese military began to participate in U.S.-led global military operations and to develop missile defense capabilities jointly with the United States. Japanese leaders also sought to play a greater role in regional and global security affairs, facilitated by U.S. efforts to encourage Japan's military to assume broader responsibilities. As China's economy and trade grew, it sought a regional leadership role on economic affairs—a role long coveted and carefully fostered by Japan. These parallel trends have fostered a de facto competition for regional leadership between China and Japan. As a result, China's Japan policy and its broader regional diplomacy are now concerned about maintaining a position of strength in East Asia relative to Japan.[34]

---

[33] For an excellent study on this point, see Phillip C. Saunders and Erica Strecker Downs, "Legitimacy and the Limits of Nationalism: China and the Diaoyu Islands," *International Security*, Vol. 23, No. 3, Winter 1998/1999, pp. 114–146.

[34] Minxin Pei and Michael Swaine, *Simmering Fire in Asia: Averting Sino-Japanese Strategic Conflict*, Policy Brief No. 44, Washington, D.C.: Carnegie Endowment for International Peace, November 2005; Peter H. Gries, "China's 'New Thinking on Japan,'" *China Quarterly*, Vol. 32, No. 184, December 2005b, pp. 831–850; and Benjamin Self, "China and Japan: A Facade of Friendship," *Washington Quarterly*, Vol. 26, No. 1, Winter 2002–2003, pp. 77–88.

Domestic political dynamics in China and Japan accentuated this emerging competition and contributed to its volatility. Internal changes in the politics of both nations created space and opportunity for anti-Chinese voices in Japan and anti-Japanese voices in China to assert themselves. Unlike before, public opinion began to play a greater role in both countries' policymaking toward the other. In China, there have been several debates about the direction of its Japan policy, which revolved around the relative importance of "the history issue" in Sino-Japanese relations. As the domestic context changed, territorial disputes and lingering historical problems came to the fore, which in turn further accentuated the sense of an emerging race for regional preeminence. In some cases, these domestic dynamics constrained the ability of political leaders to stabilize relations.[35]

Ironically, during this process, trade and investment continued to grow rapidly. Between 1996 and 2006, Japanese trade with China (including Hong Kong) grew by an explosive 239 percent, whereas Japan's overall global trade grew by only 45 percent (excluding trade with China). Japan-U.S. trade grew by only 12 percent in this period. In 2006, Japan's trade with China constituted 17 percent of Japan's global trade, including 14 percent of its exports and 21 percent of its imports. As distinct from much of Japan's trade with the United States, its trade with China is relatively balanced and highly complementary. This growth in exports contributed to the momentary recovery of the Japanese economy from its decade-long recession in the 2005–2008 period, an outcome not unnoticed in Beijing.[36]

What do these seemingly contradictory trends portend for China's approach to Japan and Sino-Japanese relations? China is moving from a position of unconditionally maintaining a positive relationship with Japan (to accrue economic gains) to one in which Beijing continues to seek continued trade and investment but is also far more willing

---

[35]   Minxin Pei and Swaine, 2005; Gries, 2004, 2005.

[36]   These data are from Evan S. Medeiros, Keith Crane, Eric Heginbotham, Norman D. Levin, Julia F. Lowell, Angel Rabassa, and Somi Seong, *Pacific Currents: The Responses of U.S. Allies and Security Partners in East Asia to China's Rise*, Santa Monica, Calif.: RAND Corporation, MG-736-AF, 2008, pp. 33–35.

to assert itself on key disagreements on historical and territorial issues. China is less economically dependent on Japan, more confident in its economic strength and regional influence, and more wary of Japan's intentions. China publicly campaigned against Japan's bid to join the U.N. Security Council. It has deployed naval vessels to the East China Sea to police its disputed claims to hydrocarbon resources there (e.g., the Chunxiao gas field) and has moved ahead with oil drilling in these contested areas. In bilateral relations, China is more willing to assert itself and to push for a Japanese accommodation of Chinese interests.

Yet there are multiple indications that China's approach to relations with Japan is changing, gradually but with important consequences. Chinese leaders recognized that the downward spiral that occurred during the 2001–2005 period generated domestic political risks and imposed acute diplomatic and economic costs. As a result, since 2006 Chinese leaders have made a major effort to stabilize bilateral relations; both Hu Jintao and Wen Jiabao have visited Japan and hosted return visits by prime ministers Fukuda, Abe, and Aso. Wen Jiabao delivered an address to the Japanese parliament in May 2007, which was broadcast simultaneously in both countries and in which he acknowledged Japan's political and economic achievements since World War II. This speech signaled Beijing's desire to move past historical issues. More concretely, despite having completed gas platforms near contested areas of the East China Sea, China has refrained from initiating full-scale production and has instead negotiated a tentative framework for managing the dispute. Chinese leaders may be more constrained by anti-Japanese nationalism than before as well.

It is not a foregone conclusion that the two countries' relationship will become even more competitive and drift into an outright rivalry. Expanding bilateral economic relations and fostering greater economic integration in East Asia are substantial common interests for Beijing and Tokyo and provide reason and momentum for maintaining stable Sino-Japanese relations. Significantly, Beijing has moved to restrict the activities of potentially troublesome anti-Japanese agitators (e.g., groups asserting sovereignty over the Diaoyu Islands). Beijing was quick to arrest unofficial strike leaders in Japanese factories during the April 2005 anti-Japanese disturbances. And China has moved ahead with a trilateral investment agreement with Japan and South Korea designed to improve the investment climate and protections for those countries' businesses in China. China also agreed in 2007 to support the initiation of a trilateral diplomatic dialogue among the United States, China, and Japan.

As of mid-2009, leaders in both nations are trying to forge a framework for bilateral political ties that would facilitate stability amid growing competition and anxieties in each country. Both sides still face real challenges in forging such a framework: enmity at the popular level in both nations remains strong, none of the complex territorial issues are close to resolution and are intimately tied to the general sense of regional competition, and the domestic political dynamics that fed a deterioration in relations in the late 1990s and early 2000s could reemerge under new leadership in either nation. Thus, whether Beijing and Tokyo succeed in reconstructing stable ties able to endure in the longer term depends on whether leaders on both sides continue to make that effort a priority and are willing to expend the necessary political capital when confronted with a flare-up in tensions.

Europe[37]

China's approach to relations with the EU and its member states has evolved substantially since the mid-1990s. The EU is a large market for China's exports and a key source of investment and advanced manufacturing equipment and technology (including potentially for military modernization). The EU, after adding several members, became China's top trading partner in 2004.[38] European countries continue to be important sources of development aid for China. Many European

---

[37] This section draws broadly from these Western and Chinese sources: *Guoji Zhanlue yu Anquan Xingshi Pinggu 2004–2005*, 2005, pp. 181–200; *Zhongguo Guoji Diwei Baogao 2004*, 2004, pp. 136–143; *Zhongguo Guoji Diwei Baogao 2007*, 2007, pp. 265–271; *Zhongguo Guoji Diwei Baogao 2008*, 2008, pp. 207–213; and several chapters in David Shambaugh, Eberhard Sandschneider, and Zhou Hong, eds., *China-Europe Relations: Perceptions, Policies and Prospects*, New York: Routledge, 2008.

[38] Crossing this threshold was, in part, a function of the addition of several countries to the EU on May 1, 2004. The new members included the Czech Republic, Estonia, Hungary, Latvia, Lithuania, Poland, Slovakia, Slovenia, and the islands of Malta and Cyprus.

leaders support, at least rhetorically, China's vision of a more "multipolar" international order, but interpretations of this goal differ. These features have led China to seek more from this relationship over the past decade, albeit with mixed results for Beijing.

China-EU relations have become more complex and contentious as they have developed, especially as mutual expectations have grown. Economic interactions, which were historically the foundation of a friendly and stable relationship, are now plagued by a proliferating variety of disputes over market access, large and growing trade deficits, and China's exchange rate policy. Growing economic pressure on and from European labor forces have made these issues more politically salient for EU leaders. China's various human rights–related policies (e.g., Tibet) have resurfaced in public debates as well as certain diplomatic practices (e.g., aid in Africa). Spurred by domestic politics, EU leaders are now more willing to confront China over these and other disputes. For both China and the EU, their relations with the United States loom largely over EU-China ties, often frustrating China's effort to shape EU policymaking.[39]

A Three-Phase Evolution. Beginning with the establishment of China's relations with the then–European Community (EC) in 1975, China's ties with Europe have evolved in three phases.[40] Each one reveals Chinese objectives and policies and their relative effectiveness.

During the first phase, from 1975 to 1995, relations were neither well developed nor a priority for either. Europe was a secondary,

---

[39] Bates Gill, "The United States and the China-EU Relationship," in Shambaugh, Sandschneider, and Hong, 2008, pp. 270–286; Bates Gill and Gudrun Wacker, eds., *China's Rise: Diverging U.S. and EU Perspectives and Approaches*, Berlin: Stiftung Wissenschaft und Politik, August 2005; David Shambaugh, "The New Strategic Triangle: U.S. and European Reactions to China's Rise," *Washington Quarterly*, Vol. 28, No. 3, Summer 2005, pp. 7–25.

For a very direct EU approach to China policy, see John Fox and Francois Godement, *A Power Audit of EU-China Relations*, Brussels, Belgium: The European Council on Foreign Relations, 2009.

[40] The European Community became the European Union after the signing of the Maastricht Treaty in 1993.

if not an occasionally tertiary, concern for China.[41] Common interests expanded amid few policy differences, led mainly by merchandise trade, which blossomed in the 1980s. China's approach focused on the European provision of development assistance, business investment, and technology transfers. Many European policymakers sought to foster China's economic development in the search for new markets, and some were motivated by the belief that development would lead to political reform—a belief China was happy to benefit from. For China, EU nations were an important source of investment, associated equipment, the technology needed to build or renovate key industrial sectors, such as automobiles (e.g., from Volkswagen), and light and heavy manufacturing (e.g., from Siemens). EU nations had a commercially driven approach to China focused on expanding trade and investment opportunities and encouraging China to join the WTO. The EU issued its first strategy paper on China in 1995, 20 years after formal relations had been established. (Several major EC/EU member states had diplomatic ties with China dating to the 1950s.)

A second phase can be identified from 1995 to 2005, which involved a sustained and qualitative expansion in EU-China relations. In this ten-year period, goods trade grew rapidly, especially following China's WTO accession 2001. The European Commission issued four "communications" on overall EU relations with China (in 1995, 1998, 2001, and 2006) and two "country strategy papers" (in 2002 and 2007). The commission's development aid joined with the aid given by the EU member states amounted to billions of euros in assistance to China. The political portfolio of the European Council (the highest political organization within the EU) became infused with issues involving China, such as nonproliferation, human rights, energy policy, and climate change. The portfolio of the commission increased to over

---

[41] On this and earlier periods, see Michael B. Yahuda, "China and Europe: The Significance of a Secondary Relationship," in Thomas W. Robinson and David Shambaugh, eds., *Chinese Foreign Policy: Theory and Practice*, Oxford, UK: Clarendon Press, 1994, pp. 266–282.

27 "sectoral dialogues" and, as a result, the commission's interactions with its Chinese government counterparts proliferated accordingly.[42]

China made a dedicated effort in the early 2000s to expand ties with the EU; China saw an opportunity as a result of trans-Atlantic tensions (especially after the Iraq War) and sought to capitalize on this apparent opening. In 2003, several unique events occurred. China issued its first policy paper on relations with the EU; it designated a minister in charge of EU relations; the annual China-EU summit was attended, for the first time, by President Hu Jintao; at the summit, China and the EU formed a "comprehensive strategic partnership"; and China also began pushing the EU to lift its 1989 embargo on arms trade with China.

The third, sobering phase in relations began in 2005 and continues to the present. It is characterized by the end of the previous honeymoon phase in relations and the arrival of several disputes about unresolved economic and diplomatic issues.[43] In 2005, the Multi-Fiber Agreement expired and the EU reintroduced import quotas on Chinese textile imports to prevent a flood of them coming into EU ports. Resolution of this tense dispute required successive and confrontational trade negotiations, some of the first for the EU and China. Also by 2005, China's effort to prod the EU into lifting its arms embargo had become intense but ultimately failed. Relying on support from France and Germany, China ran into strong opposition from the United States, a variety of Scandanavian and East European countries, and eventually the UK.

These tensions set the stage for a series of subsequent economic policy disputes about market access, China's undervalued currency, the growing trade deficit, and China's poor standards for food and product safety. British Labour Party politician Peter Mandelson became

---

[42] Franco Algieri, "It's the System That Matters: Institutionalization and Making of EU Policy Toward China," in Shambaugh, Sandschneider, and Hong, 2008, pp. 65–83.

[43] Shambaugh, Sandschneider, and Hong, 2008; and May-Britt Stumbaum, *The European Union and China: Decision-Making in EU Foreign and Security Policy towards the People's Republic of China*, DGAP Schriften zur Internationalen Politik, Berlin, Germany: Nomos Publisher, 2009. For a changing Chinese assessment on China-Europe relations, see *Zhongguo Guoji Diwei Baogao 2008*, 2008, pp. 207–213.

European Commissioner for Trade in 2005 and played a central role in taking a more assertive approach toward China in negotiations. During the November 2007 EU-China summit, for example, Mandelson and other commissioners used tough language and publicly confronted the Chinese about the myriad problems in EU-China economic relations. The 2007 summit communiqué criticized China on these issues as well as on Tibet; the communiqué was not issued until four days after the summit, as further indication of the difficulties surrounding these negotiations. In late 2008, China used the then–EU President Nicholas Sarkozy's bilateral meeting with the Dalai Lama to cancel the annual EU-China summit. These successive events led policymakers in Beijing and Brussels to recognize the limits to this relationship and the danger of false expectations, in particular China's expectations that the EU could be used to counterbalance U.S. power. As a result, China altered its strategy toward Europe, beginning to focus more on managing its bilateral relations with individual countries than with the EU; this approach allows China to return to "divide and rule," using differences among individual countries to advance Beijing's agenda and interests.

Explaining China's Motives. Several considerations explain this evolution in China's approach to Europe and EU-China relations. The economic drivers of this relationship have long provided it with momentum and direction; they will likely continue to do so, even amid growing disputes. As with the United States, Europe has long been an important and growing market for China's exports. The EU-27 is China's largest trading partner.[44] In 2007, China's most important EU trading partners were (in order) Germany, the Netherlands, the UK, France, and Italy. As a block, EU countries also provide China with a larger amount of foreign direct investment (FDI) than does the United States. China's top sources of European FDI were (in order) Germany,

---

[44] The global recession, which began in the latter half 2008, led to steep declines in Chinese exports to the EU, and Chinese policymakers see recovery in European and U.S. demand as important to recovery in China's export sector.

the Netherlands, the UK, France, and Italy.[45] EU nations remain an important source of technology transfers. Germany is China's largest supplier of machine tools, for example, followed by Japan. But there are also limits to this economic cooperation. For example, China has tried, unsuccessfully, to push Europe into granting China "market economy status" under WTO rules. China seeks this status because it could give Chinese goods easier access into European markets by making anti-dumping and countervailing duty cases more difficult to pursue. Whether and how the EU decides to grant such status to China (before the deadline specified in China's WTO accession agreement) will be a key bellwether of relations.

A consistent component of EU-China economic interactions has been European assistance to help China manage its developmental challenges. The EU and its member countries provide a significant amount of technical assistance and financial aid to the Chinese government and Chinese nongovernmental organizations. For many years, EU aid programs were focused on improving China's infrastructure and rural development. Beginning in 2002, EU aid programs shifted focus to social and economic reform, the environment and sustainable development, and good governance and the rule of law. In its prior China Country Strategy Paper for 2002–2006, the European Commission allocated 250 million euros in aid; and in the most recent China Country Strategy Paper for 2007–2013, it allocated 225 million euros in aid for the plan's seven-year period.[46]

Chinese perceptions of European countries' place in global politics have evolved significantly from the 1980s, and this has changed China's expectations about diplomatic cooperation with the EU. Once frequent Chinese references to Britain, France, and Germany's imperial and colonial past seem to have virtually disappeared from Chinese media and scholarly analyses. Although Chinese suspicions of NATO (and particularly of NATO expansion) remain, these are couched in

---

[45] Data on EU-China trade and investment relations can be found on the Web site of the European Commission.

[46] Details on EU aid programs to China can be found on the European Commission Web site.

terms of the U.S. "leadership" of NATO, which places Chinese suspicions of NATO in the same context as its dissatisfaction with U.S. unipolar or "hegemonic" tendencies.[47]

As a consequence, for China, EU countries have a unique appeal because they do not exhibit the same degree of distrust and fear of China's intentions as do many in the United States. Whereas Chinese analysts believe that the United States wants to contain China's rise, they view European policymakers as seeking to engage China and promote its stable development. In China's eyes, EU countries also do not espouse an aggressive democracy-promotion agenda or possess extensive security interests in Asia, both of which are sources of deep distrust in U.S.-China relations. Some EU members feel strongly about China's human rights situation and the Tibet issue, but these have been only occasional irritants and not permanent barriers to improving relations.

For these reasons, many in China believe that Sino-European relations are less competitive, in a strategic sense, than U.S.-China relations. China sees its relations with European countries as providing Beijing with a relatively benign Western alternative, of sorts, to the United States. For Beijing, developing closer EU-China relations has been part of its effort to diversify its sources of economic growth, security, and international legitimacy.

The quantity and quality of China-EU diplomatic interactions have expanded accordingly since the late 1990s, reflecting a clear Chinese priority. According to a U.S. study of Chinese diplomacy, Europe was the most highly visited region for China's president and premier from 2000 to 2005. In 2002 and 2004, China's foreign minister spent more time visiting Europe than any other region.[48] Chinese President Hu Jintao made one of his first overseas trips to the UK after becoming China's president in 2003; his first visit to the United States as president was not until 2006. China and the European Union hold an annual summit meeting where they engage in a structured political

---

[47] Huang Renwei, "Guoji Tixi de Gaibian yu Zhongguo Heping Fazhan Daolu."

[48] These conclusions benefited from the excellent data in Saunders, 2006, pp. 21–22.

dialogue on a range of economic and developmental issues—security and military topics are seldom addressed in detail. China and European nations also interact within the larger Europe-Asia Summit meetings among heads of states, held biannually.

China's unsuccessful effort to persuade the EU to lift its 1989 arms embargo on China reveals much about Beijing's (mis)perceptions of EU states' interests; it also taught Beijing some important lessons about the boundaries of its ties with the EU. Beginning around 2003, senior Chinese officials began to press their EU counterparts to consider lifting this prohibition on trade with China in defense-specific and dual-use goods and technologies. China was clearly trying to leverage the tensions in trans-Atlantic relations following the U.S. invasion of Iraq to push this specific goal. Relying on French and German leaders (specifically, Jacques Chirac and Gerhard Schroeder), Chinese policymakers argued that the embargo is a "symbolic barrier" to improving China-EU relations, with Beijing appealing to the goals outlined in the 2003 EU-China "comprehensive strategic partnership." China was using the latter to leverage progress on the former goal, as is often the purpose of China's strategic partnerships. Strong U.S. opposition to lifting the embargo combined with disagreement among member countries ultimately derailed China's effort in the latter half of 2005. Following China's spring 2005 passage of an Anti-Secession Law (which sought to "legalize" China's use of force against Taiwan, among other objectives), EU opposition to eliminating the embargo grew substantially and remains so today. Although EU policymakers still refer to removing the embargo as an eventual goal, opposition remains strong among numerous EU member states—both old and new.[49]

For Beijing, the failure of its effort to remove the embargo underscored several lessons: trans-Atlantic ties are deep and strong, even during periods of ardent disagreement; there are real limits to China's ability to influence the EU, in particular on issues affecting trans-Atlantic relations; it is no longer sufficient to have Germany and France on board in an EU composed of 27 member states; the EU and its

---

[49] May-Britt Stumbaum, "The Invisible Ban. EU Maintains Weapons Embargo on China," *Jane's Intelligence Review*, December 2008, pp. 52–53.

member states are wary of being drawn into Chinese-initiated efforts, implicit or explicit, to restrain the United States; and the United States continues to have much influence over European policymakers on China-related issues.[50]

Distinct from China's interactions with the European Commission and Council, Beijing has made consistent efforts to expand its relations with major EU member states. It has reached bilateral "strategic partnerships" with several major EU countries including France, Germany, Italy, Portugal, Spain, and the UK (Table 5.4). China also convenes "strategic dialogues" and security-related discussions with the UK, France, Italy, Germany, and Poland. These discussions generally focus on such issues as arms control and nonproliferation, assessments of the international security environment, human rights, and the rule of law. China in 2007 established high-level economic dialogues with the UK and the EU, modeled on a similar Chinese dialogue with the United States. Since 2005, China's bilateral diplomacy with EU countries has become a prominent feature of its Europe strategy, and this remains so today. China became frustrated with its failed interactions with the EU in Brussels and realized that it gained more leverage by working bilaterally, including by playing European capitals off one another.

On balance, Beijing does not treat the EU or individual countries as important actors on global or Asian security issues, aside from the UK and France by dint of their status as permanent members of the U.N. Security Council. Beijing would prefer to keep European countries out of the Taiwan issue. China has chafed at EU involvement in Taiwan, such as during the contentious negotiation of the final communiqué from the 2007 EU-China summit. As a consequence, China's security and defense dialogues with European countries are rather thin in content, even though they have grown in number. Beijing views such interactions as a way to shape EU perceptions of China and as providing a limited window into U.S. thinking and policies; Chinese policymakers continue to debate how much practical cooperation can result from them. On issues for which Beijing deems European nations

---

[50] Interviews with Chinese officials and scholars, Beijing, 2005, 2006, and 2008.

to be international leaders, such as aid to Africa and nonproliferation, Chinese policymakers appear to be giving European views greater attention and weight.

Even when China has shared diplomatic goals with major EU countries, substantive policy coordination was limited. Under the Chirac government, Beijing's closest diplomatic relationship in the EU may have been France. Beijing and Paris shared displeasure with the George W. Bush administration's perceived efforts to circumvent international institutions in favor of unilateral actions. Even in this situation, substantive cooperation was thin. France was far more willing to confront the United States than was Beijing, such as over U.S. Iraq policy in 2002 and 2003. French President Nicholas Sarkozy distanced his government from Chirac's intense affinity for and cooperation with China; then a series of bilateral controversies over Sarkozy's attendance at the 2008 Beijing Olympics' opening ceremony and France's Tibet policy accelerated this divergence in 2008.[51]

Several European countries, especially the Scandinavian countries, remain critical of China's human rights record; yet for many years, European countries were unwilling to support U.S. efforts to criticize China's human rights practices in the U.N. Many European countries conduct bilateral human rights dialogues with China (as does the commission), but few states are willing to confront China over policy differences. This may be changing, however. In 2008, the leaders of Germany and the UK were willing to confront China on its Tibet policy by having these nations' top leaders meet with the Dalai Lama, albeit in uncoordinated actions. Notably, German Chancellor Angela Merkel was the subject of intense criticism from Beijing and a temporary one year downgrading of relations occurred after Merkel's September 2007 meeting with the Dalai Lama. In spring 2008, several EU leaders—most notably Sarkozy of France—openly debated conditionalizing their attendance at the 2008 Olympics opening ceremony on changes

---

[51] On Sarkozy's China policy, see Willem Van Kemenade, "Between Beijing and Paris: From Abnormally Good to More Normal," *China Brief*, The Jamestown Foundation, Vol. 7, No. 15, July 27, 2007.

in Chinese policies on the treatment of Tibetans. And, as noted above, China canceled the EU-China summit in December 2008 following Sarkozy's meeting with the Dalai Lama.

China's historically strong ties with East European countries (e.g., the Czech Republic, Albania, Romania, and Hungary) have weakened significantly as many of them have drawn closer to the United States, joined NATO, and supported the United States on such controversial security questions as the arms embargo on China and U.S. missile defense policies. Most notably, in 2006, Albania, a longtime friend of China during the Cold War, accepted several Chinese Muslim Uighurs who were released from the Guantanamo Bay terrorist detention center. Beijing unsuccessfully pressed Washington for Uighurs to be returned to China for prosecution. Most East European countries also have comparatively minor economic and trade relationships with China, although China's exports of consumer goods to their markets have been growing rapidly.

China's military-to-military diplomacy with European countries has expanded, in quality and quantity, since 2000. This behavior is driven, in part, by the acceleration of PLA modernization and the growing needs of the PLA. Interactions with European militaries are of special value to the PLA because they hold the prospect of learning about the doctrine, training, tactics, and procedures of advanced European militaries and possibly also about NATO operations. These interactions include high-level policy discussions and professional military training and education exchanges. Some EU nations, such as France and the UK, have conducted very basic and scripted military exercises with the PLA, largely focused on maritime security (e.g., search-and-rescue operations). As China's defense industry modernizes and the PLA's need for advanced weapon systems grows, Europe's defense industry will continue to have appeal. No longer seeking to purchase complete weapon systems, the PLA and Chinese defense enterprises see European firms as potential sources of advanced weapon subsystems and technologies useful in building next-generation Chinese-designed weapon systems.[52]

Regional Diplomacy in Asia

China's interactions with its Asian neighbors constitute the policy area of greatest activity and innovation in its international behavior. China's ties with those on its periphery are critical to all five of its foreign policy objectives, especially the core national priority of economic development. The origin of China's current "regional diplomacy" (*zhoubian waijiao* 周边外交) dates back to the early 1990s, just after Tiananmen, when China sought to reestablish its international legitimacy.[53] Since then, China has substantially expanded the scope and content of its regional diplomacy and, thus, has improved its relations with most nations in East, South, and Central Asia. The depth of China's links with its Asian neighbors can hardly be overstated. To be sure, this is not meant to imply that China has been uniformly successful in improving ties with every country in Asia or that it has unrivaled political influence. Doubts about China's growing economic and military power and its future aspirations linger below the surface for many countries on China's periphery, fostering a tentative quality to these nations' engagement with Beijing.[54]

East Asia

Throughout all of Asia, China's expansion of its relationships with East Asian nations has been the most extensive. This effort has been driven

---

[52] On the future of China's defense industry, see Evan S. Medeiros, Roger Cliff, Keith Crane, and James C. Mulvenon, *A New Direction for China's Defense Industry*, Santa Monica, Calif.: The RAND Corporation, MG-334-AF, 2005.

[53] Suisheng Zhao, "The Making of China's Periphery Policy," in Suisheng Zhao, ed., *Chinese Foreign Policy: Pragmatism and Strategic Behavior*, Armonk, New York: M. E. Sharpe, 2004, pp. 256–275; and Suisheng Zhao, "China's Periphery Policy and Its Asian Neighbors," *Security Dialogue*, Vol. 30, No. 3, 1999, pp. 335–346.

[54] Medeiros et al., 2008.

by several objectives: to expand China's access to markets and investment, to reassure regional nations that China's rise does not threaten them economically or militarily, to broaden access to natural resources and technologies for further development, and to undermine any and all efforts, U.S.-led and otherwise, to constrain China's economic, diplomatic, and military influence. In this sense, China's regional diplomacy in East Asia has arguably received pride of place in Beijing's overall international strategy in the last decade.

Beginning in the early 1990s following the Tiananmen incident, China developed an initial set of strategies and policies to engage East Asian nations more fully—an effort that gradually expanded throughout the 1990s and into this decade. It first adopted a policy of "good and friendly neighbor diplomacy" (*mulin youhao waijiao* 睦邻友好外交) to generate support for China at a time when it was experiencing relative international isolation.[55] To implement this policy, China, in the early 1990s, established formal diplomatic relations with several East Asian nations (especially in Southeast Asia) to begin the process of breaking out of its relative isolation; it also began to join some regional organizations, such as APEC. Since 2000, this regional diplomacy has received new and invigorated emphasis, which came to be called China's "great peripheral diplomacy" (*da zhoubian waijiao* 大周边外交).

China's calculated embrace of East Asia in the 2000s has a particularly extensive policy basis and, uniquely, has been discussed and approved at the highest levels of China's leadership.[56] The 2002 report of the 16th Party Congress articulated a key, eight-character "guideline" (*fangzhen* 方针) for China's regional diplomacy: "building good-neighborly relationships and partnerships with our neighbors"

---

[55] The "policy" of *mulin youhao waijiao* was the main content of the broader "strategy" of *zhoubian waijiao*.

[56] The following discussion is drawn from these sources: Wang Yi, "Jiaqiang Huxiang Hezuo, Cujin Gongtong Anquan" [Strengthen Mutual Trust and Cooperation, Promote Collective Security], speech at the Conference on East Asian Security, Beijing, China, December 15, 2003; and Wang Yi, "Quanqiuhua Jincheng Zhong de Yazhou Quyu Hezuo" [Asian Regional Cooperation Under Globalization], speech at the Foreign Affairs College Conference on "The East Asian Community," Beijing, China, April 2004; Wang Yi, "Wang Yi Tan Zhongguo de Guoji Diwei He Waijiao Zhengce," 2004.

(*yulin weishan, yilin weiban* 与邻为善，以邻为伴). According to Ambassador Wang Yi, one of the foreign ministry's top Asia experts, this was the first time that the theme of regional cooperation was mentioned in a high-level CCP report. To implement this guideline, according to Ambassador Wang Yi, China's leaders then adopted the more specific policy of "amicable neighbor, secure neighbor, and prosperous neighbor" (*mulin, anlin, fulin* 睦邻，安邻，富邻) to foster enhanced "cooperation and coordination" (*hezuo yu xietiao* 合作与协调) among China and its Asian neighbors. The specific manifestations of these important policies are enumerated below; whether and how these guidelines and policies might change will indicate the future direction of China's diplomacy in East Asia.

China's economic interactions with East Asian nations have taken off in the last ten years and have been the leading edge of its engagement with the region. In 2008, before the global financial crisis and the rapid drop in global trade flows, half of China's total trade volume was intraregional (driven by a regional network of processing trade), and the proportion had been growing annually. China-ASEAN merchandise trade grew from $6 billion in 1991 to $202.5 billion in 2007. China's trade with Southeast Asian nations had also been growing faster than U.S. trade with the region. Many projected that China would become ASEAN's top trading partner.[57] In 2004, China became both Japan's and South Korea's top trading partner, and in 2007 it became Australia's top trading partner, overtaking Japan. Both China's exports to East Asian nations and its imports from them had been growing, which is a far less controversial and more sustainable pattern than China's unbalanced trade with the United States and the EU.[58]

One of China's most extensive trade initiatives was the 2002 launching of the China-ASEAN Free Trade Agreement, which is expected to come into force in 2010 and by 2015 to remove all relevant

---

[57] Bruce Vaughn and Wayne Morrison, *China-Southeast Asian Relations: Trends, Issues and Implications for the United States*, Congressional Research Service, Washington, D.C.: Library of Congress, April 14, 2006, pp. 12–13.

[58] On trade figures, see Kerry Dumbaugh, *China's Foreign Policy and 'Soft Power' in South America, Asia, and Africa*, Congressional Research Service Washington, D.C.: Library of Congress, April 2008, pp. 91–97; World Bank, 2007.

tariffs among members.[59] It may eventually encompass an area of more than 1.7 billion people, with a combined GDP of $2 trillion. The process of tariff liberalization within the FTA member countries began in late 2004 with the adoption of "Early Harvest" measures that called for the lowering of tariffs on select agricultural goods. The China-ASEAN trade volume is projected to expand to $1.2 trillion under the FTA; this would be the world's third-largest market after the North American Free Trade Agreement and the EU.

Beyond trade, China's outward direct investment in Southeast Asia has grown substantially, which is consistent with the global growth in Chinese outward investment. According to Chinese data, annual investment flow increased from $150 million in 2005 to $970 million in 2007, and China's total investment stock in ASEAN states grew from $1.2 billion in 2005 to $3.9 billion in 2007.[60] This is impressive, given the paucity of China's global outward FDI ten years ago: In 1996, China's global ODI flow for the year was about $300 million. However, these amounts pale in comparison to the investment stock of the United States, Japan, and EU member states. In 2006, China's investment in ASEAN (according to ASEAN data) accounted for only 1.8 percent of regional investment stock, whereas U.S. investment accounted for about 7.4 percent, Japan accounted for 20.6 percent, and EU nations accounted for 25.5 percent.[61]

---

[59] Discussions about the FTA were launched in 2001. In 2002, China and ASEAN leaders signed the "Framework Agreement on China-ASEAN Comprehensive Economic Cooperation." The document committed the parties to begin negotiations on an FTA by early 2003, with the goal of completing the agreement by 2004 and establishing the FTA for trade in goods for the original six ASEAN countries by 2010 and by 2015 for newer ASEAN members with less-developed economies. The negotiated FTA was signed in November 2004 during the China-ASEAN meeting. The 2004 Chinese ASEAN agreements are the "Agreement on Trade in Goods of the Framework Agreement on Comprehensive Economic Co-operation between ASEAN and the People's Republic of China" and the "Agreement on Dispute Settlement Mechanism of the Framework Agreement on Comprehensive Economic Co-operation between ASEAN and the People's Republic of China."

[60] *2007 Nian Zhongguo Dui Wai Zhijie Touzi Tongji Gongbao*, 2008, p. 12.

[61] "Top Ten Sources of ASEAN Foreign Direct Investment Inflow," ASEAN Secretariat Web site, undated.

China has also been expanding its subregional cooperation with mainland Southeast Asia. China is an active member in the Greater Mekong Subregion (GMS) development project that is forging a variety of new water rights accords and transportation agreements among nations within the GMS. The issue of water rights has also emerged as a source of tension, as southern Chinese provinces consider building dams on rivers that feed into mainland Southeast Asia.[62] China's private trade and migration into Laos and northern Burma are extensive, and China's investment in transportation infrastructure in these countries is particularly notable. Such transportation links provide China with improved access to Southeast Asian markets as well as to its sea ports, which possess economic as well as strategic value for China.[63]

On security and foreign policy issues, Beijing has taken a series of calculated steps to fully engage East Asian nations at a consistent pace and in novel ways, an approach popularly called China's "charm offensive."[64] China has done so with two main objectives in mind: reassurance and countercontainment. In both bilateral and multilateral settings, China has promoted conceptions of national security that go beyond classic military security to include questions of economic stability and national development. These broader conceptions resonate

---

[62] The Asian Development Bank defines the GMS as comprising Cambodia, the People's Republic of China, Lao People's Democratic Republic, Myanmar, Thailand, and Vietnam. In 1992, with the bank's assistance, the six countries entered into a program of subregional economic cooperation, designed to enhance economic relations among the countries. The program has contributed to the development of infrastructure to enable the development and sharing of the resource base and promote the freer flow of goods and people in the subregion. It has also led to the international recognition of the subregion as a growth area. This text is from Asian Development Bank, undated.

On the issue of water rights, see Vaughn and Morrison, 2006, pp. 30–32; Alex Liebman, "Trickle-Down Hegemony? China's 'Peaceful Rise' and Dam Building on the Mekong," *Contemporary Southeast Asia*, Vol. 27, No. 2, 2005, pp. 281–304.

[63] Mathew Wheeler, "China Expands Its Southern Influence," *Jane's Intelligence Review*, June 2005, pp. 40–44; and Bronson E. Percival, "China's Influence in Southeast Asia: Implications for the US," testimony before the U.S.-China Economic and Security Review Commission on "China's Global Influence: Objectives and Strategies," July 22, 2005.

[64] Joshua Kurlantzick, *Charm Offensive: How China's Soft Power Is Transforming the World*, New Haven, Conn.: Yale University Press, 2007.

strongly with Southeast Asian nations and provide China with a way to reassure them that China shares their views of national security challenges. These ideas also allow China to draw a contrast with U.S. foreign policy goals which, under the Bush administration, have focused on counterterrorism missions and the military dimensions of national security.[65]

China's embrace of multilateral security institutions in East Asia represents one of the most significant and enduring elements of its East Asia policy and a change from past practice. In the early 1990s, China was wary of such forums, viewing them as venues that others would use to criticize and gang up on China; Beijing now views participation as a way to shape international rules, improve relations with neighboring countries, manage concerns about expanding Chinese capabilities, and limit what it perceives as U.S. efforts to constrain Chinese influence. China has joined all the key regional organizations in East Asia including the ASEAN Regional Forum, the APEC forum, ASEAN+1 (China), ASEAN+3 (China, South Korea, and Japan), and the EAS (Table 5.2). In the case of the EAS, China agreed—after much deliberation—to let the ASEAN states take the reins of this new multilateral gathering, despite China's initial aspirations to play a leading, if not the leading, role. In 2006, China co-hosted in Southern China a major China-ASEAN summit to commemorate 15 years of relations, as partial testament to the success of Chinese diplomacy. At the meeting, Prime Minister Wen Jiabao heralded that China and ASEAN have "together gone through the experience of eliminating suspicions and developing dialogue as well as promoting mutual trust," leading to his conclusion that relations were now at their "historic best."[66]

China's efforts at reassurance have also focused on managing past tensions with ASEAN states. China has resolved numerous border disputes and has also deferred resolution of other territorial conflicts, both

---

[65] Bronson Percival, *The Dragon Looks South: China and Southeast Asia in the New Century*, Oxford, UK: Praeger Security International, 2007; and Ian Storey, *The United States and ASEAN-China Relations: All Quiet on the Southeast Asian Front*, Carlisle, Pa.: U.S. Army War College, October 2007, pp. 1–11.

[66] This quotation is from Storey, 2007, p. 7.

land and maritime ones.[67] China agreed, in November 2002, to sign ASEAN's Declaration on the Conduct of Parties in the South China Sea aimed at preventing escalation of ongoing maritime territorial disputes over the Spratly Islands. (The agreement notably does not cover the Paracel Islands, over which China and Vietnam have competing claims.) Beijing in 2003 also signed the Treaty of Amity and Cooperation, signaling its nominal acceptance of ASEAN's security norm of peaceful settlement of disputes. China was the first non-ASEAN state to take this step; India followed. Also in 2003, China and ASEAN signed a "Joint Declaration on a Strategic Partnership," to signal China's commitment to long-term cooperation on regional security issues.

These commitments, to some degree, have been reflected in China's actual behavior. In addressing maritime territorial disputes, China agreed in 2004 to conduct joint seismic investigations of underwater resources with the Philippines in the South China Sea, and Vietnam joined this three-year research investigation in 2005. Beijing also agreed to conduct joint patrols of sea areas that have been agreed on and demarcated, such as with Vietnam in the Gulf of Tonkin.[68]

China's ultimate aims with these efforts remain unclear. It may be drawing the Philippines and Vietnam into bilateral management of these disputes as a way to lessen the influence of ASEAN's goal to ensure that maritime territorial conflicts are managed multilaterally, such that these smaller states collectively have more sway over Beijing. China's other offshore territorial disputes, such as with Japan regarding the Senkaku/Diaoyu Islands and natural gas deposits in the East China Sea, are far from resolution and have even flared up in recent years. These remain potential flash points for armed conflict.

China has been a key supporter of a nascent effort to create an organization for managing Northeast Asian security issues, potentially modeled on the Six Party process to denuclearize North Korea. A working group on establishing such a regional security mechanism for Northeast Asia was established within the Six Party process in Febru-

---

[67] Fravel, 2005.

[68] "Philippines, China, Vietnam to Conduct Joint Marine Seismic Research in South China Sea," *Xinhua*, March 14, 2005. Also see Storey, 2007, pp. 24–27.

ary 2007.[69] China has been active on other issues regarding regional architecture. It was initially a strong supporter of convening an East Asia Summit as a first step toward building an East Asian Community. China's initial enthusiasm for this meeting (which was based on Beijing's stated support for expanding pan-Asia regionalism) waned as various ASEAN states asserted themselves in summit planning, reducing China's relative influence in shaping this new institution. Southeast Asian nations in concert with Japan chose the venue, set the agenda, and expanded the participants list to include India, Australia, and New Zealand. The initial summit was convened in December 2005 in Kuala Lumpur and occurred at the same time at the ASEAN+1 and ASEAN+3 ministerial meetings.[70]

Moreover, China has made a concerted effort to forge "strategic partnerships" as part of its effort to improve the quality of its bilateral relationships in the region. Although such actions are part diplomatic window-dressing, they are the basis of China's effort to raise the level of its diplomatic and security dialogue in ways that appeal to regional actors, and, ultimately, to reassure them. The substance of such strategic partnerships now includes annual high-level exchanges (or "strategic dialogues" in some instances) on traditional and nontraditional security topics among top diplomats and senior political leaders.

China's emphasis on nontraditional security challenges has been a central part of its effort to reassure its Asian neighbors about "the China threat," to draw a contrast with U.S. foreign policy, and to enhance the areas of security cooperation in these relationships. The collective aim of these efforts is to augment China's appeal, to expand its influence, and to further inject China into all regional security discussions.[71]

---

[69] Cao Huayin, "Shixi Dongbeiya Anquan Xin Kuangjia" [A Humble Analysis of the New Framework for Northeast Asian Security], *Gaige Luntan Xuebao* [China Reform Forum Journal], No. 10, 2004, pp. 27–36; this idea is also raised in Wang Jisi, 2005.

[70] Alan Romberg, "The East Asia Summit: Much Ado About Nothing—So Far," *Freeman Report*, Washington, D.C.: Center for Strategic and International Studies, January 2006.

[71] These goals are reflected in Zhang Youwen and Huang Renwei, 2004, pp. 327–337; and *Guoji Zhanlue yu Anquan Xingshi Pinggu 2003–2004*, 2004, pp. 235–241.

Corresponding with China's effort to improve the quality of its regional relationships, the PLA has stepped up its military-to-military interactions with China's East Asian neighbors.[72] This is part and parcel of China's effort to manage regional perceptions and to reassure Asian militaries that PLA modernization does not threaten their security. For example, beginning in 2008, Chinese military leaders have begun to sensitize its neighbors about its plans to deploy an aircraft carrier. The PLA also likely uses these dialogues to gather information on these nations' interactions with the U.S. military, especially for U.S. allies in Asia, for which training and arms transfers with the United States are quite extensive.

China's military-to-military diplomacy with the region is increasingly diverse and robust. It now has high-level exchanges with most countries in Northeast and Southeast Asia; it has allowed military officials from neighboring countries to watch Chinese military exercises; it has invited a few to participate in joint exercises, a first for the PLA; PLA Navy ships' visits to the region are more common; academic and functional exchanges between China and Asian militaries are growing in number; and China has offered favorable arms sales packages to Cambodia, Indonesia, and the Philippines, among others in the region.

Central Asia[73]

China's relations with Central Asia have undergone a gradual but important evolution in the last decade; this subregion has become more significant to China's domestic economic and security interests. As a result, China has been investing greater diplomatic and financial resources to improve its access to natural resources, to limit U.S. (and to some extent Russian) influence, to combat terrorism, and to generally reduce regional instability.

---

[72] Ken Allen, "China's Foreign Military Relations: 2003–2004," *Chinese Military Update*, Royal United Services Institute, Vol. 2, No. 5, December 2004.

[73] In this section, Central Asia refers only to Kazakhstan, Uzbekistan, Turkmenistan, Tajikistan, and Kyrgyzstan.

Beginning in the early 1990s following China's establishment of relations with these former Soviet nations, China's ties with them were a relatively low priority. Beijing's policy was principally focused on improving regional stability, border security, and gaining access to energy resources. China in the early 1990s negotiated border agreements with Kazakhstan, Kyrgyzstan, and Tajikistan that resolved outstanding territorial conflicts by demarcating their respective borders; in some cases, China reached agreements in which it received 50 percent or less of the disputed territory.[74] As China became a net oil importer in 1993, it began to seek more foreign sources of crude oil and natural gas. China pitched its engagement as creating mutually beneficial economic opportunities for these transition economies. Counterterrorism did not emerge as a policy driver until the late 1990s when China sought the cooperation of Central Asian nations in cracking down on Muslim Uighur separatists who trained and lived in the region.

In contrast to China's relations with East Asia, trade between China and Central Asian nations has always been quite modest and remains so today. Economic ties are gradually expanding, led by resource trade. China's total trade with the five Central Asian nations has increased from very low levels before the fall of the Soviet Union to more than $30 billion in 2008. Between 2004 and 2008 alone, the value of trade between China and Central Asia increased more than four times, albeit from a small baseline. Even with current increases, China's trade with Central Asia currently constitutes only about 1.3 percent of its total foreign trade. China's top trading partner in the region is Kazakhstan, which accounts for 90 percent of its total imports from the region (more than 50 percent of which is crude oil). China's exports to the region, mainly consumer goods, are almost four times greater than its imports.[75] Although non-energy trade with Central Asia may

---

[74] In China's negotiations with Tajikistan over the Pamir Mountains, China received 1,000 km of the 28,000 km of contested area. M. Taylor Fravel, *Strong Nation, Secure Borders*, Princeton, N.J.: Princeton University Press, 2008.

[75] In 2006, Kazakhstan's top export markets were Germany, Russia, and China, and its top two sources of imports were Russia and China. Dumbaugh, 2008; Vladimir Paramonov, *China & Central Asia: Present & Future of Economic Relations*, Conflict Studies Research Centre, Surrey, UK: Defence Academy of the United Kingdom, May 2005.

not be that important for China, it is very valuable to Central Asian economies. China is a top export market for all of them, and it is the only viable non-Russian export route to the rest of the world via Chinese roads, railways, and ports. This reduces their reliance on Russia.

Infrastructure development in the transport, communications, and energy sectors has been and remains the focus of China's investment in Central Asia. China has contributed to building oil and gas pipelines in Kazakhstan and Turkmenistan, railways in Kazakhstan and Kyrgyzstan, and various road, bridge, and hydroelectric projects in Tajikistan and Uzbekistan. China has used such infrastructure investments to gain access to resources and to lubricate various commercial interactions with the region. Beijing also seeks to revitalize Eurasian trade routes to diversify its trade partners and thereby better integrate western China, especially Xinjiang Province, into its economy. For Central Asian nations, Chinese investment is especially appealing because it invests in government-backed projects as a means of generating good will, regardless of these projects' actual contributions to economic development. Western investors are far less willing to do so, further enhancing China's relative appeal.[76]

Since 2001, Chinese diplomacy has given greater attention to Central Asia. Beijing now emphasizes, on the one hand, improving trade and investment links and, on the other hand, enhancing China's regional involvement to reduce U.S. and Russian influence. China remains concerned about Muslim terrorists training and operating in Central Asia. China has modestly expanded its security and military cooperation with the Central Asian states to prevent regional unrest from overflowing into Xinjiang.[77]

---

[76] Dumbaugh, 2008, p. 72.

[77] Robert Sutter, "Durability in China's Strategy Toward Central Asia—Reasons for Optimism," *China and Eurasia Forum Quarterly,* Vol. 6, No. 1, 2008, pp. 3–10; Matthew Oresman, "Repaving the Silk Road: China's Emergence in Central Asia," in Joshua Eisenman, Eric Heginbotham, and Derek Mitchell, eds., *China and the Developing World* Armonk, N.Y.: M. E. Sharpe, 2007, pp. 60–83; and Niklas Swanstrom, "China and Central Asia: A New Great Game or Traditional Vassal Relations?" *Journal of Contemporary China,* Vol. 14, No. 45, November 2005, pp. 569–584.

Energy security and countering U.S. influence became top priorities in China's Central Asia diplomacy after two key events: U.S. military deployments to the region after 9/11 and the U.S.-led intervention in Iraq in 2003. China sought to diversify its reliance on imported oil and gas from Middle Eastern suppliers; this made Central Asia far more appealing because of its relative proximity to China and the availability of land routes to transport energy to the mainland. In addition, Chinese analysts began to argue that U.S. military presence in Central Asia "creates an unfavorable strategic environment" for China and that China should ensure that the region does not fall under U.S. domination or that of any single great power (e.g., Russia).[78] For many Chinese, the U.S. military presence in Central Asia facilitates both coalition operations in Afghanistan as well the U.S. pursuit of regional hegemony. Chinese military commentators regularly raise the prospect that U.S. military presence in the region will endure so that the United States can further contain China. PLA officials specifically raised this possibility with then–Secretary of Defense Donald Rumsfeld during his first visit to China as defense secretary in fall 2005. Among the PLA, there is a general sense that greater U.S. military involvement in Central Asia could be used to put pressure on China, especially during a crisis. However, how the United States could do this or why is seldom articulated.

Following the U.S. invasion of Iraq in 2003 and political instability in Central Asia in 2004, Chinese analysts began expressing particular concern about the U.S. presence. The "color revolutions" in Ukraine, Georgia, and Kyrgyzstan heightened this anxiety because many believed that these events were facilitated, if not sponsored, by the United States. Many Chinese feared such revolutions could spread throughout Central Asia. Some in China argued that the presence of U.S. government and nongovernmental organizations in Central Asia could be used to export such movements to China.[79]

---

[78] Zhao Huasheng, "Can China, Russia and the United States Cooperate in Central Asia," *Zhanlue yu Guanli* [Strategy and Management], March 2004, pp. 34–107, as translated by FBIS.

[79] Interviews with Chinese scholars, Beijing, 2007.

China has used and continues to use a mix of bilateral and multilateral initiatives to broaden its presence and expand its influence. It has begun to upgrade its bilateral political relationships in Central Asia after neglecting them since the early 1990s. A high-profile manifestation of China's efforts was the state visit of Uzbekistan's President Karimov to Beijing in May 2005, less than two weeks after Uzbek government security forces opened fire on anti-regime protestors in the town of Andijon. During this visit, the Andijon incident was not mentioned, and China and Uzbekistan signed a treaty (vice the more common joint statement) outlining their "friendly cooperative partnership," which was the first treaty the two had signed since normalization of relations in 1992.[80] During this trip, China and Uzbekistan also signed a $600 million agreement for China to help develop oil fields in Uzbekistan.[81] In taking these steps, China presented Uzbekistan's leaders with political and economic opportunities at a time when that country was under international pressure over the Andijon incident. For regional policymakers, China's treatment of Uzbek leaders represented a particularly stark contrast with U.S. criticism of their management of the Andijon incident and its generally poor human rights record.

China has made a major effort to improve political and economic relations with Kazakhstan and with much success. China's bilateral activities have focused on leveraging improved political relations to secure access to Kazakh energy resources. Several of China's top leaders met numerous times with their counterparts from Kazakhstan in 2004 and 2005; in particular, Hu Jintao has met with Kazakhstan's president at least three times since 2004. During Hu's July 2005 trip to Kazakhstan, the leaders upgraded bilateral relations to a "strategic partnership" (the first for a Central Asian nation), and they reached commercial agreements on building a joint oil pipeline and expanding trade relations. China in 2005 succeeded in purchasing a stake in a large natural gas field in Kazakhstan, after being outbid in past years.

---

[80] Most of these "friendly cooperative partnerships" are noted in joint statements, but in the case of Uzbekistan's, it is noted in a treaty dated May 25, 2005.

[81] Andrew Yeh, "Uzbekistan Signs $600m Oil Deal with China," *Financial Times*, May 25, 2005.

The China National Petroleum Corporation agreed to buy PetroKazakhstan, a regional business competitor, for $4.18 billion. This is one of China's biggest cross-border investments.[82] In May 2006, a Chinese-financed 970-km pipeline from central Kazakhstan began delivering crude oil to western China, with plans to triple its size to deliver oil from the Caspian Sea. The pipeline is designed to eventually carry 20 million tons of oil, which was almost 10 percent of Chinese crude oil imports in 2007.[83]

Leadership diplomacy has been a key Chinese mechanism for developing bilateral relations with Central Asian states. In addition to the visits noted above, Wen Jiabao visited Russia, Uzbekistan, and Turkmenistan in 2007 and concluded major economic deals during those trips. Hu Jintao made state visits to Kyrgyzstan and Kazakhstan in 2007 and to Tajikistan and Turkmenistan in 2008; both visits were linked to his annual participation in the summit of the Shanghai Cooperation Organization. It is significant that the Chinese president attends the Shanghai Cooperation Organization summit each year, providing an occasion to conduct state visits to key countries in the region.

Beyond bilateral diplomacy, China developed and expanded the SCO to advance its regional interests. The SCO has functioned as one of China's main vehicles for entry into Central Asia's economic and security politics. It has sought to use the SCO to restrict U.S. advances and to limit Russian influence. This has manifested in China's consistent material support for the SCO and activism within the organization. In 2003, China provided financial support for the SCO secretariat to be established in Beijing; this was the first such support offered since the SCO was founded in 2001.[84] During the June 2004

---

[82] Enid Tsui and Francesco Guerrera, "China's CNPC Agrees to Buy PetroKaz for $4.2bn," *Financial Times*, August 22, 2005.

[83] Isabel Gorst and Richard McGregor, "Kazakh Oil Arrives in China," *Financial Times*, May 26, 2006.

[84] The SCO began in 1996 as the "Shanghai Five," whose mandate was to address border security and counterterrorism issues. Pan Guang, "Shanghai Cooperation Organization: Challenges Opportunities and Prospects," *SASS Papers*, Vol. 9, Shanghai, China: Shanghai Academy of Social Sciences, Shanghai Academy of Social Sciences Press, 2003, pp. 99–109.

SCO summit, Hu Jintao pledged $900 million in preferential export buyer credits to SCO members and noted that China would establish a special fund for the training, in China, of 1,500 students from other SCO member countries. Hu also called on the SCO to move beyond the institutional development stage; he advocated that the organization "shift its focus" to establish "specific objectives" and adopt "effective measures." These words and actions strongly indicated that China seeks to build the SCO into a strong regional organization with a role in managing all regional economic and security questions.[85] In 2005, China took several steps to improve further the international standing of the SCO. India, Pakistan, and Iran were given observer status; the SCO was made an observer at the U.N. General Assembly; and the SCO signed a memorandum of understanding with ASEAN.

China has had to balance multiple objectives as it operates in the SCO. Most controversially, the joint communiqué from the 2005 SCO summit called for a timetable for the U.S. military to withdraw from its bases in Central Asia when "active" counterterrorism operations end in Afghanistan. As an indication of SCO members' concerns, the SCO statement was preceded by a Russia-China summit statement on "the 21st Century World Order," which also strongly criticized U.S. use of its power and the perceived U.S. disregard for multilateral organizations. Although Uzbekistan and Russia instigated the call for the timetable for U.S. withdrawal, China likely supported the request—or at least made no obvious effort to oppose it. In that same year, China and Russia conducted a large-scale joint amphibious assault exercise off China's coastline, which they rhetorically linked to the SCO's counterterrorism mission. As a further indication of China's balancing act, the language of the 2006 SCO summit declaration was noticeably less confrontational than in 2005. But, the 2006 document still referenced similar themes opposing U.S. human rights policies in the region and the Bush administration's democracy-promotion agenda. It stated: "difference in cultural traditions, political and social systems, values and model of development . . . should not be taken as pretexts to interfere

---

[85] "Hu Jintao Proposes SCO Focus on Security, Economy," *Xinhua*, June 17, 2004.

in other countries' internal affairs" and then bluntly stated: "models of social development should not be exported."[86]

China has also sought to limit Russian influence in Central Asia, albeit with mixed success. This effort has been in response to Russia's attempts to dominate the SCO and to restrain Chinese prerogatives. Given the Sino-Russian "strategic partnership," the countries' military-technical relationship, and their shared interest in constraining U.S. unilateralism, limiting Russian influence is a subtle Chinese goal. China does not want to provoke Russia but does not want it to dominate Central Asia either. The SCO helps China to balance these objectives by allowing Beijing to engage Central Asian states in a multilateral format. Russia, unlike the United States, is much more able to manage Chinese influence in the region given its long-standing links to the former Soviet Republics and its willingness to use confrontational tactics. This situation creates multiple layers of competition and cooperation between Russia and China in Central Asia.

Two examples capture the complexity of Chinese interests as they relate to Russia—the push and pull of a subtle competition for regional influence. Beijing, for years, resisted having the Russian-led Collective Security Treaty Organization (CSTO)—which includes many SCO member states—be linked formally to the SCO. Russia had been pushing for this. China and other SCO members opposed it for fear that it would allow Russia to define the SCO as an anti-Western security institution, rather than one with both economic and security agendas. Some reports indicate that Russia seeks to link the CSTO and SCO to form a Eurasian version of NATO. China resists because it does not want the SCO to assume such a confrontational identity and a Russian-led security agenda.[87] China's efforts initially failed in October 2007 when the CSTO signed an agreement with the SCO to facilitate cooperation on a range of such regional security questions as drug trafficking and organized crime. In 2008, SCO mem-

---

[86] "Declaration on Fifth Anniversary of Shanghai Cooperation Organisation," the Shanghai Cooperation Organisation Web site, June 15, 2006.

[87] Interviews with Chinese scholars, Beijing, 2006 and 2008; also see John C.K. Daly, "Sino-Russian Split at Regional Summit," *Asia Times Online*, November 15, 2007.

bers were more successful at resisting Russian pressure. The 2008 joint statement of the annual SCO summit did not endorse Russia's position on the independence of the Georgian enclaves South Ossetia and Abkhazia; the statement only expressed understanding for Russia's position but did not go any further, much to Moscow's frustration.

Collectively, China's multilateral and bilateral diplomacy in Central Asia indicates a growing interest in the region, with a focus on investing in infrastructure, gaining access to natural resources, expanding political influence, and supporting counterterrorism activities. China's diplomacy is primarily focused on establishing a regional economic role that affords it choice access to regional markets and natural resources. Concerns about U.S. military and diplomatic presence in the region will persist, as will nagging anxieties about Russian assertiveness. China will continue to build up the status and capabilities of the SCO to create an environment in which U.S. influence, at a minimum, is constrained and, at a maximum, will eventually decline. China also sees the SCO as a way to prevent Russia from monopolizing regional security agendas and debates. China eventually seeks a security environment in which it plays a leading role; that is, no major issue can be resolved without Chinese consent. China will likely stop short of being an active challenger to U.S. interests, especially given that other countries have been willing to publicly confront and criticize the United States. Beijing's relative tolerance of a U.S. presence may wane if its concerns persist about U.S. democracy-promotion efforts and the potential spillover effects on Chinese political stability.

Looking forward, China's approach to Central Asia will likely reflect continuity and durability. Its regional interests are long-term and enduring, most of which directly support the CCP's top goals of internal stability and economic development. Also, many of the instabilities and uncertainties in China's interests in East Asia, such as the Taiwan issue or relations with Japan, do not affect China's Central Asia policy. And the U.S. presence in Central Asia is far more limited than in East Asia, lessening the degree to which U.S. policy could undermine China's regional interests. Checking Russian influence, while preventing outright confrontation with Moscow, will remain long-term objectives as well.

South Asia

The major event in China's South Asia policy is the historic renovation and rapprochement taking place in Sino-Indian relations. China has undertaken a dedicated effort since 2001 to expand its political, military, and economic relations with India. Moreover, Beijing has done so while also seeking to manage its increasingly complex and costly, but traditionally close, ties with Pakistan. There are inherent tensions in China's approach.

China's initiation of such a dramatic policy shift toward India is motivated by three main goals: to stabilize China's southern periphery to prevent the emergence of threats (such as a highly competitive or even hostile India), to expand opportunities for bilateral trade and investment, and to minimize India's alignment with the United States and the possibility that Washington and Delhi could constrain Chinese power. Regarding the last motivation, Chinese analysts since early in this decade have expressed growing concerns about the expansion of U.S.-Indian security and military relations, which many Chinese see as a U.S.-led effort to balance Chinese power. China has sought to forestall or limit such a possibility by expanding diplomatic, military, and economic relations with India. It is no coincidence that China's effort to upgrade relations with India (especially military exchanges) coincided with the qualitative shifts in U.S.-India relations in the 2001–2002 period, in particular the George W. Bush administration's expansion of the U.S.-India defense relationship.[88] John Garver nicely explained the totality of Chinese motivations as they relate to India:

> China's broad strategic objective is to persuade India to look benevolently on an open-ended and expanding Chinese economic, political, and military presence in South Asia and the Indian Ocean; to eliminate suspicion in Sino-Indian relations; and to transform India into China's partner. In this way the rise of China in Asia will not lead to Indian efforts to countervail China in coalition with the United States. But the conversion of India to friendship with China is to be done without making con-

---

[88] "Washington Draws India in Against China," *People's Daily Online*, English ed., July 7, 2005 (originally in *Global Times*, July 1, 2005, in Chinese).

cessions to India on the status of Tibet, the Sino-Pakistan strategic link, or by restricting China's expanding military, security, and transportation ties with other South Asian nations.[89]

In contrast to China's foreign policy in East Asia, China's diplomacy in South Asia has principally been bilateral, partly because of the lack of a strong multilateral organization in the subcontinent. Chinese policymakers have conducted numerous high-level and high-profile exchanges with their Indian counterparts, many of which have resulted in agreements or targets for expanding economic interactions and security dialogues.

Three such high-level visits have been particularly important to this rapprochement. First, in June 2003, China invited Indian Prime Minister Atal Bihari Vajpayee to visit China. (This visit followed an important one in April that year by controversial Defense Minister George Fernandez, who publicly linked India's nuclear modernization to security threats from China.) During Vajpayee's visit, both sides agreed to a basic plan to upgrade bilateral relations in a joint statement called "Principles for Relations and Comprehensive Cooperation." This was an important step for both countries because their leaders indicated, at least rhetorically, that neither viewed the other as a threat and, thus, they opened a new phase in relations. At the summit, Vajpayee also called the relationship "stable and forward looking" and both sides agreed to designate "special representatives" to negotiate border issues. Although most of this meeting's documents and major statements were similar to those made during Jiang Zemin's ice-breaking visit in 1996 and Zhu Rongji's 2002 trip, Vajpayee's visit finally normalized Sino-Indian relations after the political tensions following the May 1998 nuclear tests. This trip was important in that it provided a roadmap for expanding Sino-India ties, which both sides acted on in subsequent years.[90]

---

[89] John W. Garver, "China's South Asian Interests and Policies," testimony before the U.S.-China Economic and Security Review Commission on "China's Growing Global Influence: Objectives and Strategies," Washington, D.C., July 21–22, 2005.

[90] Garver, 2005; Waheguru Pal Singh Sidhu and Jing-Dong Yuan, *China and India: Cooperation or Conflict*, Boulder, Colo.: Lynne Reinner Publishers, 2003.

Second, the April 2005 visit of Premier Wen Jiabao marked a watershed in Sino-Indian relations. During Wen's visit (the first of a Chinese premier since Zhu Rongji's 2002 trip), both sides agreed to upgrade their relationship to a "strategic and cooperative partnership for peace and prosperity" from the "cooperative and constructive partnership" initially articulated in 1996 (and reiterated during Vajpayee's 2003 visit to China). This new and important formulation was a culmination of the growing diplomatic, economic, and military exchanges since Vajpayee's 2003 trip, which included the first ever Sino-Indian "strategic dialogue" in January 2005. Also, Chinese scholars indicated that Chinese media seemed to provide greater coverage of Wen's visit than of Zhu Rongji's in 2002—and to the Pakistan leg of Wen's South Asia trip as well.[91]

The economic and security content of Wen's trip was particularly significant. Both leaders noted that between 2001 and 2004, bilateral trade had quadrupled from $3.6 billion to $13.6 billion, which exceeded earlier goals.[92] Both leaders also agreed to begin a feasibility study on a free trade agreement. Just before Wen's trip China published a map acknowledging Indian sovereignty over Sikkim, and the joint statement from the meeting stated that Sikkim was part of India. This was China's first acknowledgment of India's claim; since 1975, China had refused to recognize the incorporation into India of Sikkim that year. Indian and Chinese policymakers also signed an important document that outlined "guiding principles" for resolution of the border dispute. Premier Wen noted during his trip that this was the first time since the resumption of border negotiations in 1981 that such "political guidance" for negotiations had been mutually agreed on.

As a further sign of China's commitment to improving bilateral ties, Hu Jintao conducted his first visit to India in November 2006. This was the first visit of a Chinese head of state to India in over ten

---

[91] Interviews with Chinese scholars, Beijing, 2005.

[92] Although this amount of trade is by far China's greatest in South Asia, it pales in comparison to China's trade with Japan, South Korea, ASEAN, and the United States. Interestingly, in 2003 China ran a $1 billion trade deficit with India as a result of large purchases of natural resources and industrial products.

years. (Jiang Zemin visited India in 1996.) During this summit meeting, Hu outlined a "five point proposal" for further developing Sino-India relations, perhaps as an effort to resolve such lingering problems as the relative lack of progress on resolving the border question. Both sides agreed to launch a joint feasibility study on a bilateral FTA. Interestingly, Hu's trip was followed by his visit to Pakistan of equivalent length.

The changing nature of Sino-India relations is further reflected in growing bilateral interactions on security and military issues. Through such activities, Beijing has sought to reassure India of China's cooperative intentions, to demystify the PLA, and to reduce New Delhi's willingness to work with the United States to balance Chinese power. India's defense minister traveled to China in April 2003 and the Chinese reciprocated in 2004. In late 2004, the Indian Army's chief of staff visited China (after a ten-year hiatus), and his trip was reciprocated in May 2005 when his Chinese counterpart, General Liang Guanglie, visited India; this was the first such trip for a PLA chief of staff in seven years. Indian media reports have also indicated that India's military intelligence chief visited China in June 2005. Later that year, in December 2005, China and India conducted their first joint maritime search-and-rescue exercise. In May 2006, China and India signed their first memorandum of understanding on defense cooperation, which referenced a variety of future activities including "frequent exchanges . . . an annual defense dialogue . . . and joint military exercises." During India's Chief of Staff J. J. Singh's May 2007 visit to China, both sides decided to conduct a joint army counterterrorism drill in October 2007 (in China) and then in December 2008 (in India).[93]

Beyond military interactions, diplomatic cooperation on security issues is broadening. China and India initiated, in early 2005, an annual "strategic dialogue" at the vice foreign minister level. China supported having both India and Pakistan join the SCO as observers, and China gained observer status in SAARC. An important event

---

[93] Jagannath P. Panda, "The Impact of Sino-India Army Exercise on Bilateral Relations," *China Brief,* The Jamestown Foundation, Vol. 7, No. 15, July 2007, pp. 7–10.

to note from Wen Jiabao's 2005 trip was his indication that China would look favorably on—but did not explicitly endorse—India's bid to become a permanent member of the U.N. Security Council. Later in 2005, Beijing also sought to communicate to New Delhi that its effort to oppose expansion of the UNSC was directed at Japan and not India.[94]

China and India face long-standing and new challenges to their bilateral relationship. India's unease and suspicion of Chinese intentions—resulting from the 1962 conflict, the unresolved border dispute, and the competitive dynamics associated with their positions as rising powers in Asia—serve as natural brakes on the development of closer security ties. China's continued military support for Pakistan, which India sees as an effort to check Indian power in South Asia, is a source of enduring tension; although China has taken some steps to inject greater balance into Indo-Pakistani relations, few Indian strategists see it that way. (China did not support Pakistan during the Kargil crisis in 1999, for example.) Furthermore, as the need for imported energy grows in both nations, tensions are fostered as they compete for access to foreign oil and gas resources, including in areas close to both, such as in Burma.[95] China's rapidly expanding trade with India has also been a source of friction; among Indian trading companies, almost half of India's anti-dumping cases have resulted from deals with Chinese firms. For their part, Chinese software manufacturers are concerned about competition from Indian software exports. Whether Beijing and New Delhi agree to pursue FTA talks and can then successfully negoti-

---

[94] Specifically, Wen Jiabao said, "China reiterates that we attach great importance to the important role of India in international affairs. India is a very populous country and is also a very important developing country. We fully understand and support the Indian aspirations to play an even bigger role in international affairs including in the UN." "China Non-Committal on Backing India at UNSC," *Press Trust of India*, April 12, 2005; and interviews with Chinese diplomats, Beijing, 2006.

[95] One recent example of such competition was the rival bids by Chinese and Indian energy companies to buy PetroKazakhstan, a Canadian company that controls large oil fields in Kazakhstan. Keith Bradsher, "China and India Vie for Company with Oil Fields in Kazakhstan" *New York Times*, August 16, 2005; and Tsui and Guerrera, 2005. China and India have also competed for access to oil supplies in Africa.

ate an FTA will indicate their ability to manage the increasingly competitive dimensions of their economic relationship.

Diplomacy Beyond Asia

Africa and Latin America

China's foreign relations with Africa and, to a lesser extent, Latin America have a unique historical lineage. Dating back to the days of Mao's revolutionary foreign policy and his pro–developing nation orientation, China provided much material support (such as grants for large infrastructure projects) to revolutionary movements and pro-China leaders throughout Africa. China had very little economic and political ties to Latin America, far less than in Africa. In both regions, China's diplomacy was primarily driven by its efforts to undermine support for U.S. "imperialism" and Soviet "revisionism" (during the Cold War) and, importantly, to isolate Taiwan. Unlike the Soviet Union, Beijing was less interested in spreading a specific Chinese communist model of political and economic development—even with close regional states such as Tanzania. Although China claimed the moral high ground by opposing colonialism throughout Africa and Latin America, Beijing's goals were always based far more on self-interest than is suggested by its revolutionary rhetoric.[96] China's extensive material assistance to Africa, and to a lesser degree Latin America, declined dramatically beginning in the late 1970s as Deng Xiaoping reduced the most ideological manifestations of Chinese foreign policy and began to divert national resources toward domestic development.

China's current relations with countries in Africa and Latin America represent an evolution in China's reform-era foreign policy, albeit with links to past interests and policies. China's diplomatic and economic engagement with Africa and Latin America has been far more extensive in this decade than throughout the 1980s and 1990s. Chinese diplomacy has been driven by four motivations: to diversify China's access to natural resources, especially oil and minerals (mainly

---

[96] The classic case for this argument is made in Van Ness, 1970.

oil); to expand access to markets in Africa and Latin America, which increasingly purchase Chinese consumer goods, cars, and conventional weapons; to generate support for China's effort to promote multilateralism and to build a multipolar world; and to further isolate Taiwan diplomatically in Africa, Latin America, and the Caribbean, where majority support for Taiwan still remains.[97]

China's Economic Goals. There is a consistent economic logic to China's activism in sub-Saharan Africa.[98] China's merchandise trade with sub-Saharan Africa increased from just $3 billion in 1995 to $45.4 billion in 2006, with annual increases of about 40 percent since 2004.[99] China's imports from Africa grew from $4.5 billion in 2001 to $26.31 billion in 2006, increasing by 485 percent. Over those five years, about 90 percent of China's African imports, in terms of value, consisted of crude oil, iron ore, raw timber, raw cotton, rough diamonds, re-imports of previously exported goods, metals, bulk stainless steel supplies, and raw tobacco. Not only are China's imports from Africa mostly raw materials, but they also come from a small group of countries. Imports from seven countries—Angola, South Africa, Sudan, the Democratic Republic of the Congo, Equatorial Guinea, Gabon, and Nigeria—constituted about 90 percent of China's imports between 2001 and 2006. Most of China's imports from these countries

---

[97] As of June 2009, 16 of the 23 nations that currently recognize Taiwan are in Africa and Latin America. The 16 include Belize (1989), the Dominican Republic (1957), El Salvador (1961), Guatemala (1960), Haiti (1956), Honduras (1965), Nicaragua (1990), Panama (1954), Paraguay (1957), Saint Kitts–Nevis (1983), Saint Lucia (1984–1997, 2007), Saint Vincent and the Grenadines (1981), Burkina Faso (1994), Gambia (1995), São Tomé and Príncipe (1997), and Swaziland (1968).

[98] On China's relations with Africa, see Chris Alden, *China in Africa*, London, UK: Zed Books, 2007; Princeton Lyman, "China Rising Role in Africa," testimony before the U.S.-China Economic and Security Review Commission on "China's Growing Global Role: Objectives and Influence," July 21, 2005; and David H. Shinn, "China's Approach to East, North and the Horn of Africa," testimony before the U.S.-China Economic and Security Review Commission on "China's Growing Global Role: Objectives and Influence," July 21, 2005.

[99] Dumbaugh, 2008, p. 119.

consisted of crude oil, with the exception of South Africa, from which most of the imports consisted of metals.[100]

Furthermore, China's exports to Africa increased from $4.42 billion in 2001 to $19.04 billion in 2006, an increase of over 330 percent. Its major exports were woven cotton fabrics, motorcycles, footwear, synthetic fabrics, batteries, broadcasting equipment, telephone equipment, tires, embroidery, and mixed component fabrics.[101] Sub-Saharan African nations, like many nations in other parts of the world, are fast becoming major export markets for Chinese consumer goods. According to U.S. government officials, "Small, private Chinese investors have invested millions of dollars into opening enterprises in Africa that operate in textiles, light manufacturing, construction and agriculture."[102]

The growth in China-Africa trade is impressive but needs to be evaluated in the context of China's total world trade and global economic trends. China's trade with sub-Saharan Africa remains of limited importance to China's overall trade volume. In 2006, its trade with sub-Saharan Africa accounted for 2.6 percent of China's total world trade. According to U.S. government data,

> As of 2006, the value of China's trade with Africa was lower than China's trade with the Middle East or Latin America and was a minute percentage of its trade with the rest of Asia. On the investment side, China's investment flow into Africa constituted only 2.9% of China's global outward direct investment. China's total direct investment stock in Africa accounted for only 1% of global foreign direct investment in Africa.[103]

China's trade with African nations possesses several attributes. First, its imports and exports to Africa have both been growing sig-

---

[100] Dumbaugh, 2008, p. 121.

[101] Dumbaugh, 2008, pp. 124–125.

[102] Thomas J. Christensen, Deputy Assistant Secretary of State for East Asian and Pacific Affairs and James Swan, Deputy Assistant Secretary for African Affairs, statement before the Subcommittee on African Affairs of the Senate Foreign Relations Committee on "China in Africa: Implications for U.S. Foreign Policy," June 5, 2008.

[103] Christensen and Swan, 2008.

nificantly. Second, the *value* of China's imports from Africa, mainly Angola, is large because of oil imports. (In 2007, oil imports from Angola accounted for more than 50 percent of the value of all Chinese imports from sub-Saharan Africa; and four of China's top five trade partners in sub-Saharan Africa are oil suppliers.) Third, the growth in Sino-African trade is characterized by much volatility, largely in China's oil imports and resulting from variations in world oil prices. Fourth, China's exports to Africa have consistently grown and some sub-Saharan African nations now run a trade deficit with China. As a result, China's exports to Africa have not always fostered a "win-win" situation, as Chinese commentaries suggest, and have resulted in political frictions with disenfranchised African nations. For example, China's global textile exports have hurt numerous African nations, causing textile-producing factories to close in Kenya, Lesotho, South Africa, Swaziland, and Kenya. In some cases, China's textiles exports are a "double whammy" for African manufacturers: Chinese exports destroy both domestic and foreign demand for African textiles.

China's investment in Africa has grown dramatically as trade has become a major component of China's economic interactions with Africa. According to Chinese government data, annual investment flow to the entire African continent grew from $74 million in 2003 to $1.5 billion in 2007; the total stock of Chinese investment increased from $491 million in 2003 to $4.4 billion in 2007.[104] But China's official data seem to miss some major investments, so it is unclear how comprehensive those data are. More than 800 Chinese state-owned enterprises have investment projects in 40 Africa countries. As of late 2008, China's largest cross-border investment was its 2007 purchase of a 20 percent stake in Standard Bank of South Africa, a deal reported to be worth $5.5 billion.[105]

An important and underexamined component of Chinese investment in Africa is its infrastructure projects. China's financial commitments to African infrastructure projects grew from about $1 billion

---

[104] *2007 Nian Zhongguo Dui Wai Zhijie Touzi Tongji Gongbao* [2007 Statistical Bulletin of China's Outward Foreign Direct Investment], Beijing, China: Ministry of Commerce of the People's Republic of China, September 27, 2008, pp. 60–65.

[105] Christensen and Swan, 2008.

a year in 2001–2003 to $4.5 billion in 2007—with a peak of $7 billion in 2006. About 70 percent of Chinese infrastructure investment has been in just four countries: Nigeria, Ethiopia, Angola, and Sudan. The majority of China's projects cover two sectors: power generation (principally hydropower) and transport (principally rail). China also financed and provided equipment for the creation of national telecommunication backbone systems in Ethiopia, Sudan, and Ghana. China's focus on infrastructure investment in Africa has allowed a natural economic complementarity to flourish: Africa's infrastructure deficit is one of its biggest development challenges, and China's construction sector is one of the world's largest and most competitive. This complementarity suggests that the current pattern of Chinese infrastructure investment will continue to grow.[106]

China's largest investments in Africa, by far, have been in resource extraction (mainly oil), but the scale, mechanics, and consequence of these investments are often exaggerated. According to a World Bank study of Chinese investments in Africa, between 2001 and 2005, China made about $10 billion in oil sector investment across 15 African nations, with the largest investments in Angola and Sudan. Yet, this investment pales in comparison to the $168 billion that other international oil corporations have already invested in Africa. In 2006, 55 percent of African oil exports went to the United States and the EU, whereas only 15 percent went to China. China's non-oil investments in Africa are estimated at about $2 billion and focused on mineral extraction (e.g., copper and iron ore) in such countries as the Democratic Republic of the Congo, Gabon, Guinea, Zambia, and Zimbabwe. Interestingly, a World Bank study argues, contrary to some current research, that only about 7 percent of Chinese infrastructure investment is directly linked to resource extraction, where Chinese companies make a net-negative infrastructure investment to facilitate access to resources for export to China. A more common pattern of Chinese

---

[106] The information in this section on the patterns of Chinese investment in Africa is drawn from Vivien Foster, William Butterfield, Chuan Chen, and Nataliya Pushak, *Building Bridges: China's Growing Role as Infrastructure Financier for Africa*, Washington, D.C.: The World Bank, 2008.

investment is known as "the Angola model," in which natural resources are used as repayment for the loan used to finance Chinese infrastructure development. For example, in 2007, China gave the Democratic Republic of the Congo a $9 billion package of loans and investments, which will be repaid in cobalt and copper from Congolese mines.[107] These deals are commonly done through China's Export-Import Bank rather than a Chinese development agency. The World Bank report also found that government loans to Chinese companies for these and other infrastructure projects "compare favorably with private sector lending to Africa [with a grant element of 36 percent] but they are not as attractive as ODA, which tends to provide a grant element of around 66 percent to Africa."[108]

China also provides much classic development aid to African nations in the form of grants and technical assistance (as opposed to state-subsidized financing for investment projects). In November 2006, at the China-Africa Cooperation Forum, China pledged an extensive package of development aid that included grants, loans, and technical assistance; it was China's largest commitment of aid to Africa in decades. One U.S. analysis explained the appeal of China to African nations: China offers a "complete package" to African nations: money, technical assistance, and influence in international organizations to protect the host from international sanctions.[109] The World Bank report underscored these sentiments by noting the appeal of China's approach to development aid: "African leadership has typically welcomed China's fresh approach to development assistance, which eschews any interference in domestic affairs, emphasizes partnership and solidarity among developing nations, and offers an alternative development model based on a more central role for the state."[110]

China's trade, aid, and investment in Africa has at least three implications for China's foreign policy and Western diplomacy in Africa.

---

[107] Christensen and Swan, 2008.

[108] Foster et al., 2008, p. x.

[109] Lyman, 2005.

[110] Foster et al., 2008, p. vii.

First, China's varied economic interests and historical relations with countries in Africa have led it to support regimes with dubious human rights records, such as Sudan and Zimbabwe. China's aid and assistance has helped shield such regimes from Western pressure, including multilateral sanctions. This has constrained the ability of Western diplomacy, in recent years, to effect change in these African nations.

However, growing international attention may also be precipitating a gradual change in China's diplomacy in Africa. Beijing's support for Sudan has not been unqualified, but only in the face of U.N. and international pressure; for example, Beijing did not obstruct (and in some cases supported) U.N. efforts to impose limited sanctions on Sudan, albeit grudgingly. The early 2007 effort by international nongovernmental organizations to link the 2008 Beijing Olympics to China's current support for the Sudanese government by labeling the 2008 Olympics the "genocidal" or "Darfur Olympics" appears to have galvanized Chinese leaders to become more involved in resolving the humanitarian crisis in Darfur. More generally, negative reactions among African publics to Chinese business practices prompted leaders in Beijing to sensitize both diplomats and business leaders to the possible effect on China's image of Chinese business practices and political relationships in Africa and other regions.[111]

A second challenge is that China's economic assistance has diminished the ability of Western pressure, such as International Monetary Fund limitations on aid or investment, to improve the governing practices of certain African nations. A third challenge is that the Chinese government's support for investments in Africa creates unfair competition for Western businesses that cannot afford to make unprofitable investments or offer various types of aid and assistance (as the Chinese do) to successfully bid on contracts. In business competition in Africa, such instruments of Chinese influence are often not available to Western businesses.[112]

---

[111] Glaser, 2007, pp. 2–5.

[112] Report of an Independent Task Force, *More Than Humanitarianism: A Strategic U.S. Approach Toward Africa*, New York: Council on Foreign Relations, November 2005, pp. 39–52.

China's expanding involvement in Latin America is primarily (but not exclusively) driven by economic considerations: gaining access to markets, investments, and resources. The growth in China's merchandise trade and investment in the region offers strong evidence of China's economic motives. Trade between China and Latin America and the Caribbean has rapidly increased over the last several years, and as a result, this region has become more important to China. From 1999 to 2006, total merchandise trade increased from $8.2 billion to close to $70 billion, an almost tenfold increase. In 2006, Latin America and the Caribbean accounted for 4 percent of China's total world trade, increasing its share by 1.7 percent since 1999.

Between 1999 and 2006, China's regional imports increased from close to $3 billion to nearly $34 billion. In terms of value, Brazil, Chile, Argentina, Peru, and Venezuela supplied most of China's imports in 2006. China's primary regional imports included iron, copper, lead and other ores, soybeans, crude oil and other mineral fuels, and electrical machinery. China's imports from any single country in Latin America and the Caribbean primarily comprise only one or two commodities. From 1999 to 2006, China's exports to Latin America and the Caribbean increased from $5.3 billion to $35.8 billion, with the primary markets being Mexico, Brazil, Panama, Chile, and Argentina. During this period, China primarily exported electrical machinery, appliances, apparel, footwear, and organic chemicals.[113]

China's trade with Latin America is a mixed blessing for the region. It offers opportunities for nations with rich natural resources, such as Brazil and Argentina, and presents harsh competition to those who produce low-end manufactured goods, such as Mexico. Mexico's textile and apparel industry, in particular, has been hurt by China's emergence as a major global textile and apparel producer, undercutting Mexico's competitiveness in other countries' textile markets.[114]

---

[113] Dumbaugh, 2008, pp. 20–21.

[114] These data are taken from the IMF's *Direction of Trade Statistics*, 2004. Also see Claudio Loser, "China's Rising Economic Presence in Latin America," testimony before the U.S.-China Economic and Security Review Commission on "China's Growing Global Role: Objectives and Influence," July 21, 2005.

China's investments in Latin America are growing as well. China currently has projects in Argentina, Brazil, Chile, Cuba, the Dominican Republic, Guyana, and Venezuela, among other nations. China's investments in Brazil, Argentina, Chile, and Venezuela are mainly focused on facilitating access to such natural resources as iron ore, copper, and oil (in the case of Venezuela); as such, its investments have been in the mining, transportation, manufacturing, and petroleum sectors. From 2003 to 2007, China's annual investment flow grew from $1 billion to $4.9 billion, and its cumulative stock of investment grew from $4.6 billion to $24.7 billion. However, China's investment in the region may not be nearly as high as it appears on paper. In 2007, the destinations for about 95 percent of Chinese FDI in this region were the Cayman Islands and the British Virgin Islands—countries known to be tax havens. As a large amount of FDI in China comes from these three countries, it is possible that Chinese investors reinvest the money in China as foreign capital to benefit from provisions for foreign investors (e.g., round-tripping). As for other parts of the region, in 2007, China's nonfinancial FDI was primarily directed at Mexico, Peru, Argentina, Brazil, and Venezuela. China's nonfinancial investment in Latin America has been primarily devoted to resource extraction and production but some has been directed at manufacturing assembly, telecommunications, and textiles.[115]

China's Diplomatic Goals. Beyond trade and investment, China's activities in both Latin America and Africa reflect specific diplomatic objectives as well. First, Chinese diplomacy is heavily oriented toward reducing support for Taiwan. Of the 23 countries with formal diplomatic relations with Taiwan, 12 are in Latin America. This number shrank from 14 in 2004, after Costa Rica (2007), Grenada (2005), and Dominica (2004) changed diplomatic recognition to Beijing (and St. Lucia switched back to Taiwan in 2007).[116] Four of the 23 nations

---

[115] Dumbaugh, 2008, pp. 22–23.

[116] Taiwan's official relations in Latin America include one South American country (Paraguay), six Central American countries (Belize, El Salvador, Guatemala, Honduras, Nicaragua, and Panama), and six Caribbean countries (the Dominican Republic, Haiti, St. Lucia, St. Kitts–Nevis, St. Vincent, and the Grenadines). These data were taken from the Ministry of Foreign Affairs, People's Republic of China, Web site.

with diplomatic relations with Taiwan are in Africa; this number has been gradually shrinking as countries such as Malawi (2008), Chad (2006), Senegal (2005), and Liberia (2003) established diplomatic ties with China.[117]

Chinese diplomacy in Latin America and Africa has sought for decades to persuade, coerce, and bribe countries to switch their diplomatic allegiance; China's efforts have received new intensity in recent years as its ability to offer aid, investment, and other creative financial enticements has increased.[118] For example, China, in a secret deal that was revealed in 2008, agreed in June 2007 to purchase $300 million in Costa Rican government bonds as part of a larger package to entice Costa Rica to switch its diplomatic recognition to mainland China. China has been making active efforts to push Paraguay, Guatemala, and Panama to do the same. As an indication of the new and less publicly confrontational tone in China's approach to appeal to the region, Beijing agreed in 2004 to contribute police forces to a U.N. Peacekeeping Operation in Haiti, despite Haiti's diplomatic relations with Taiwan.

Second, China seeks to build and maintain bilateral relationships to secure access to markets and natural resources in Africa and Latin America. China has used extensive high-level diplomacy in the last three to five years to pursue these goals. In 2004 alone, Hu Jintao and Wu Bangguo, the Communist party's two most senior officials, both visited Latin America. Chinese leaders also regularly meet with their Latin American counterparts in Beijing.

China's leadership diplomacy in Africa has been even more intensive than in Latin America (Table 6.1). The Chinese leadership has used such visits to manage its increasingly complex economic and political agenda with African nations and the implications of its

---

[117] Taiwan's official relations in Africa include four countries: Burkina Faso (1994), Gambia (1995), São Tomé and Príncipe (1997), and Swaziland (1968). These data were taken from the Ministry of Foreign Affairs, People's Republic of China, Web site.

[118] For example, China offered Dominica $122 million in aid over six years, which trumped Taiwan's $9 million in annual assistance to the small country. Kerry Dumbaugh and Mark P. Sullivan, *China's Growing Interest in Latin America*, Congressional Research Service, Washington, D.C.: Library of Congress, April 2005.

Table 6.1
Chinese Leaders' Visits to Africa, 1996–2009

Date	Chinese Leader	Countries Visited
May 1996	President Jiang Zemin; his first trip as president	Egypt, Ethiopia, Kenya, Mali, Namibia, Zimbabwe
May 1997	Premier Li Peng	Cameroon, Gabon, Mozambique, Nigeria, Seychelles, Tanzania, Zambia
January–February 1999	Vice President Hu Jintao: his first trip as vice president	Côte d'Ivoire, Ghana, Madagascar, South Africa
October–November 1999	President Jiang Zemin	Morocco, Nigeria
April 2000	President Jiang Zemin; the first Chinese president to visit South Africa, which switched diplomatic ties to China from Taiwan in 1998	Egypt, South Africa
April 2002	President Jiang Zemin	Libya, Nigeria, Tunisia
April 2002	Premier Zhu Rongji	Egypt, Kenya
August–September 2002	Premier Zhu Rongji	Algeria, Cameroon, Morocco, South Africa
December 2003	Premier Wen Jiabao: he attended the first meeting of the China-African Cooperation Forum	Ethiopia
January–February 2004	President Hu Jintao	Algeria, Egypt, Gabon
June 2004	Vice President Zeng Qinghong	Benin, South Africa, Togo, Tunisia,
April 2006	President Hu Jintao	Kenya, Morocco, Nigeria
June 2006	Premier Wen Jiabao	Angola, Egypt, Ghana, Democratic Republic of the Congo, South Africa, Tanzania
January–February 2007	President Hu Jintao	Cameroon, Liberia, Mozambique, Namibia, Seychelles, Sudan, Zambia
February 2009	President Hu Jintao	Mali, Mauritius, Senegal, Tanzania

SOURCES: Numerous media reports.

Africa policy for its broader international image (e.g., the humanitarian crisis in Darfur, Sudan). As noted above, since 2003, Hu Jintao has visited Africa four times and a total of 18 countries, an unprecedented amount for a Chinese leader in such a short period. This clearly reflects a top diplomatic priority on this continent.

In February 2007, Hu Jintao made a major state visit to eight African nations, including making controversial stops in Sudan and Zimbabwe. Notably, during the Sudan visit, Hu made his first public statements encouraging the Sudanese government to resolve the humanitarian crisis in Darfur, including a call for Sudan to allow U.N. and African Union peacekeepers into Darfur. In 2006, Hu Jintao and Wen Jiabao separately visited a total of 11 African nations; in 2005, Wen Jiabao and another Politburo Standing Committee member visited eight African nations; and in 2004, Hu Jintao and three other Politburo Standing Committee members visited 12 African nations. A key goal of these leaders' visits is gaining access to African resources: Hu Jintao's African tours in 2004 and 2006 both included stops in such oil-rich nations as Nigeria and Angola. But Hu's more recent visit, to four nations in early 2009, was to nonresource-rich countries to signal that China is committed to Africa's long-term political and economic development.

A third Chinese diplomatic goal in Africa and Latin America is promoting the interests of developing nations and forging common causes with them in international institutions. China regularly touts itself as the "largest developing nation" and, thus, as a natural protector of these nations' rights. China rhetorically promotes a common vision by advocating such diplomatic principles as equality, sovereignty, "win-win" cooperation, economic development, and noninterference in internal affairs. This approach redounds to China's economic and geopolitical benefit. China presents a "soft alternative" to U.S. and Western aid and lending policies, which at times has provided China with preferential access. China also uses common cause with African and Latin American nations to execute specific diplomatic goals. Developing nations can be a powerful voting block in international organizations. They can help to prevent votes against China, such as in the former U.N. Human Rights Commission. China's maneuverings with developing nations in the U.N. are discussed in more detail below.

China has pursued its political goals through both intensive bilateral and multilateral diplomacy. In Africa, China has established "strategic partnerships" with South Africa, Nigeria, and Angola, as well as with the region as a whole. In 2003 and 2004, China forged strategic partnerships with Argentina, Brazil, Mexico, and Venezuela (Table 5.4). Beijing may seek to use these partnerships in Latin America to signal implicitly to the United States that Beijing possesses influence in a region traditionally dominated by the United States.

Given that China's pro-development, pro-sovereignty, and pro-multilateralism diplomacy resonates with many Latin American and African capitals, relations with China provide them with some diplomatic and economic leverage in the face of the occasionally unappealing diplomacy by the United States and other Western nations. Hugo Chavez in Venezuela and, to a lesser extent, Luiz Inácio Lula da Silva in Brazil have used their ties with Beijing to manage their own relations with the United States. Chavez has successively—but not successfully—sought to draw China, using appeals of greater access to crude oil, into a coalition to oppose U.S. power. Although China has accepted offers of preferential access to crude oil and related investments, it has rejected Chavez's efforts to become part of an anti-U.S. partnership.[119]

Chinese foreign policy in these regions has a growing multilateral element as well, in both its goals and its execution. In 2000, China established the China-Africa Cooperation Forum to jointly discuss regional economic development initiatives and "to reach a broad consensus about establishing a fair and just international political and eco-

---

[119] Dumbaugh, 2008, pp. 16–30; William Ratliff, "The Global Context of a Chinese 'Threat' in Latin America," Miami, Fla.: China-Latin American Task Force, Center for Hemispheric Policy, University of Miami, June 2006b; William Ratliff, "Pragmatism over Ideology: China's Relations with Venezuela," *China Brief,* The Jamestown Foundation, Vol. 6, No. 6, March 15, 2006a, pp. 3–5; Amaury de Souza, "Brazil and China: An Uneasy Partnership," Miami, Fla.: China-Latin American Task Force, Center for Hemispheric Policy, University of Miami, June 2006; and Cynthia A. Watson, testimony before the U.S.-China Economic and Security Review Commission on "China's Growing Global Role: Objectives and Influence," July 21, 2005.

nomic order in the 21st century."[120] This forum has allowed China to bolster its political influence among African leaders; for example, China often uses the CACF meetings to launch major aid and trade promotion packages, such as in November 2006.[121] China joined the Organization of American States in May 2004 as an observer and has used its position to hinder Taiwan's effort to do likewise. China in 2008 finally reached an agreement to join the Inter-American Development Bank, which expands its ability to bid on lucrative development projects in Latin America.[122]

The Middle East

China's economic and security interests in the Middle East are expanding and diversifying. It is no longer a region of tertiary interest and occasional attention from Chinese policymakers. China's involvement in the Middle East has grown accordingly. In the last decade, China has been upgrading its diplomatic, economic, cultural, and military relations with several countries in the region. China's growing demand for energy is an important driver of this but it is not the only one. China's bilateral and multilateral diplomacy in the Middle East is also motivated by a search for overseas markets and investment opportunities, by a desire to foster stability in a region increasingly important to Beijing, and by a wish to generate leverage in its multilateral diplomacy beyond the Middle East.[123]

---

[120] "China-Africa Cooperation Forum: Past, Present and Future," December 11, 2003; the first ministerial meeting was in October 2000 and the second was in December 2003 in Addis Ababa, Ethiopia.

[121] Report of an Independent Task Force, 2005, pp. 39–52.

[122] The OAS currently has 35 members and 60 permanent observers. The resolution suggesting China's observer status was sponsored by Argentina, Bolivia, Brazil, Chile, Colombia, Mexico, Peru, Uruguay, and Venezuela. "OAS Accepts China as Permanent Observer," *People's Daily Online*, English ed., May 4, 2004; on the IADB, see Inter-American Development Bank, "People's Republic of China and Inter-American Development Bank Sign Memorandum of Understanding for Possible Admission to Membership into the IDB," news release, March 18, 2007.

[123] Very little has been written on China's relations with the Middle East. A recent and comprehensive study is John Alterman and John Garver, *The Vital Triangle: The United States, China and the Middle East,* Washington, D.C.: Center for Strategic and International Stud-

Chinese policymakers also remain wary of getting drawn into regional politics, especially the Israel-Palestine issue. China has sought and achieved a greater voice, but it will aver deep involvement, even when pulled by regional actors. This is emerging as a new tension in its effort to expand its presence and influence in the Middle East.

China's growing engagement with the Middle East is starting from a low baseline. China seldom devoted major political or diplomatic resources to Middle Eastern affairs before the 2000s. It lacked extensive expertise in the region, having nowhere near the levels of expertise it has on the United States or East Asia. China's strong rhetorical support (largely under Mao) for Palestinian and Arab causes changed as China toned down the ideological elements of its foreign policy in the 1980s and, more practically, as it sought to build better relations with Israel to gain access to conventional weapons and related technology imports. (Since the 1980s, Israel has become one of the top external arms suppliers to the Chinese military.)[124]

Moreover, the Middle East was never a region of high strategic value to China and certainly had nowhere near the levels of importance as East and South Asia. Instability in the Middle East seldom prompted concern among Chinese leaders, as indicated in part by their proclivity to introduce destabilizing weapon systems into regional conflicts. In the 1980s and 1990s, a main feature of China's Middle East diplomacy was arms sales to the region, aside from rhetorically touting Arab causes. This was largely for profit, except in the case of Iran, in which China also used such transfers to maintain some regional influence and generate leverage in dealings with the United States.[125] Examples of

---

ies, 2007. Also see Geoffrey Kemp, "The East Moves West," *National Interest,* No. 84, September 2006, p. 75; and Lillian Craig Harris, "Myth and Reality in China's Relations with the Middle East," in Thomas W. Robinson and David Shambaugh, eds., *Chinese Foreign Policy: Theory and Practice,* Oxford, UK: Clarendon Press, 1994, pp. 322–347.

[124] Interestingly, China began importing weapons from Israel in the 1980s, but Israel and China did not normalize relations until 1992. On the China-Israel arms linkage, see Yitzak Shichor, "Israel's Military Transfers to China and Taiwan," *Survival,* Vol. 40, No. 1, Spring 1998, pp. 68–91.

[125] John W. Garver, *China and Iran: Ancient Partners in a Post-Imperial World,* Seattle, Wash.: University of Washington Press, 2007, pp. 136–230; Evan S. Medeiros, *Reluctant*

major Chinese arms exports include sales of conventional weapons and cruise missiles to both Iraq and Iran during their conflict in the 1980s; sales of medium-range missiles to Saudi Arabia (1987–1988); civilian nuclear cooperation with Iran, which reportedly ended in 1997; and long-standing and extensive assistance to Iran's ballistic missile and cruise missile programs.[126]

Since the 1980s, China's relations with Iran have been the most high-profile and controversial aspect of its Middle East policy—to the extent that Beijing had a clear and coherent "policy" toward this region. Sino-Iranian relations have always loomed large for Beijing because of the complications they created for China's relations with the United States; in other words, China-Iran interactions were (and are) strongly influenced, in China's eyes, by the implications for U.S.-China ties. The stark differences in Chinese and U.S. views about Iran's intentions as a regional actor and as an aspiring proliferator fueled recurring tensions in U.S.-China relations. Whereas U.S. policymakers viewed Iran as a prime source of regional instability (because of its funding of terrorism and pursuit of WMD), China sought stable and amicable relations with Iran on the basis of their mutually beneficial arms trade relationship, their common views about both nations being great civilizations, their joint efforts to foster a more multipolar international system, and their mutual suspicion of the United States.[127] Beijing also frequently used its ties with Iran to generate leverage in U.S.-China relations, in particular to register opposition to such U.S. policies as arms sales to Taiwan. Some of these dynamics persist today.[128]

Restraint: The Evolution of Chinese Nonproliferation Policies and Practices 1980–2004, Stanford, Calif.: Stanford University Press, 2007, pp. 97–174.

[126] John Calabrese, "The Risks and Rewards of China's Deepening Ties with the Middle East," *China Brief*, The Jamestown Foundation, Vol. 5, No. 12, May 24, 2005. For more on some of these sales, see Evan S. Medeiros and Bates Gill, *Chinese Arms Exports: Policy, Players, and Process*, Strategic Studies Institute, Carlisle, Pa.: U.S. Army War College, 2000; and Yitzhak Shichor, "Decisionmaking in Triplicate: China and the Three Iraqi Wars," in Andrew Scobell and Larry M. Wortzel, eds., *Chinese National Security Decisionmaking Under Stress*, Carlisle, Pa.: Strategic Studies Institute, 2005.

[127] Garver, 2007.

[128] Medeiros, 2007, pp. 131–174.

In contrast to its past approach to the Middle East, China has increased its multilateral and bilateral interaction with regional nations, and Beijing is a far less passive actor than before. China forged "strategic partnerships" with two key countries—Saudi Arabia (1999) and Iran (2000), and it has frequent and expanding diplomatic exchanges with both. China's dedicated effort to grow its ties with the Saudis is a prime example of its goal to diversify its political and economic influence in the region. China established the Sino-Arab Cooperation Forum in 2004 to encourage cooperation on regional politics, trade, science, education, culture, and health care between China and Arab countries. Beijing maintains a dialogue with the Arab Gulf Cooperation Council; Hu Jintao met with the GCC's leadership in April 2006. In the wake of the 9/11 terrorist attacks on the United States, China appointed a special envoy to the Middle East who has sought to "promote reconciliation and facilitate dialogue" on the Middle East peace process, although China has avoided substantive involvement in that process.[129] In October 2006, following the Israel-Lebanon conflict earlier that summer, China pledged to expand to 1,000 the number of Chinese engineering troops that were supporting the U.N.'s Interim Force in Lebanon peacekeeping operation; China's commitment notably came as the U.N. faced problems finding contributors (even among the UNSC permanent member states) to the expanded peacekeeping activity in southern Lebanon.[130]

To increase its general political influence and economic leverage (i.e., its ability to win contract bids), China has provided development aid and infrastructure support to numerous Middle Eastern nations, most notably the Palestinian Authority and Iran. China has engaged actively in multilateral discussions about Iraq's future. It contributed to Iraq's reconstruction by agreeing, in June 2007, to forgive billions in

---

[129] Bai Jie and Cao Jia, "China's Special Envoy on the Middle East Issue Sun Bigan: China Hopes That Palestine Would Strengthen Internal Unity," *Xinhua*, August 2, 2007, as translated by OSC.

[130] "Commander Highlights Chinese Peacekeeping Force Role in Lebanon," *China Daily*, October 2, 2006.

Iraqi debt and offering millions in humanitarian aid.[131] In mid-2008, a Chinese national oil company was given the Iraqi government's first foreign contract to develop an Iraqi oil field. This pattern of using development aid to facilitate market access is similar to that used in Africa, as noted above.[132]

What has driven these policy shifts? China's Middle East diplomacy is increasingly, but not exclusively, influenced by its need for oil and natural gas. In 2008, about 50 percent of China's crude oil imports came from the Middle East, which makes it the region on which China relies most for imported oil. That figure has remained static for years, whereas China's imports from other regions, notably Russia and Africa, have grown substantially.[133] China's oil demand is rising and will likely be met by increased imports, including from this region. The International Energy Agency projects that China's dependence on imported oil will increase from 46 percent of total demand in 2004 to 63 percent in 2015 and 77 percent in 2030.[134] More than half of these imports are likely to continue coming from the Middle East, although estimates vary.[135] Already, China runs a trade deficit with major oil-producing countries in the Middle East, especially Saudi Arabia, Iran, and Oman.[136] Together, these three countries supplied China with 37 percent of its crude oil imports in 2007.[137] Not surprisingly, oil, and not exports of Chinese goods, dominates China's trade relationships with many Middle Eastern nations. Israel, the Levant,

---

[131] "China Agrees to Cancel Iraqi Debt," *China Daily*, June 21, 2007.

[132] Mao Yufeng, "Beijing's Two-Pronged Iraq Policy," *China Brief*, The Jamestown Foundation, Vol. 5, No. 12, May 14, 2005.

[133] Tian Chunrong, 2007, pp. 14–21.

[134] International Energy Agency, *World Energy Outlook 2006*, Paris, France: Organisation for Economic Co-operation and Development/International Energy Agency, 2006, p. 101.

[135] The U.S. Energy Information Administration has projected that 53 percent of China's oil imports in 2030 will come from members of the Organization of the Petroleum Exporting Countries. U.S. Energy Information Administration, *International Energy Outlook 2006*, June 2006, p. 34.

[136] International Monetary Fund, *Direction of Trade Statistics Yearbook*, 2005, p. 135.

[137] Tian Chunrong, 2007, p. 16.

Egypt, and the United Arab Emirates are exceptions to this trend. The United Arab Emirates for many years has been the biggest importer of Chinese goods in the region.[138] The Middle East may become a more lucrative export market for China as countries import Chinese technology, which is already the case in Egypt.[139]

The relative importance of energy is reflected in China's regional diplomacy. China continues to work assiduously to secure oil and natural gas trade and investment deals with Iran and Saudi Arabia as a way to secure long-term access.[140] A Chinese state-owned oil company, Sinopec, in December 2007, signed a $70 billion to $100 billion deal to develop the giant Yadavaran oil field in Iran (in exchange for pledges to purchase natural gas from Iran), although this agreement has yet to be finalized.[141] In December 2006, another Chinese state-owned company, China National Offshore Oil Corporation, signed a memorandum of understanding with Iran to invest $16 billion in the development of the North Pars gas field and the construction of gas liquefaction facilities. In Saudi Arabia, Sinopec, in January 2004, also secured a natural gas exploration block in Rub al-Khali in an auction that failed to attract the interest of most major international companies. In March 2006, Sinopec, Saudi Aramco, Exxon Mobil, and the Fujian provincial government finalized joint venture agreements to expand the capacity of the Fujian refinery, which will primarily process Saudi crude oil.

---

[138] International Monetary Fund, *Direction of Trade Statistics Yearbook*, 2000, p. 164; and International Monetary Fund, 2005, p. 135.

[139] "Egypt Seeks Stronger Trade Ties with China," *Asia Pulse*, September 11, 2006.

[140] Saudi Arabia does not allow foreign companies to invest in its upstream (exploration and production) oil sector, but it has allowed them to invest in the upstream gas sector. Iran allows upstream investment but does not permit foreign companies to have equity stakes. Thanks to Erica Downs for providing this information.

[141] The deal was initially valued at $70 billion (and later $100 billion) because it was originally linked to Sinopec's purchase of 250 million tons of liquefied natural gas over 25 years, and the estimated value of these gas purchases constituted the bulk of the $70 billion to $100 billion estimate. The Yadavaran field and liquefied natural gas purchases have since been unlinked. Steven Weisman, "Politeness of China Talks Can't Disguise the Discord," *New York Times,* December 15, 2007.

China's desire for greater access to Middle Eastern energy supplies should not be overstated as a driver of its regional diplomacy. Although China's reliance on oil imports is growing and it imports much crude oil from the Middle East, it has also initiated a national energy diversification strategy that eventually could moderate the growth in imports. Also, China is diversifying its sources of energy imports, especially from such politically volatile and diplomatically complex regions as the Middle East. China is concerned about its reliance on energy shipments through vulnerable sea lanes, through which much Middle Eastern oil travels. China is looking for both alternative suppliers and alternative routes for transporting energy resources to China. Its crude oil imports from Russia are large (9 percent in 2007) and rising rapidly (a 25 percent increase in 2007). China is investing in numerous projects within Central Asia (notably in Kazakhstan) that would facilitate land transport of oil and natural gas resources.[142] This effort is already reflected to some extent in Chinese crude imports: The growth in China's imports from the Middle East slowed to 9 percent in 2006, and the growth in imports from Africa and Eurasia were 19 percent and 30 percent, respectively.

Beyond energy security, Beijing is concerned about the rise of Islamic extremism in the Middle East, fearing that it could embolden and materially assist Muslim Uighur separatists in Xinjiang Province. Such concerns about extremism and transnational terrorist networks are one reason that Chinese policymakers, more frequently than in past years, express concerns about regionwide instability. These concerns motivate China's efforts to foster stability through more aid and diplomatic involvement. China created a special envoy to the region and has even participated in peace process negotiations, such as the 2007–2008 Annapolis Process. At the same time, a distinct objective for Chinese policymakers is to avoid getting drawn deeply into Middle East politics, which they view as too complex to resolve and as sapping China's diplomatic resources. Last, China's Middle East policymaking is part and parcel of Beijing's broader effort to promote its view of

---

[142] Kemp, 2006, p. 75; and Don Lee, "China Barrels Ahead in Oil Market," *Los Angeles Times*, November 14, 2004.

building a more multipolar international system in which Beijing can forge coalitions among developing countries to advance China's positions in major multilateral organizations such as the U.N.[143]

China's approach to the Middle East continues to be shaped by its relations with the United States and Chinese perceptions of U.S. objectives in the region. Chinese leaders recognize that U.S. presence in the Middle East is considered by Washington as a strategic interest, that U.S. diplomatic and military presence will persist for decades, and that U.S. policy is critical to regional stability—as well as being a source of much instability. Chinese policymakers harbor deep suspicions that the long-term U.S. intention is to dominate the region, and Chinese leaders often disagree with the specific policies that the United States has used to pursue perceived American objectives (notably the 2003 intervention in Iraq). Chinese strategists also recognize that the U.S. involvement in Iraq has so heavily preoccupied U.S. leaders (and so drawn on U.S. diplomatic and military resources) that it has created welcome breathing space in U.S.-China relations and diverted U.S. attention away from East Asia.[144]

Chinese views about the U.S. regional role manifest in a balancing act in China's Middle East diplomacy—one that is becoming more complex for Beijing as its interests expand. China seeks to maintain positive relations with both Sunni and Shia Arab states, on the one hand, and with Israel and Arab states, on the other hand. China also seeks to avoid actions that will place it in direct confrontation with the United States, such as large and high-profile arms sales or a close association with Iran. At the same time, Beijing wants to build and main-

---

[143] Li Shaoxian and Tang Zhichao, "China and the Middle East," *Contemporary International Relations,* English ed., Vol. 17, No. 1, January/February 2007, pp. 22–31; *Guoji Zhanlue yu Anquan Xingshi Pinggu 2003–2004,* 2004, pp. 20–41; and *Guoji Zhanlue yu Anquan Xingshi Pinggu 2004–2005,* 2005, pp. 21–42, 223–241.

[144] Li Shaoxian and Tang Zhichao, 2007, pp. 22–31; Hua Liming, "Yilan He Wenti yu Zhongguo Waijiao de Xuanze" [The Iran Nuclear Questions and the Choices for Chinese Diplomacy], *Guoji Wenti Yanjiu* [China International Studies], No. 1, 2007, pp. 58–62; *Guoji Zhanlue yu Anquan Xingshi Pinggu 2003–2004,* 2004, pp. 20–41; *Guoji Zhanlue yu Anquan Xingshi Pinggu 2004–2005,* 2005, pp. 21–42, 223–241; and interviews with Chinese scholars, Beijing, 2007.

tain political relationships that will ensure access to resources and markets, even when this involves preserving ties with controversial nations such as Iran. Beijing is also pursuing policies that would prevent the United States from restricting China's ability to exercise political and economic influence; this manifests in China's regional aid, expanding diplomatic relationships, and continued pursuit of energy deals and weapons technology exports to Iran despite U.S. protests. China's "middle-man" approach to UNSC deliberations on Iran's nuclear weapons program similarly further reflects China's effort to balance these multiple regional objectives, specifically its interests in nonproliferation and regional stability, on the one hand, and access to energy supplies and stable relations with Iran, on the other.

Overall, China's evolving policymaking toward the Middle East is focused on diversifying its political and economic relationships to protect its equities in the region. China's desire for access to energy supplies plays a leading role, but not an exclusive one, in Beijing's calculations. As these material interests expand, China's stake in fostering regional stability will likely increase as well; indeed there is already evidence of this. This development, in turn, may precipitate heretofore avoidable tradeoffs in China's Middle East diplomacy that lead Beijing to contribute to regional or international processes to moderate state behaviors (such as Iran's support for terrorism and weapons proliferation).[145] These trends aside, the broader context of Chinese Middle East diplomacy should not be lost: Chinese foreign policy will continue to give priority to China's Asian neighbors and its relations with major powers. Even among China's ties with developing nations, the Middle East does not appear to garner as much of China's political and economic resources as do China's ties with Africa, even though Beijing's attention to and activities in the Middle East are expanding.

---

[145] For example, Chinese policymakers increasingly recognize the dangers of Iran possessing nuclear weapons. Hua Liming, 2007, pp. 58–62.

Multilateral Diplomacy

Since the mid-1990s, Chinese views on the value of multilateral organizations evolved from passivity and skepticism to active embrace of them. Chinese policymakers now see multilateral organizations as central to the Chinese goals of advancing "multipolarization," fostering the emergence of a "just and rational international order," and "building a harmonious world." The importance of multilateralism has grown. Beginning around 2002, Chinese leaders, policymakers, and state media started *reducing* their classic calls for greater "multipolarity" and less "hegemony and power politics"; instead, they began emphasizing the role of multilateral organizations in addressing global economic and security challenges.[146]

This change in rhetoric was more than just symbolism. In 2004, China's top leaders elevated explicitly the concept of "cooperation," along with the core ideas of "peace and development," as three defining principles in China's diplomacy.[147] The addition of this third term underscored China's commitment to multilateralism as a mechanism of reassurance and also as an indication of China's growing comfort with and use of such institutions. Thus, there is a firm policy basis for this priority in China's official diplomacy—one that is sanctioned at the highest levels of the CCP. Most notably, multilateralism has become a pillar of Hu Jintao's foreign policy and a way for his administration to distinguish (albeit modestly) its diplomatic approach from that of Hu's predecessors.[148]

---

[146] This shift is apparent in a comparison of the 2000 and 2002 Chinese national defense white papers.

[147] For the current official foreign policy lexicon, see Yang Jiechi, 2008.

[148] Interviews with Chinese officials and scholars, Beijing and Shanghai, 2005. Official Chinese commentary regularly highlights peace, development, and *cooperation* as the core principles in Chinese foreign policy. These three themes were reiterated at an important August 2006 Central Party Conference on Foreign Affairs work; "Adhere to Peaceful Development Road, Push Forward Building of Harmonious World," 2006; and "Central Foreign Affairs Meeting Held in Beijing," 2006.

For earlier references, see Li Zhaoxing "Heping, Fazhan, Hezuo: Xin Shiqi Zhongguo Waijiao de Qizhi," August 22, 2005; and Ministry of Foreign Affairs, the People's Republic of

China in the U.N.

China's behavior in the United Nations is a leading indicator of its affinity for using multilateral organizations to advance its objectives. China has been more involved and assertive in its U.N. activities, including in the UNSC and U.N. affiliate organizations, such as the International Atomic Energy Agency (IAEA) and the Conference on Disarmament (CD). For Beijing, the U.N. is the center of its support for multilateralism and building a multipolar international system. As Chinese President Hu Jintao stated during a speech at the U.N.'s 60th anniversary in 2005, "[We should] uphold multilateralism to realize common security. . . . The United Nations, as the core of the collective security mechanism, plays an irreplaceable role in international cooperation to ensure global security. Such a role can only be strengthened and must not in any way be weakened."[149]

China pursues several goals in its U.N. activities.[150] First, it seeks to bolster the U.N.'s standing as the premier multilateral organization that can promote China's vision of "democracy in international affairs" and building a "just and fair international order."[151] With China being a veto-wielding, permanent member of the U.N. Security Council, such goals are not communitarian altruism but directly advance China's foreign policy objectives. In practical terms, what that means is that China uses its position to change U.N. actions it opposes and to advance the ones it supports. China, for example, hails the U.N. as a citadel of

China, "Foreign Minister Li Zhaoxing Delivers a Speech to UN General Assembly," 59th U.N. General Assembly, September 28, 2004.

[149] Hu Jintao, "Build Towards a Harmonious World of Lasting Peace and Common Prosperity," speech at the Plenary Meeting of the United Nations' 60th Session, New York, United Nations, September 22, 2005.

[150] Samuel S. Kim, "China and the United Nations," in Elizabeth Economy and Michel Oksenberg, eds., *China Joins the World: Progress and Prospects*, New York: Council on Foreign Relations Press, 1999, pp. 42–89.

[151] Yang Jiechi, 2008; for past accounts, see Li Zhaoxing, "2006 Nian Guoji Xingshi he Zhongguo Waijiao Gongzuo" [International Situation and China's Diplomatic Work in 2006], *Qiushi* (online), January 2007; and Li Zhaoxing, "Wei Renmin Fuwu de Xin Zhongguo Waijiao" [New China's Diplomacy of Serving the People], *Qiushi* (online), October 2004.

multilateral cooperation but, for all practical purposes, it opposes the expansion of the permanent membership of the U.N. Security Council to include Japan, India, or Brazil. China's use of the U.N. to promote its worldview is increasingly reflected in Chinese efforts to constrain or alter U.S. positions in the U.N. Security Council on such controversial security issues as North Korea, Iran, Sudan, and Burma.

Second, China has historically seen the U.N. as a prime venue in which to reduce international support for Taiwan and to prod nations to transfer their formal diplomatic relations to Beijing. Of China's six UNSC vetoes to date, two have been related to denying U.N. peace-keeping support to nations that recognized Taiwan. China has become more subtle in its Taiwan-related U.N. diplomacy, but this motive is still prominent.

Third, China uses the U.N. to validate and bolster its image as a major power worthy of respect and deference; in recent years, it has used its UNSC actions to demonstrate that it is a "responsible major developing nation" that seeks to address such common, global security challenges as WMD proliferation and terrorism.[152] This Chinese goal has meant that the quality of its participation in U.N. activities has improved, and it has become slightly more transparent as a government. This motivation is most strongly reflected in China's substantial contributions to U.N. peacekeeping operations; it has contributed more than any other permanent member of the Security Council. Also, China has begun to participate in U.N.-led processes to improve transparency on defense issues. This requires that it report its annual defense expenditures to the U.N., and in 2008 it restarted its annual reporting to the U.N. Register on Conventional Arms Exports, which was suspended in 1997 over a dispute about how to classify U.S. arms sales to Taiwan.

Last, a central, but more subtle, driver of China's U.N. diplomacy is to constrain the U.S. assertion of its power and minimize U.S. ability to impose its solutions on international problems. Many Chinese analysts see the U.N. as a mechanism to moderate U.S. "unilateralism"

---

[152] In Wen Jiabao's 2008 speech to the U.N. General Assembly, he referred to China as a "responsible major developing nation."

by bolstering the organization's ability to constrain the prerogatives of the United States and its allies.[153] This is most evident in topics related to human rights, humanitarian questions, and imposition of penalties and sanctions. Seldom mentioned in Chinese public statements, this objective is evident in numerous Chinese actions at the UNSC (detailed below) and is a reflection of contrasting U.S. and Chinese visions of state sovereignty and involvement in other states' internal affairs.

In this decade, China has been more openly resistant to U.S. policies that directly affect China's economic and security interests, such as U.S. efforts to impose economic sanctions on Sudan, or the U.S. push for nonproliferation-related sanctions against North Korea or Iran. Chinese cooperation with Russia in shaping U.N. debates, especially opposing U.S. positions, on these issues has grown substantially in the latter half of this decade.

This is a complex and shifting objective for Beijing, largely because of the competing foreign policy objective of not confronting or openly antagonizing Washington. This latter dynamic was evident in China's low-key but "principled opposition" to U.S. efforts to seek U.N. authorization for the 2003 military intervention in Iraq; Beijing let Moscow and Paris lead the charge in opposing U.S. actions. Since then, China's tolerance for disagreeing with the United States at the U.N. seems to have grown. Beijing has shown increased willingness to assert itself in high-profile UNSC debates and to openly contradict Washington. This is largely a function of several factors: China's growing confidence in its own capabilities; its willingness to tolerate negative U.S. reactions and a related view that the United States needs China more than before; Beijing's perception that the U.S. image and influence were in decline during the Bush administration; its expanding global economic interests; and China's ability to work with other nations, such as Russia, to avoid isolation in its disagreements with the United States.

---

[153] Interviews with Chinese officials and scholars, Beijing and Shanghai, 2005.

U.N. Security Council Activities

China's involvement, activism, and assertiveness in the U.N. are evident in its UNSC-related activities. Several examples are provided below: U.N. peacekeeping operations, Somalia, Sudan, Taiwan, and other UNSC debates.

Peacekeeping Operations. China has quantitatively and qualitatively expanded its participation in U.N. peacekeeping operations (UNPKOs) in the last five years. As of 2008, China is the largest contributor to UNPKOs among the five permanent members of the U.N. Security Council and almost the largest contributor among other NATO member states. In 2008, China was the 12th largest contributor to U.N. peacekeeping operations among all U.N. members. China currently deploys 1,861 troops, 88 military observers, and 208 police to 12 U.N. peacekeeping operations worldwide (Table 6.2).[154]

China first began participating in UNPKOs in 1990 but, throughout that decade, its contributions were limited to providing a few military observers and civilian police to some U.N. operations. In the 2000s, China dramatically expanded its contributions, which have increased 20 times since 2000 (whereas those of the United States, Russia, and the UK have declined or not grown). About 75 percent of China's contributions are to UNPKOs in Africa, and this number is set to increase as China augments its deployments to UNPKOs in the Darfur region of Sudan, Liberia, and the Democratic Republic of the Congo. China's contributions are commonly in the functional areas of engineering, medical services, and transportation. China is also the second-largest contributor of civilian police (from the Ministry of Public Security) to UNPKOs.

The quality of China's involvements in UNPKOs has improved as well. In September 2007, the U.N. for the first time appointed a Chinese General, Zhao Jingmin, as the primary commander for the U.N. Mission for the Referendum in Western Sahara (MINURSO).

---

[154] Bates Gill and Chin-hao Huang, "China's Expanding Presence in UN Peacekeeping Operations and Implications for the United States," in Roy Kamphausen, David Lai, and Andrew Scobell, eds., *PLA Missions Other Than Taiwan*, Carlisle, Pa.: U.S. Army War College, April 2009, pp. 99–126.

Table 6.2
Contributions to U.N. Peacekeeping Operations

U.N. Peacekeeping Mission	Date	Noncombatant Troops (Current/ Historical Total)	Military Observers and Staff Officers (Current/ Historical Total)	Police (Current/ Historical Total)
U.N. Truce Supervision Organization	April 1990–present		2/89	
U.N. Iraq-Kuwait Observer Mission	April 1991–October 2003		0/164	
U.N. Mission for the Referendum in Western Sahara	September 1991–present		13/314	
U.N. Transitional Authority in Cambodia	April 1992–September 1993	0/800	0/97	
U.N. Operation in Mozambique	June 1993–December 1994		0/20	
U.N. Observer Mission in Liberia	November 1993–September 1997		0/33	
U.N. Special Mission in Afghanistan	May 1998–January 2000		0/2	
U.N. Observer Mission in Sierra Leone	August 1998–December 2005		0/37	
U.N. Department of Peacekeeping Operations	February 1999–present		2/11	
U.N. Mission in Ethiopia and Eritrea	October 2000–August 2008		0/49	
U.N. Mission in Bosnia and Herzegovina	January 2001–January 2002			0/20
U.N. Mission in the Congo (Kinshasa)	April 2001–present	218/1,962	16/101	
U.N. Mission of Support in East Timor	May 2002–April 2005			0/207
U.N. Mission in Liberia	October 2003–present	558/3,906	7/70	8/83
U.N. Assistance Mission in Afghanistan	January 2004–May 2005			0/3

Table 6.2—continued

U.N. Peacekeeping Mission	Date	Noncombatant Troops (Current/ Historical Total)	Military Observers and Staff Officers (Current/ Historical Total)	Police (Current/ Historical Total)
U.N. Operation in Côte d'Ivoire	March 2004–present		7/33	
U.N. Mission in Kosovo	April 2004–present			18/73
U.N. Stabilization Mission in Haiti	May 2004–present			143/916 (anti-riot police)
U.N. Operation in Burundi	June 2004–September 2006		0/6	
U.N. Mission in the Sudan	May 2005–present	435/1,740	23/88	18/47
U.N. Interim Force in Lebanon	March 2006–present	335/1,187	9/24	
U.N. Integrated Mission in Timor-Leste	October 2006–present		2/7	21/30
U.N. Integrated Office in Sierra Leone	February 2007–February 2008		0/1	
African Union–U.N. Hybrid Operation in Darfur	November 2007–present	315/315	7/7	
Total (2,157)		1,861	88	208

SOURCES: *China's National Defense in 2008*, 2009, Appendix III (data as of November 30, 2008); The Central People's Government of the People's Republic of China, "Zhongguo Weihe Budui" [China's Peacekeeping Forces], 2008; and United Nations Peacekeeping, Monthly Summary of Contributors of Military and Civilian Personnel, 2008.

According to Bates Gill and Chin-hao Huang, "There are now at least three Chinese nationals serving in the Force Generation Unit, Military Planning Service Office and the Operations Office for the Asia and Middle East Division at U.N. headquarters."[155]

In addition, China has become more politically flexible in the operations it supports. In 2004, it initially contributed 130 police officers to the UNPKO in Haiti, even though Haiti recognizes Taiwan, and then expanded the contribution to 143 by early 2009.[156] This was the first time that China has taken such a step; in the late 1990s, it vetoed UNSC resolutions authorizing such peacekeeping operations in nations that recognize Taiwan (Guatemala in 1997 and Macedonia in 1999).[157] Gill and Chin-hao Huang argue that even on a highly sensitive issue that directly affects China's international image, such as the humanitarian crisis in Darfur, "Beijing has adopted a more active approach, supporting the need for political reconciliation and a hybrid African Union/United Nations peacekeeping force to address the humanitarian crisis. In early 2008, China dispatched some 140 engineering troops to Darfur to help prepare the way for the larger U.N. force envisioned by the international community."[158]

Somalia. In 2003 and 2004, China led the charge in UNSC deliberations on the Somalia peace process. In 2003, it took the unusual step of chairing a resolution on the peace process in which it was designated as the lead and thus "held the pen" on drafting relevant statements and resolutions. In 2004, China prodded the UNSC to frequently issue UNSC presidential statements on Somalia—nearly doubling the number from previous years. China also insisted—during an unusual UNSC meeting held in Nairobi, Kenya (convened to address the Darfur crisis in Sudan)—that the council members address the Somalia issue first. China successfully pushed for Somali leaders to

---

[155] Gill and Chin-hao Huang, 2009.

[156] These are official Chinese numbers taken from China's 2006 national defense white paper.

[157] Sally Morphet, "China as a Permanent Member of the Security Council: October 1971–December 1999," *Security Dialogue*, Vol. 31, No 2, 2000, pp. 151–166.

[158] Gill and Chin-hao Huang, 2009.

speak to the UNSC meeting in Nairobi *before* it discussed the Sudan issue. As a result of China's efforts, the UNSC issued five presidential statements on Somalia and an equivalent number of UNSC resolutions. Chinese motivations for assuming such an active role are not clear, as China has no major economic or diplomatic stakes in Somalia. A possible explanation is that Beijing sought to improve China's standing with East African nations, an area in which Taiwan has some diplomatic relations and the United States has traditionally been isolated.[159]

Sudan. China's diplomatic activism in the UNSC has been most prominent and public in deliberations about Sudan's Darfur crisis. China consistently used its position on the UNSC to shield the Sudanese government from sanctions and other international opprobrium (Table 6.3).

Beginning in early 2004, China initially sought to keep the Darfur issue off the UNSC agenda, even as Kofi Annan and other senior U.N. officials were raising public awareness of the emerging humanitarian crisis there.[160] Once the Darfur issue was put onto the UNSC agenda, China opposed several draft resolutions that would impose economic penalties on the government in Khartoum for its support of Janjaweed militia activities in Darfur. In UNSC deliberations, Beijing threatened to veto several such resolutions, even after Washington declared Khartoum's activities to constitute "genocide." China actively argued against resolutions that placed sanctions on Sudan's petroleum sector (e.g., UNSC 1564), imposed an arms embargo on Sudan (e.g., UNSC 1556), expanded the scope of the arms embargo to all parties operating in Darfur and imposed additional measures including a travel ban and an assets freeze on individuals designated by the UNSC Sudan Sanctions Committee (e.g., UNSC 1591), and referred the Sudan issue to the International Criminal Court (e.g., UNSC 1593). Also, China (working often through Pakistan and Syria, perhaps to deflect criticism from itself) sought to lessen the scope of

---

[159] Interviews with U.S. diplomats at the U.S. mission to the U.N., New York, April 2005.

[160] James Traub, "The World According to China," *New York Times Magazine*, September 3, 2006, pp. 24–29.

Table 6.3
China's U.N. Security Council Votes on Sudan

U.N. Security Council Resolutions	Key Aspects of UNSC Resolutions on Sudan	China's Vote
	2004 Votes	
1. 1547 June 11, 2004	This was the first UNSC resolution to address the Darfur issue.	Yes
	The Security Council unanimously voted to send an advance team to Southern Sudan. This team, UNAMIS, had the mandate to facilitate contacts with concerned parties and to prepare for the introduction of a U.N. peace support operation.	
	The resolution welcomed the North-South peace agreement and called on involved parties to "bring an immediate halt to the fighting in the Darfur region."	
2. 1556 July 30, 2004	The resolution imposed an arms embargo on all nongovernmental combatants in Darfur, including the Janjaweed militias.	Abstain (with Pakistan)
	The council threatened to "consider further actions" under Article 41 of the U.N. Charter if the Sudanese government failed to disarm the Janjaweed within 30 days. (Article 41 gives the council a wide range of nonmilitary powers including "complete or partial interruption of economic relations.")	
	The resolution also endorsed the deployment of a protection force by the African Union to monitor the April 2004 cease-fire in Darfur.	
3. 1564 September 18, 2004	The resolution pointed out the Sudanese government's failure to disarm the Janjaweed militia, provide security for civilians, and bring perpetrators of violence to justice.	Abstain (with Algeria, Russia, and Pakistan)
	The resolution called on member states to support an expanded African Union mission in Darfur and requested an international commission of inquiry into genocide.	
	The council again threatened to "consider additional measures," possibly involving the petroleum sector, should the Sudan government fail to comply.	

Table 6.3—continued

U.N. Security Council Resolutions	Key Aspects of UNSC Resolutions on Sudan	China's Vote
4. 1574 November 19, 2004	The Security Council held an extraordinary meeting in Nairobi to encourage progress in peace talks between Khartoum and the Sudanese Liberation Army.	Yes
	Unable to impose sanctions, the council sought to tempt the Sudanese government and rebel forces into ceasing all violence in Darfur by offering international aid.	
	This resolution called on the African Union to expand its mission in Darfur and stressed the need for human rights monitors in the region.	
2005 Votes		
5. 1585 March 10, 2005	Extended the mandate of UNAMIS.	Yes
6. 1588 March 17, 2005	Extended the mandate of UNAMIS.	Yes
7. 1590 March 24, 2005	The Security Council established UNMIS, which consisted of 10,000 U.N. forces, to work together with the African Union Mission in Sudan.	Yes
	The U.N. peacekeepers oversaw the implementation of the cease-fire and monitored the North-South Comprehensive Peace Agreement, which called for "disarmament, demobilization and reintegration" of armed forces.	
	The U.N. decided not to deploy troops to Darfur to address human rights violations.	
8. 1591 March 29, 2005	In response to the failure of all armed parties in Sudan to comply with previous Security Council resolutions, the council ordered a travel ban and a freeze on all assets for human rights violators in Sudan.	Abstain (with Algeria and Russia)
	The resolution did not include an oil embargo on Sudan, which China would almost certainly have vetoed.	
	The document is a modified version of an earlier U.S. draft resolution, which called for the establishment of a U.N. peacekeeping mission for Darfur as well as imposition of sanctions, including a freeze on the country's "economic resources."	

Table 6.3—continued

U.N. Security Council Resolutions	Key Aspects of UNSC Resolutions on Sudan	China's Vote
9. 1593 March 31, 2005	The Security Council decided to refer perpetrators of human rights abuses in Sudan's Darfur region to the International Criminal Court, bringing an end to a long-standing discussion between council members and overcoming the threat of a U.S. veto. The adoption of Resolution 1593 marked the first time the Security Council referred a case to the International Criminal Court.	Abstain (with the United States, Algeria, and Brazil)
10. 1627 September 23, 2005	Extended the mandate for UNMIS.	Yes
11. 1651 December 21, 2005	Emphasized the need to respect the provisions of the charter concerning privileges and immunities, and the Convention on the Privileges and Immunities of the United Nations. Extended the mandate for the Panel of Experts.	Yes
2006 Votes		
12. 1663 March 24, 2006	The resolution asked Secretary General Kofi Annan to "expedite the necessary preparatory planning for transition" from the African Union peacekeeping mission in Darfur to a U.N. operation by April 24, 2006. The council also requested that UNMIS intensify its efforts to coordinate closely with the African force during the transitional period. The council called on Annan to recommend ways to deal more effectively with the Lord's Resistance Army, the Uganda-based rebel group that the council condemned for human rights abuses.	Yes
13. 1665 March 29, 2006	Extended the mandate for the Panel of Experts.	Yes
14. 1672 April 25, 2006	The resolution imposed sanctions on four Sudanese nationals accused of war crimes in Darfur. China, Russia, and Qatar abstained from voting, arguing that sanctions would interfere with the Abuja peace negotiations.	Abstain (with Qatar and Russia)

Table 6.3—continued

U.N. Security Council Resolutions	Key Aspects of UNSC Resolutions on Sudan	China's Vote
	The U.S.-sponsored resolution placed restrictions on the assets and international travel of two rebel leaders, a former Sudanese air force chief, and the leader of a pro-government militia.	
	Although the council ordered sanctions against human rights violators in March 2005, the vote marked the first time that sanctions were applied against individuals directly involved in the Darfur conflict.	
15. 1679 May 16, 2006	The resolution sought to speed up the transition of the African Union peacekeeping mission in Darfur to a larger U.N. force.	Yes
	The U.S.-drafted resolution threatened sanctions against any group that attempted to hinder or prevent implementation of the peace agreement between the Sudanese government and the Sudan Liberation Army.	
16. 1706 August 31, 2006	Acting under Chapter VII of the U.N. Charter, the Security Council expanded the mandate of UNMIS to use all necessary means within its capabilities to protect civilians from violence.	Abstain (with Qatar and Russia)
	According to the resolution, the U.N. should deploy 17,000 peacekeepers in Darfur.	
	While confronted with Khartoum's refusal to have international troops in its territory, the UNSC invited the consent of the Sudanese government.	
17. 1709 September 22, 2006	With a unanimous vote, the Security Council extended the mandate of UNMIS until October 8, 2006, with the intention of further renewal.	Yes
	The resolution came after Secretary General Kofi Annan's earlier warning that Darfur was heading for disaster. In extending the mandate, the council affirmed that the situation in Sudan constitutes "a threat to international peace and security," language invoking the U.N. Charter's Chapter VII.	
18. 1713 September 29, 2006	Extended the mandate for the Panel of Experts.	Yes

Table 6.3—continued

U.N. Security Council Resolutions	Key Aspects of UNSC Resolutions on Sudan	China's Vote
19. 1714 October 6, 2006	Extended the mandate for UNMIS.	Yes
2007 Votes		
20. 1755 April 30, 2007	Calls on the parties to the Comprehensive Peace Agreement, the Darfur Peace Agreement, the N'Djamena Humanitarian Ceasefire Agreement, the Eastern Sudan Peace Agreement, and the communiqué of March 28 to respect their commitments and implement fully all aspects of those agreements without delay. Calls on those parties that have not signed the Darfur Peace Agreement to do so without delay and not to act in any way that would impede the implementation of the agreement.	Yes
21. 1769 July 31, 2007	Established the African Union/ United Nations Hybrid operation in Darfur (UNAMID); UNAMID shall monitor whether any arms or related material are present in Darfur in violation of Resolution 1556.	Yes
22. 1779 September 28, 2007	Extends the mandate for the Panel of Experts.	Yes
23. 1784 October 31, 2007	Extends the mandate for UNMIS.	Yes

SOURCES: The summaries of these resolutions are drawn from the text of the UNSC resolutions as well as summaries provided by the Global Policy Forum, the United Nations Security Council, and the U.S. State Department.

these sanctions. China eventually abstained on all four of these UNSC sanction resolutions, after moderating the language of many of them, including eliminating references to Chapter VII of the U.N. Charter. Beijing reluctantly agreed to UNSC Resolution 1590, which called for creation of a U.N. Mission in the Sudan (UNMIS) and deployment of 10,000 military personnel. In August 2006, Beijing abstained on another key UNSC vote on resolution 1706, which expanded the size of the original UNMIS force and called for its deployment to Darfur. Khartoum opposed 1706 as well. Beijing's position was that

Khartoum's consent is required to deploy the U.N. forces to Darfur—consent that was not forthcoming until mid-2007.[161]

Beginning in late 2006, China began to play a more active role in resolving the Darfur situation, including putting pressure on the Sudanese government. According to the joint congressional testimony of two deputy assistant secretaries of state, Thomas Christensen and James Swan,

> Since late 2006 China has shown an increased willingness to engage with the international community on Darfur, and has applied diplomatic pressure on the Government of Sudan to change its behavior, as well as to engage in a political process for a peaceful negotiation to the Darfur conflict. China voted for UNSC Resolution 1769 that created the hybrid United Nations African Mission in Darfur, but has at times acquiesced in the Government of Sudan's opposition to its full implementation. China has pledged up to 300 military engineers, of whom 140 have been dispatched, making China the first non-African Troop Contributing Country to deploy in Darfur. China has also become more involved in responding to the humanitarian crisis, providing some direct assistance and donating $1.8 million U.S. dollars to the Darfur region and the African Union Special Mission.[162]

Chinese diplomats and analysts have been relatively clear, in both public and private, about the symbolic and material motivations for Beijing's actions on the Darfur crisis. Publicly, Chinese diplomats raise the banner of China's long-standing opposition to external interference in the internal affairs of other countries, especially on the basis of human rights violations or a humanitarian crisis. Many Chinese fear

---

[161] These data on Chinese policymaking are based on interviews with U.S. officials involved in UNSC affairs, New York, April 2005. In all cases of Chinese abstentions, China was never alone but rather was joined by at least two other nations. On UNSC 1556, the abstentions were China and Pakistan; on 1564, the abstentions were Russia, Algeria, China, and Pakistan; on UNSC 1590, there were no abstentions; on UNSC 1591, the abstentions were Russia, Algeria, and China; and on UNSC 1593, the abstentions were Algeria, the United States, Brazil, and China. Also see Traub, 2006.

[162] Christensen and Swan, 2008.

that such justifications for imposing sanctions or the use of force could be directed at China in the future. At a more basic level, senior Chinese scholars argue that Chinese leaders are simply agnostic about the domestic political activities of China's international partners; for them, there is no universal value system that should be applied by the U.N. or bilaterally. The prevailing value for Chinese leaders is fostering economic growth and development; issues of regime legitimacy and governance practices are not a priority for China in its bilateral relations.[163]

Such issues become relevant to Chinese leaders and diplomats only when China's agnostic approach toward humanitarian issues affects its international image and its ability to foster long-term bilateral economic relations. There are many indications that China's position on the Darfur crisis began to change because of such calculations. There is a rough correlation between China's willingness, in late 2006, to put pressure on the Sudanese government to allow peacekeepers into Darfur and the escalation in the campaign led by nongovernmental organizations to criticize China for its support of Khartoum, such as by labeling the 2008 Beijing Olympics the "Genocide Olympics." Another likely influence on China's change in approach to the Darfur issue was the concerns about Darfur expressed by numerous African leaders during the November 2006 China-Africa summit in Beijing.[164]

Moreover, Chinese diplomats note privately that China has had a substantial economic stake in relations with Sudan, given its deep involvement in Sudan's petroleum sector. In 2004 and 2005, the years of the critical U.N. debates on Darfur, Sudan was one of China's top ten suppliers of crude oil imports (about 5 percent). Sudan was also China's largest source of foreign oil production (followed by Kazakhstan) as a function of the large equity investment of two large national oil companies, Sinopec and the China National Petroleum Corporation. As a result, Chinese policymakers were reluctant to alienate a key

---

[163] Interviews with senior Chinese scholars and analysts of international relations, Beijing and Shanghai, 2005, and Washington, D.C., 2006.

[164] Wang Meng, "Daerfuer Weiji: Zhongguo Waijiao Zhuanxing de Tiaozhan yu Qiji" [The Darfur Crisis: The Challenge and Turning in the Transformation of Chinese Diplomacy], *Shijie Jingji yu Zhengzhi* [World Economics and Politics], No. 6, 2005; and interviews with Chinese scholars, 2007 and 2008.

supplier of energy resources at the very time they felt in desperate need to increase access to imported oil.[165]

Taiwan. China's effort to isolate Taiwan and to reduce its international space has historically been a consistent driver of its activities at the U.N. Since 1971, three of China's six UNSC vetoes have been to block U.N. assistance to states with formal ties to Taiwan.[166] China's recent anti-Taiwan diplomacy in the U.N. reflects a greater sophistication and less-confrontational approach. Without using the veto option (or even threatening to veto), China has creatively calibrated its support for U.N. peacekeeping operations to reduce Taiwan's international space—and thus the number of countries that recognize Taiwan.

China is no longer vetoing such operations (which otherwise usually garner unanimous UNSC support), but rather China is taking a more low-profile (and seemingly effective) approach. In 2003, China complicated the U.N.'s ability to deploy a peacekeeping stabilization force to Liberia until Beijing was assured that the new host government would shift recognition to China. (The old government, run by Charles Taylor, had diplomatic relations with Taiwan since 1997.) When the UNSC initially agreed to establish a mission and send a stabilization force to Liberia after the fall of Charles Taylor's regime, China supported only a three-month mandate for the operation even though at least six months were necessary for the initial mobilization and deployment of the peacekeeping force. China then persuaded the U.N. to intervene to ensure that the post-Taylor government would recognize China. A month after the September 2003 UNSC resolution (1509) authorizing for 12 months the stabilization force in Liberia, China and Liberia reestablished diplomatic relations (on October 11, 2003).[167]

In contrast to this episode, China has also been willing to support and send troops to U.N. peacekeeping operations in Haiti, even though the government there has formal diplomatic relations with Taiwan. This arrangement has not been trouble-free for Beijing, given

---

[165] The author would like to thank Erica Downs for providing the data on the latter points.

[166] By contrast, between 1972 and 2006, the United States has used its veto over 50 times (excluding multiple resolutions on the same issue).

[167] Interviews with U.S. officials at the U.S. Mission to the U.N., New York, 2005.

some statements by Haitian officials that Beijing deemed provocative, but China's support has continued.

UNSC Expansion. In early 2005, China's UNSC activism and influence were readily apparent in its response to a proposal to expand Security Council membership. Although China has been fairly passive in past U.N. discussions about such reform (by endorsing most of the Group 77's suggestions), China staunchly opposed the formal April 2005 proposal to expand the Security Council to include Germany, India, Brazil, and Japan. It was Japan's inclusion that most motivated Beijing's opposition, with China arguing that Japan's perceived unwillingness to face up to and properly atone for the brutality of its occupation of China and other Asian nations in World War II invalidated Tokyo for such a position on the Security Council. Supporters of Japan argued that Japan's U.N. contributions justify its membership: Japan pays 19 percent of the U.N.'s budget and the United States pays about 21 percent. China contributes 2 percent.

China used a variety of creative diplomatic approaches to block this proposal. Chinese diplomats lobbied their U.N. counterparts to initially not sponsor the resolution and then to reject it. China leveraged its growing political relations with African nations to successfully kill the proposal. China encouraged African diplomats to insist that at least two African nations join the original proposal for UNSC membership *and* be given veto power. The latter requirement guaranteed the death of the expansion proposal, which occurred in August 2005.[168]

For China, there was a domestic component to its opposition as well. Japan's bid for council membership prompted a massive Internet-based petition opposing Japanese membership; these events, among others, incited a series of anti-Japan riots in Beijing and Shanghai in spring 2005 that caused millions of dollars in destruction—including to Chinese businesses. It is unclear whether the Chinese government initiated such public activities, facilitated them once started, or simply did not strongly oppose them. Government authorities eventually intervened to halt the Shanghai riots after a few days, indicating that, although the government may have found these riots useful, it

---

[168] On this latter account, see Traub, 2006.

ultimately worried that they could spin out of control and change to antigovernment protests.

China's UNSC Assertiveness. In addition to the specific Chinese behaviors described above, a more general trend is apparent in China's UNSC behavior—a growing assertiveness and a related policy coordination with Russia. Since 2007, China has vetoed two UNSC resolutions, which is unique behavior given that, beforehand, Beijing had issued only four vetoes in about 30 years, dating back to when it joined the U.N. in 1971 (Table 6.4). Both vetoes, one related to Burma (2007) and the other to Zimbabwe (2008), were in response to UNSC resolutions censuring these two countries for their human rights practices and calling for political change. In both cases, China argued that the human rights issues are not the purview of the Security Council because they do not pose a "threat to international peace and security," referring to the language in the U.N. Charter. In both cases, Russia and China issued joint vetoes, a first for them since the early 1970s. To be sure, Bush administration officials pushed these resolutions even though they knew that they were highly controversial, and Chinese diplomats had signaled that they would be opposed by China, Russia, and other nations.[169]

Chinese and Russian coordination on other Security Council issues has increased as well. In 2006 and 2007, a high correlation is evident in Chinese and Russian votes on many UNSC resolutions. On Sudan, Russia joined China in abstaining on almost every resolution involving imposition of sanctions, even after China successfully lessened the penalties (e.g., UNSC 1564, 1591, and 1672). In particular, a rough division of labor appears to have developed on the North Korea and Iran nuclear issues: On Iran, Russia takes the lead and China follows; on North Korea, China takes the lead and Russia follows. This

---

[169] On the Burma resolution, China, Russia, and South Africa issued vetoes with the Democratic Republic of the Congo, Indonesia, and Qatar abstaining. Colum Lynch, "Russia, China Veto Resolution on Burma Security Council Action Blocks U.S. Human Rights Effort," *Washington Post*, January 13, 2007, p. A12.

On Zimbabwe, China, Russia, South Africa, Libya, and Vietnam also voted against the resolution. Indonesia abstained. Colum Lynch, "U.N. Zimbabwe Measure Vetoed by Russia, China," *Washington Post*, July 12, 2008, p. A09.

cooperation has most often been used to alter or modify U.S.- and UK-led efforts in the Security Council to impose sanctions on or otherwise penalize Iran and North Korea for their continued development of nuclear weapons.[170] A clear motivation of Sino-Russian coordination is to constrain U.S. efforts to advance punitive solutions to the Iran and North Korea issues.

China's assertiveness in the UNSC has also manifested in a greater willingness to confront other nations and, in this sense, its actions have been more in line with U.S. policy goals. Since 2006, China has supported limited sanctions on both North Korea and Iran for their continued nuclear weapons development: UNSC 1695 and 1718 in the case of North Korea and UNSC 1737, 1747, and 1803 in the case of Iran. In some cases, these resolutions even included sanctions referencing Chapter VII of the U.N. Charter. In April 2009, following a North Korean rocket launch, China notably supported a tough-minded UNSC presidential statement against Pyongyang's actions even though it opposed a binding UNSC resolution. The statement was robust and sent a strong signal; however, it "condemned" North Korea's rocket launch, called it a violation of 1718 (closing a loophole for satellite launches), called for no more launches, and tightened sanctions on Pyongyang. All of these actions represent stark breaks from past Chinese approaches to UNSC deliberations on nonproliferation.[171]

U.N.-Related Nonproliferation Affairs. China has become heavily involved in U.N.-related forums on arms control and nonproliferation affairs, such as the Conference on Disarmament in Geneva and International Atomic Energy Agency in Vienna. China has used such forums to register its opposition to U.S. security policies (such as U.S. missile defense programs), to limit U.S. influence on key issues and to promote the Chinese position on nonproliferation and arms control.

In the late 1990s and early in the 2000s, China used the CD as its main venue in which to oppose U.S. missile defense plans. China essen-

---

[170] This analysis is based on interviews with U.S. diplomats, Washington, D.C., 2007 and 2008, and on an assessment of Chinese and Russian voting patterns in the UNSC since 2004. U.S. Department of State, *Voting Practices at the United Nations*, various years.

[171] Christensen, 2008.

tially froze the activities of the CD until the United States agreed to a "mandate" to begin negotiations on a treaty banning the weaponization of space; the United States had long opposed this step, favoring informal "talks" instead. China sought to use its position in the CD to generate international opposition to U.S. missile defense plans and to push the United States to agree to limits on its development of missile defense capabilities. China finally dropped this stance in 2003 when it realized that it had been ineffective and that China had stalled CD activities for years.[172]

China's actions within the IAEA have had an increasingly cooperative flavor and been more in line with U.S. nonproliferation goals. China has sought to moderate other members (often the United States) who pushed the IAEA for both stronger safeguards and greater attention to noncompliance with the Nuclear Nonproliferation Treaty (NPT) and IAEA safeguard agreements. For example, China for years opposed the IAEA Board of Governors' "reporting" of cases of noncompliance to the UNSC, arguing that such issues should be handled within the IAEA. China feared that once such cases reached the UNSC, certain nations, such as North Korea and Iran, would be the subject of possible sanctions and penalties. China believed that sanctions would be counterproductive to a negotiated solution—a long-held Chinese view of sanctions.

China's approach began to change around 2003, however. In February 2003 and March 2004, as the North Korea situation escalated, China supported a consensus resolution of the IAEA Board of Governors on reporting North Korean noncompliance to the UNSC. Beijing had been reluctant to take such a position against Pyongyang throughout the 1990s. In September 2005 and February 2006, respectively, China abstained and then voted "yes" in roll call votes on two resolutions that reported Iranian noncompliance to the UNSC. These changes in China's behavior are a result of growing concerns about North Korean and Iranian intransigence, greater attention to the effect of nuclear proliferation on stability in Northeast Asia and the Middle East, and, perhaps, a recognition that international concerns about

---

[172] Medeiros, 2007, pp. 205–209.

Table 6.4
China's U.N. Security Council Vetoes

Date	Contents	Reason for Veto	Other States' Vetoes
1972 S/10771	Application by Bangladesh to join the U.N.	China considered Bangladesh to be a breakaway province of Pakistan.	None
1972 S/10786	Amendments to a UNSC resolution (10784); amendments deplored terrorist acts in the Middle East and called for their cessation.	China was supporting Arab states and the Palestine Liberation Organization; China did not feel the resolution was balanced in not naming Israel for violence against Arabs.	None
1997 S/1997/18	To attach military observers to a U.N. verification mission in Guatemala.	Guatemala has diplomatic ties with Taiwan and supported Taiwan's bid for U.N. membership.	None
1999 S/1999/201	Extending the U.N. Preventive Deployment Force in Macedonia.	Macedonia had diplomatic ties with Taiwan.	None
2007 S/2007/14	Call for end to violence against ethnic minorities and for political freedom in Burma.	Burma's problems do not "pose a threat to international peace and security" and thus are outside the UNSC mandate.	Russia, South Africa
2008 S/2008/447	Sanctions against Zimbabwe; arms embargo and travel and financial restrictions on top military and government officials.	Zimbabwe's internal problems are outside the UNSC mandate; sanctions would interfere with negotiations and cause the situation to worsen.	Russia, South Africa, Libya, Vietnam

SOURCES: United Nations Security Council Web site; Samuel S. Kim, *China, the United Nations, and World Order,* Princeton, N.J.: Princeton University Press, 1979; Morphet, 2000; and Yitzhak Shichor, "China's Voting Behavior in the UN Security Council," *China Brief,* The Jamestown Foundation, Vol. 6, No. 18, September 6, 2006.

nuclear proliferation were growing more acute and that China was increasingly out of line with mainstream international assessments.[173]

Another example of changing Chinese nonproliferation activities in U.N. bodies was its support for UNSC resolution 1540 on combating WMD proliferation. During the drafting of 1540, the Chinese strongly supported calling WMD proliferation "a threat to international peace and security," which refers to Chapter VII of the U.N. Charter. Yet, it was reluctant to let the resolution include any language that would provide a legal basis for proliferation-related interdiction activities, which the Chinese government felt would violate international law. With the input of China and other countries, UNSC 1540 evolved from essentially a counterproliferation initiative (that did not ban interdiction) to one that created binding legal obligations on member states to prevent proliferation, a reporting requirement for member states on their domestic nonproliferation controls, and a mechanism for multilateral nonproliferation cooperation.[174]

In sum, China is getting better at maneuvering within the U.N. and using U.N. processes to pursue its increasingly global foreign policy interests, even when they conflict with the United States and other major powers. Beijing's willingness to take the lead on issues appears to be growing as well. Beijing's cooperation with Moscow has afforded it added room to pursue its foreign policy objectives without appearing to be isolated or out of step with international public opinion. China has opposed U.S. initiatives and has sought to moderate U.N. actions that directly impinge on China's material interests, such as in the cases of Sudan and Iran. China will continue to take steps to promote its own view of global order and, when possible, to constrain U.S. exercise of its diplomatic and military power in the future—especially when it undercuts Chinese interests.

---

[173] On such changes in Chinese views on nonproliferation, see Medeiros, 2007, pp. 89–96. Also see Patricia McNerney, Principal Deputy Assistant Secretary, International Security and Nonproliferation, testimony before the U.S.-China Economic and Security Review Commission on "China's Nonproliferation Practices," May 20, 2008.

[174] Merav Datan, "Security Council Resolution 1540: WMD and Non-state Trafficking," *Disarmament Diplomacy,* No. 79, April/May 2005.

CHAPTER SEVEN

Challenges Facing Chinese Diplomacy

Beijing confronts several challenges to achieving its five foreign policy objectives. Some of them stem from domestic circumstances that constrain effective statecraft, and others stem from external reactions to China's growing capabilities. China's ability to manage these challenges will serve as an important indicator of its diplomatic power and influence.

Domestic Transition and Foreign Policy Decisionmaking

In examining the evolution of China's international behavior, one consideration is central: China is experiencing far-reaching changes in its economic, social, and—to a limited degree—political affairs. The resulting shifts in the structure and functioning of the Chinese economy, society, and polity are affecting the substance of its foreign policy and related decisionmaking processes. The influence of these internal dynamics on China's international behavior is substantial and will only strengthen in the future.

The linkages in China between foreign policy and domestic social, economic, and political transformation are difficult to specify and quantify, but they regularly manifest themselves. Some recent examples include the influence of corporate interest groups and nationalist sentiments (e.g., national oil companies and anti-Japan nationalist groups) on foreign policymaking.[1] Given the brittle legitimacy of the Communist Party, Chinese leaders can no longer pursue policies with minimal regard for the views of interest groups (both those within and those outside the CCP) or public opinion. Popular sentiments can and have constrained the foreign policy decisions of Chinese leaders, especially when such popular views on controversial foreign policy questions are used as instruments by those in the highest levels of the Chinese Communist Party to jockey for power among a "collective leadership." Such policy opportunism for narrow political gain within the CCP has been common among China's top leaders for decades—it may be even more so today given that no individual Chinese leader has supreme authority.[2]

In this period of rapid social and economic transition, a related challenge for Chinese policymakers is how to accurately assess the domestic costs and benefits of foreign policy decisions. As China's economic reforms evolve and Chinese industry and society diversify, it is becoming increasingly difficult for Chinese policymakers to conduct cost-benefit types of calculations regarding policy decisions. This

---

[1]   For specific examples of the role of corporate interests on energy policy, see Erica Downs, "Business Interest Groups in Chinese Politics: The Case of the Oil Companies," in Cheng Li, ed., *China's Changing Political Landscape: Prospects for Democracy,* Washington, D.C.: Brookings Institution Press, 2008, pp. 121–141; Trevor Houser, "The Roots of Oil Investment Abroad," *Asia Policy,* No. 5, January 2008, pp. 141–166. For the role of business interests on nonproliferation policy, see Medeiros, 2007.

On the role of domestic politics in China's Japan policy, see Susan L. Shirk, *China: Fragile Superpower,* Oxford, UK: Oxford University Press, Chapter Six, 2007, pp. 140–180; and, generally, Gries, 2004; Downs, 2004.

On the general relationship between Chinese public opinion and foreign policy, see Joseph Fewsmith and Stanley Rosen, "The Domestic Context of Chinese Foreign Policy: Does Public Opinion Matter?" in David M. Lampton, ed., *The Making of Chinese Foreign and Security Policy,* Stanford, Calif.: Stanford University Press, 2002, pp. 151–190.

[2]   A classic volume on the domestic-foreign linkage is Michael Swaine, *China: Domestic Change and Foreign Policy,* Santa Monica, Calif.: RAND Corporation, MR-604-OSD, 1995; on the changing domestic political dynamics in China, see Joseph Fewsmith, *Elite Politics in Contemporary China,* Armonk, New York: M. E. Sharpe, 2001; and Kenneth Lieberthal, *Governing China: From Revolution Through Reform,* 2nd ed., New York: W. W. Norton and Co., December 2003. On policy opportunism in the Chinese political system, see Lucian W. Pye, *The Spirit of Chinese Politics,* Cambridge, Mass.: MIT Press, 1968.

occurs because policymakers are often unaware of all the stakeholders in China (with views on specific foreign policy issues) and their respective equities, which are constantly changing as well. According to interviews with Chinese policymakers and scholars, this situation has significantly complicated the foreign policy decisionmaking process in China under Hu Jintao and led to Hu's efforts to improve interagency coordination on all types of foreign policy-related decisions, at both the central and provincial levels of government.[3]

Thus, the scope and pace of China's domestic transition in the coming years will continue to create conditions under which foreign policymaking could appear to foreign observers as uncoordinated, irrational, unpredictable, and perhaps even erratic. China's seemingly frenzied global search for oil supplies in the 2003–2006 time frame serves as one recent example of this phenomenon.[4]

These observations are meant to highlight a general and seemingly growing constraint on China's pursuit of its international interests. For foreign analysts of China, these observations provide a lens through which to evaluate future trends in China's international behavior by underscoring the importance of understanding the domestic context of decisionmaking when making analytic judgments about China's foreign policy motives.

Looming Challenges

Beijing confronts several additional challenges to effective pursuit of its international interests. First, Chinese leaders will likely face rising expectations from other states, if this is not already occurring. In the past, China has benefited from low expectation about its behaviors (e.g., its response to the 1997 Asian financial crisis), and now expectations of both China's involvement and its contributions to global economic and security affairs are growing.

---

[3] Interviews with Chinese policymakers and analysts, Beijing and Shanghai, 2008; on Hu Jintao's efforts to improve governmentwide foreign policy coordination see Glaser, 2007.

[4] Downs, 2008.

As China's global profile grows and, in Asia, as Beijing continues to position itself as central to economic and security affairs, China's neighbors and members of the international community will expect more of Beijing, especially as it proclaims itself to be a "responsible major power" engaged in a "peaceful rise." In the past, China has benefited from relatively low expectations about its behavior, but now the pendulum is swinging in the other direction.

It is not clear that China has the intention or capacity to consistently meet such expectations or that China's expectations will match those of its neighbors. Many leaders in Asia are wondering whether China's "rise" will really be peaceful. China's role in regional security is already the subject of some apprehension among East Asian states, and its ongoing military modernization may enhance such anxieties.[5] Is China willing to contribute "public goods" to the region or make the types of costly decisions that will help maintain regional stability? As China's stakes in regional stability in Asia and other regions grow, it may make such investments. But Chinese leaders have provided only limited indications of their willingness to define their national interests in a way that may sacrifice short-term gains for the sake of medium- to long-term benefits to regional stability. On the one hand, China's increase in development and humanitarian aid is a sign of Beijing's desire to make such contributions. Beyond Asia, China's 2008 military deployment of three ships to the international antipiracy effort in the Gulf of Aden is a high-profile example of China trying to act "responsibly" and contribute to a global security effort. On the other hand, the business practices of some Chinese state-run companies, especially in Africa, have generated concerns among regional nations that China is more self-interested and less supportive of regional development.

Related to the above constraint, to what extent will China's compliance with its numerous (and growing) trade and security commitments raise concerns about its ability to be a trusted rising power? China's compliance will be an important indicator of its intentions.

---

[5]   Bates Gill, Michael Green, Kiyoto Tsuji, and William Watts, *Strategic Views on Asian Regionalism: Survey Results and Analysis*, Washington, D.C.: Center for Strategic and International Studies, February 2009, pp. 4–7.

Beijing's mixed history of meeting its international trade, nonprolifera-tion, and human rights pledges suggests this will be a problem China needs to manage.[6] China's interpretation of some of its trade commit-ments has already resulted in frictions with ASEAN nations and eco-nomic partners in Africa.[7] China's relations with these and other coun-tries may be damaged if they begin to question China's reliability and, ultimately, its intentions.

Second, China's approach to the Taiwan question complicates Beijing's image. Beijing's occasionally confrontational and aggres-sive approach with other states on Taiwan issues reveals the limits of its effort to appear moderate and benign. Although this behavior is less frequent than before, there are several prominent examples of it in this decade. In 2004, Chinese officials publicly lambasted Singa-pore's incoming Prime Minister Lee Hsien Long, before he had taken office, about a pending visit to Taiwan and then berated him follow-ing his trip. China then halted all high-level dialogues with Singapore for two years. In March 2005, a Chinese diplomat publicly demanded that Australia recuse itself from involvement in a military conflict over Taiwan, despite Canberra's commitments to Washington through the Australia–New Zealand–United States Security Treaty. China's pas-sage of the Anti-Secession Law in spring 2005 contributed to the deci-sions in many European capitals to defer an impending EU decision about lifting its 1989 arms embargo on China. In spring 2006, Chi-na's then–ambassador to South Korea, Ning Fukuai, publicly advised South Korean officials to restrict the role of U.S. military forces based in Korea to the defense of Korea and not to allow them to be used for regional contingencies (e.g., Taiwan). This sparked Korean sensi-tivities to China's meddling in alliance politics, contributing to current debates about South Korea's need to reduce its economic dependence on China.[8]

---

[6] China's mixed record of compliance with its WTO pledges and various nuclear and mis-sile nonproliferation pledges is well documented in the literature on Chinese foreign policy. See various chapters in Economy and Oksenberg, 1999.

[7] Liebman, 2005.

[8] Medeiros et al., 2008, pp. 70–71.

Such actions and statements from Beijing present China's "rise" in a less benign light, and regularly remind states of China's willingness to engage in coercive diplomacy. Ultimately, any Chinese use of force (limited or major) to address the Taiwan question would heighten latent concerns, especially among Southeast Asian nations with a history of Chinese interference and coercion, that China's ascension in regional affairs could threaten their own security interests.

Third, China's acute governance challenges are directly and indirectly affecting external perceptions of China, and negatively so.[9] China's most severe governance problems—such as systemic corruption, increasing center-periphery tensions, weak environmental controls, a decrepit health care system, and growing nationalism—hinder Beijing's ability to control the multiple actors in China's large economy and expansive party-state bureaucracy. These weaknesses constrain the government's ability to effectively manage internal problems that could spill over to China's neighbors. Beijing's initially slow and dismissive response to the spread of SARS in southern China highlighted to Southeast Asian governments the degree to which China's public health crises and environmental problems can threaten their economies because of Beijing's negligence. In late 2005, the Chinese government's failure to rapidly control the chemical contamination of the Songhua River in northeastern China resulted in the spill flowing into Russia. Examples abound of foreign countries' concerns about China's inability to meet various commitments as a result of corruption, center-periphery tensions, and generally underdeveloped government controls in certain sectors.

A fourth challenge stems from weaknesses in China's national security decisionmaking system, especially those related to crisis decisionmaking. China's bureaucracy for making national security decisions is plagued with the problems of excessive secrecy; divisions between the civilian, intelligence, and military decisionmaking structures; and the lack of ways to coordinate among civilian and military

---

[9] This is a key theme of Shirk, 2007.

organizations.[10] Prominent manifestations of these weaknesses include the slow and haphazard national response to the SARS episode, the prominence of the PLA narrative in the EP-3 incident in April 2001, and the slow response and vague explanation about the January 2007 test of a direct ascent antisatellite weapon. These limitations will likely become even more problematic as the PLA improves its capabilities and conducts military activities beyond China's immediate periphery, such as submarine patrols, which will raise questions about China's regional ambitions.

A fifth challenge is China's possession and mobilization of sufficient national resources to play a more active role in East Asia—especially when compared to the resources of the United States and its allies. Although its diplomatic toolkit is expanding, China is still limited in the national resources it can use and is willing to mobilize to pursue its diplomatic agenda. The most obvious example of this constraint was the comparatively small amount of aid that China donated to tsunami victims in Southeast Asia in early 2005. China provided $83 million worth of financial and material support. Although this was the greatest amount of humanitarian aid China has ever provided, it paled in comparison to the hundreds of millions of dollars that the United States, Australia, and Japan spent on relief operations. Also, the collective military logistics capability of the U.S. military and its Asian allies (mainly India and Japan) to deliver such aid far outstrips anything that China currently possesses.

Sixth, as China "goes global" with its overseas investment and purchasing of natural resources, Beijing risks being seen as an extractive economy, taking much from developing nations and contributing little to their national development. Given the modes of operations of many Chinese companies operating abroad, in which they import Chinese labor and goods for local infrastructure projects, China is increasingly facing this very challenge. Such sentiments have already

---

[10] The weaknesses of China's crisis decisionmaking are explored in detail in Michael D. Swaine, Zhang Tuosheng, and Danielle F.S. Cohen, *Managing Sino-American Crises: Case Studies and Analysis*, Washington, D.C.: Carnegie Endowment for International Peace, 2006.

been raised in several Latin American and African nations.[11] This perception of China, if it develops further, could undermine a core feature of China's international behavior: its identity as a fellow developing nation that has long opposed such "neo-colonialist" practices as resource exploitation.

A final diplomatic challenge for Chinese leaders is the constraining effect of nationalist sentiments on foreign policy choices. Although Chinese leaders have used nationalist sentiment as a tool to shape the domestic context of policy decisions, they face the inherent constraints of trying to manipulate nationalism. The growth of anti-Japanese sentiments in China, in particular, has limited the ability of Chinese policymakers to pursue a more balanced approach to the Sino-Japanese relationship—one that better reflects Beijing's economic and security interests in stable and amicable relations with Tokyo. In periods of bilateral crises with Japan, the United States, or other nations, nationalist protests have had and will continue to have a corrosive effect on the government's ability to de-escalate the situation and reach resolution.

To be sure, Chinese leaders appear to have begun to recognize this constraint, and they now pay attention to managing public perceptions. In recent years foreign ministry and CCP statements about foreign affairs work have become replete with references to the importance of "people-centered" diplomacy and "balancing the overall international and domestic situations," which are both references to avoiding public opposition to key foreign policy decisions, including by providing opportunities for input.[12]

---

[11] Jorge I. Dominguez, *China's Relations with Latin America: Shared Gains, Asymmetric Hopes*, China Working Paper, Washington, D.C.: Inter-American Dialogue, June 2006. On a perception of exploitation in Africa, see Alden and Rothman, 2008.

[12] Yang Jiechi, 2008; "Adhere to Peaceful Development Road, Push Forward Building of Harmonious World," 2006; and "Central Foreign Affairs Meeting Held in Beijing," 2006.

CHAPTER EIGHT

Conclusions

China's domestic dynamism now clearly extends to its international behavior. China is involved in places and on topics previously marginal to its interests, and it is effectively using tools previously out of its reach. China is a truly global *actor*, with interests and influence far beyond Asia. It is both shaping and being shaped by nations, institutions, and processes all over the world. China is not yet a global *power* but it will eventually get there, depending on one's standard of measurement. And by the time China gets there, the concept of being a "global power" will likely have a very different meaning from the predominant position of the United States in the international system since the end of the Cold War.

China's global activism is being driven by a distinct set of perceptions, objectives, and policies—some are long-standing and others are more current, as documented throughout this monograph. To the extent that any nation possesses and executes a foreign policy strategy, China has one. Chinese leaders possess the long-standing goals of advancing national development, protecting China's sovereignty and territorial integrity, and securing China's status as a respected great power. And to do so, Chinese policymakers have crafted a foreign policy that seeks to accomplish five *specific objectives*: economic growth and development, reassurance, countering constraints, resource diversification, and reducing Taiwan's international space. As of summer 2009, China's traditional goals as well as its more current objectives are consistent and persistent drivers of its international behavior.

Chinese leaders continue to approach their foreign policy and foreign relations through the prism of domestic affairs: how foreign policy assists the increasingly complex tasks of economic and social development at home. This does not mean that China is an insular nation that just wants to be left alone or that Chinese leaders approach their external affairs as a secondary concern. The reality of China's international behavior could not be further from that. The linkage between domestic and international affairs for China has become stronger and assumed new dimensions in the last decade; but it is this linkage that will continue to have a defining influence on China's external behavior.

The internal-external linkage has shifted from a passive to an active logic. Domestic growth and stability require an active foreign policy. For China, acting locally now requires that it think globally. No longer is Chinese foreign policy simply focused on creating a safe and stable external environment for reform to continue, as Deng set out to do three decades ago. Now, China's foreign policy makes a critical contribution to meeting China's most pressing developmental challenges: China needs diplomacy to gain access to markets, investment, technologies, and resources—all necessary inputs to sustained growth. Indeed, more than during the first two decades of reform, China's domestic needs have become a driver of as well as a constraint on its external behavior.

This logic to China's foreign policy is widely accepted among China's policymakers and is likely to remain so. But it is also accurate to argue that China's international objectives are continually evolving. None of China's long-standing goals (e.g., sovereignty and territorial integrity) or its more current objectives (e.g., reassurance and countering constraints) are likely to change in the near future, assuming there is no major discontinuity in China's domestic or foreign affairs. China's current and next generation of leaders share the CCP's view of giving priority to increasing comprehensive national power to facilitate national revitalization; they also understand how domestic affairs drives foreign policy.

That said, Chinese interests and objectives are constantly evolving as China comes to grips with its new responsibilities and the burdens associated with global involvements, especially in such regions as the Middle East and Latin America which, for decades, were peripheral to Chinese foreign policy calculations. But these new interests and responsibilities should be viewed in the context of the widely accepted domestic logic to China's foreign policy. China knows, for example, that it needs to assume new responsibilities but it is wary of doing so for fear that it lacks the expertise to succeed and that such ventures will drain resources away from domestic development.

The changing nature of China's international behavior is further reflected in its evolution away from strict adherence to long-standing foreign policy principles, such as noninterference in the internal affairs of other nations. China's new perceptions and interests have fostered a gradual shift in its adherence to this principle—or, in Chinese terms, a "flexible interpretation" of it. China has done so to allow management of regional issues that affect its economic and security interests, as well as its reputation (such as the Darfur crisis in Sudan and political instability in Burma). As China's equities in such regions as Africa and Southeast Asia have grown and China has become more comfortable with using its influence to effect change, it has come to recognize the value in promoting political stability and reducing violence in these regions. This modification in China's approach was also catalyzed by external pressure in the form of opprobrium from the United States, African nations, and nongovernmental organizations. In the end, Chinese leaders chose to assist in the stabilization and management of these regional crises.

Implications for Regional and Global Stability

Three major implications for regional and global stability follow from this study. First, China has been largely working within the current international system to accomplish its foreign policy objectives. China is not trying to tear down or significantly revise the current constellation of global rules, norms, and institutions on economic and security affairs. Rather, on balance, it is seeking to master them to advance its international interests—an approach that has proven quite productive for Beijing.

In the main, Chinese foreign policy is heavily focused on leveraging the size, appeal, and expectations of China's economy and its deep involvement in multilateral institutions—globally and regionally—to expand Chinese influence and stature, to increase China's access to inputs to economic growth, and to reduce constraints on China's freedom of action. As China has deepened its involvement in certain regions and in multilateral institutions, it has sought to shape them in ways conducive to Chinese goals. China's role in creating the EAS and SCO and its effort to derail expansion of the U.N. Security Council are prominent examples of China's use of multilateral organizations to advance specific Chinese objectives.

China has succeeded in implementing this approach in ways that do not appear immediately aggressive or threatening to other nations in East Asia and beyond.[1] On balance, China has been effective at reassuring many Asian nations and forestalling the development of regional coalitions seeking to balance Chinese power. Since the beginning of this decade, China's strategy has allowed it to draw a particular contrast with U.S. foreign policy, which has appeared unilateral, coercive, and military-oriented to many nations. The perception among many nations that the Bush administration discounted international institutions and preferred military force aided China's efforts to appear more cooperative and predictable than the United States.

To date, China's shaping of international institutions has been limited and episodic. There are more instances of China gradually accepting international rules than objecting to and then trying to revise them (and succeeding). Globally, China has adopted numerous complex trade and nonproliferation commitments, albeit with a mixed compliance record. Even in East Asia, China's strategic periphery, it has backed down when faced with opposition from regional nations about creation of a China-directed multilateral organization (e.g., EAS). In Southeast Asia, Beijing appears, so far, to have accepted regional norms on conflict resolution and has made pledges on peacefully resolving maritime territorial disputes. Although China's ultimate behavior on

---

[1] Japan is an exception to this, as Tokyo has been the target of some Chinese efforts to expand its influence at Japan's expense.

these territorial disputes is still unfolding (including some provocative activities), its initial commitments indicate, importantly, a degree of self-binding for the sake of reassurance.

China's efforts to shape other countries' policies and preferences have been similarly limited and focused mainly on issues of particular sensitivity to China, such as the status of Taiwan and Tibet. In these instances, the costs to the target state of accommodating China were often low and the benefits were substantial. There are few instances of states making costly decisions (for their national interests) in response to Chinese policy intervention. China has been most effective at raising its profile among countries in Asia, Africa, and Latin America; states in these regions are now more aware of Chinese views and interests. But China's actual influence on the behavior of other states has been limited and episodic. Despite China's growing presence and interactions with countries and institutions all over the world, the instances of China successfully using its diplomacy to change the behavior of other states are few.

China, to be sure, is dissatisfied with some attributes of the current international system. It does not accept the current status of Taiwan; preventing the island's *de jure* separation from the mainland remains a top national security priority. However, Chinese policies on this issue do not serve as an unambiguous indicator of China's regional aspirations, such as those related to territorial acquisition. China's resolution of numerous territorial disputes on its land borders and its management in the last decade of maritime disputes serve as more consistent indicators of Chinese views on territorial acquisition. Thus, although China seeks eventual reunification with Taiwan, this goal does not *ipso facto* mean that Beijing sees territorial aggrandizement as a way to accomplish national revitalization as a great power. Chinese behaviors on maritime territorial issues bears continued watching, especially in the South China Sea.

Moreover, China is also dissatisfied with the U.S. position as the predominant global power, motivated in part by the perception that the United States has sought to use its diplomatic, economic, and military power to push a development model of free-market democracy. The Bush administration's democracy-promotion agenda was a particular concern among Chinese leaders. The Iraq War and "color revolutions" in Central Asia heightened these anxieties. The latter U.S. approach made China wary of U.S. power and fearful that this could be directed at China. This, in turn, has motivated Chinese efforts to work with other nations, especially Russia, to constrain U.S. advances, globally and in Asia.

Diversification

In part by design and in part by default, China is pursuing an international strategy of diversification. It is doing so by simultaneously broadening its sources of economic prosperity, security, and status.

China is using foreign policy to expand its access to markets, investment, technology, and resources—the key inputs to economic growth and modernization. During the early years of China's reform and opening, the external sources of growth were mainly trade and investment with a small number of large industrialized economies, such as the United States, Japan, and west European countries. Within the last decade, Chinese leaders have come to realize that the only way to sustain moderately high growth levels is to more actively go abroad in search of new markets, investments, technologies, and resources. China's extensive economic integration with East Asian nations and its growing ties with Africa, Latin America, and the Middle East lead this trend; expanding trade with the latter three regions will be key to maintaining exports during a global recession. This allows China to reduce it reliance on one or even a small number of powerful economies, such as the United States. China also uses such economic relationships to generate political influence—such as creating a perceived dependence on China—that Beijing can leverage to pursue other diplomatic priorities, such as sensitizing nations to China's preferences and interests.

China is also diversifying its sources of security by developing new and expanding existing relationships with various power centers. It is upgrading its bilateral relationships by forming "strategic partnerships" and "strategic dialogues" with both developed and developing nations, as well as with major regional groupings such as ASEAN, the EU, and the GCC. China has embraced multilateral institutions in virtually every part of the world, in some cases creating them where none previously existed. It uses these mechanisms to reassure countries about its intentions, to demonstrate the benefits of China's rise, and, ultimately, to expand its political influence—often related to gaining access to markets and resources. A natural consequence of this security diversification is that China has lessened its reliance on stable and positive relations with a few major powers, such as the United States, for its security. By dint of this security diversification process, China now generates leverage, avoids constraints on its behavior, and gains maneuverability from a variety of sources.

Last, China is diversifying its sources of international status and legitimacy. For decades, it relied on crude metrics as the basis of such status: its large size and population, long history and legacy as a great Asian power, U.N. Security Council membership, and possession of nuclear weapons. Now, it has turned to highlighting its economic successes of the last 30 years and is demonstrating a willingness to share these with others. Chinese leaders are also slowly redefining their external profile: They are shifting away from the view of international affairs as "a struggle" against "hegemony and power politics" toward a more positive view that stresses "peace, development and cooperation" in building a "harmonious world." China also remains one of the most influential advocates of the principle of nonintervention in the internal affairs of other states (even though its views have moderated in recent years), which is an important status-marker for China among developing nations. For many Chinese, hosting the 2008 Olympics was a benchmark achievement in its effort to become an accepted "member of the club" among world powers.

China's Diplomacy in Transition

China's international behavior is a deeply transitional phenomenon. China has clear and widely accepted foreign policy objectives, but they are also evolving as its economy, society, and polity change. What occurs inside China is directly linked to China's external behavior, more so than ever before, and China's domestic situation is in a constant state of flux. China's diplomacy reflects a balancing of competing internal and external demands, which are growing in number and variety. How China manages this balancing act has a direct influence on its external behavior, both facilitating and constraining its policies. For example, China's governance challenges are a barrier to efficient foreign policy decisionmaking and its effective implementation.

An added element of the phenomenon is that China's international identity is changing: It represents many things to many nations, often at the same time. China is both a developing and a developed nation to many in the international community. It is a regional power in Asia and a global actor. Chinese policymakers are groping their way forward with their newfound influence, status, and responsibilities. When should they lead and when should they follow? They are testing the effectiveness and limits of their capabilities. Although Chinese policymakers clearly have objectives in mind in their current foreign policy, they are pursuing them and then recalibrating in response to domestic imperatives, internal constraints, external reactions, and a dynamic international security environment in which threats and opportunities readily emerge. Ultimately, this process provides the international community—including the United States—with an important opportunity to influence this evolution. But it also makes it difficult for the international community to understand how China's interests will evolve over time.

Implications for U.S. Security Interests

This monograph raises numerous implications for U.S. global security interests, U.S. interests in Asia, the U.S.-China relationship, and the future of America's China policy.

Global Challenges

China does not seek to displace the United States as the global superpower. Chinese leaders do not want China to be a global power on par with the United States—a peer competitor. They view their domestic challenges as too great to assume the burdens associated with such a role, and they recognize that they lack currently the material resources to be able to project and sustain military and economic power all over the world. They also fear that playing such a role could deplete much needed resources and might foster a backlash against China. For Chinese leaders, trying to play such a role would represent a major break from Dengist orthodoxy on foreign affairs—a significant but not insurmountable political barrier to a major change in strategy. Such a course correction would likely only come about in reaction to a dramatic shift in China's external security environment—one that precipitated a complete reassessment by China's top leaders. In addition, if China were seeking to become a global competitor to the United States, its behavior would look far different than it does, as discussed below.

This does not mean that there are not competitive aspects of China's foreign policy that challenge U.S. security interests. Some of China's international behaviors are directed at eroding U.S. influence in specific regions and in certain institutions. The most competitive aspects of China's foreign policy are evident in the Asia-Pacific region. China is not currently trying to push the United States out of this region. Chinese leaders recognize the dangers and likely failure of such an approach, and some recognize the stability provided by U.S. alliances. Rather, China is trying to increase its power and influence *relative to the United States*. A core Chinese objective is to hinder the U.S. ability to constrain China; that is, China seeks to maximize its freedom of action and leverage as means of countering perceived U.S. efforts to limit Chinese choices. China seeks political influence to increase the costs, for the United States and its allies, of constraining China.

Thus, China is challenging the United States by trying to reduce its relative influence, but it does not seek to confront the United States by trying to expel it. As noted above, China is pursuing this approach by deepening economic interactions with Asian nations, joining multilateral organizations to shape regional agendas, expanding bilateral interactions to shape these nations' preferences, and generally reassuring countries on its periphery about China's intentions and capabilities. In this sense, China's approach is more gravitational than confrontational—pulling nations toward China (to bind them) rather than pushing them away from the United States or each other.

The logic, in China's eyes, of its most competitive foreign policies is essentially defensive. China seeks influence so that the United States and its allies will not work together to limit China's options. Chinese actions in the Asia-Pacific region, for example, seek to create an environment in which the United States cannot constrain China, now or in the future. Although it has tried and flirted with more offensive options, such as offering an alternative vision of a regional security order, none of these have taken hold and China has not pursued them. Rather, China has actively used economic diplomacy, multilateral interactions, and bilateral engagement to create a regional security environment in which states do not view China as a threat, are more sensitive to Chinese interests, are willing to accommodate China on some issues, and will not collectively balance Chinese power. This approach has been successful for China.

Going forward, a key challenge for China is maintaining the fine balance between challenging and confronting U.S. interests. Although China may perceive its actions as defensive (i.e., reacting to U.S. efforts as opposed to actively undermining them), some Chinese policies, depending on their manifestations, could appear confrontational to U.S. and regional policymakers. Chinese actions, such as its military diplomacy, could make competition look increasingly direct, intense, and potentially adversarial. As China becomes more globally active, U.S. and Chinese interests will increasingly collide as well as overlap. As a result, a policy challenge for both Washington and Beijing is to maximize the latter and minimize the former. To date, Washington and Beijing have managed to avoid negative outcomes, but more tests are likely.

Challenges for America's China Policy

A second major implication for U.S. interests is that China's diversification strategy is altering the U.S. ability to shape Chinese behavior and the conduct of bilateral relations. Washington, for decades following normalization, effectively leveraged Beijing's priority on stable and positive relations with the United States to elicit changes in China's policies on international economic and security issues. U.S. policy played a central role in encouraging (at times, coercing) China's acceptance of international rules related to trade and investment, arms control and nonproliferation, and regional security affairs. U.S. policy was certainly not the only factor shaping this process of post-Mao internationalization, but it often played a catalytic role by jump-starting internal debates and accelerating existing ones, including by empowering China's domestic advocates for change. Chinese foreign policy elites used to refer to U.S.-China relations as "the key of keys"—a reflection of the centrality of the United States to China's world view and its foreign policy. This dynamic is now gradually changing.

As the sources of China's prosperity, security, and status have broadened, Chinese leaders are no longer as preoccupied with American views. Over time, Beijing will become less willing to accommodate U.S. preferences and more able to resist pressure from Washington, or even generate countervailing forces. The traditional U.S. approach of relying principally on bilateral diplomacy to shape China's policies and practices now confronts new limitations.

Regional Challenges

China's ascendance in Asia is changing the nature of U.S. relations with its allies and partners in the region. As China becomes more relevant to the economic, financial, and military affairs of U.S. allies and partners, their needs and their demands on Washington will change. As China looms larger in their economic development and regional security planning, this could complicate Washington's ability to "set the agenda for cooperation" with other nations in the Asia-Pacific region. For example, this could also result in unwanted policy choices or constraints on U.S. security cooperation with these nations; challenges in the middle part of this decade in the U.S.-South Korean alliance are instructive in this regard, although they appear to have been resolved under the new Korean leadership. These trends are highly relevant to U.S. defense planning for a possible conflict over Taiwan. U.S. friends and allies in Asia will increasingly need to balance the competing visions and demands of Washington and Beijing. This ongoing process presents U.S. Asia strategy with an enduring challenge.

In Africa and Latin America, similar but less intensive shifts in bilateral dynamics are already materializing. In Africa, China's trade and investment policies are challenging (and in some cases undermining) Western efforts to improve human rights and governance practices. China has effectively leveraged its improved diplomatic ties with

African states to advance its goals in multilateral forums, such as in U.N. debates about Security Council reform. China's growing trade and financial interactions with such states as Brazil, Venezuela, and Bolivia offer these nations choices and options not available when they relied heavily on economic interactions and security commitments from the United States. This alters their discourse with Washington in ways that complicate U.S. diplomacy. Venezuela's embrace of China as a poke at the United States (and as a perceived alternative source of oil demand) is a prominent example of this latter phenomenon.

China's regional involvements are not only changing the regions but are shaping Chinese behaviors as well. China's increased interactions with African nations have sensitized Beijing to the consequences of its policies, leading China to recognize the value of improving corporate governance in Africa and encouraging resolution of the Darfur crisis in Sudan. These regional interactions, for example, have led China to moderate its previously staunch adherence to the principle of "noninterference in the internal affairs of other states."

A broader challenge for the United States is monitoring the nature, scope, and pace of China's global activism. How and where is China accumulating influence, beyond merely a greater presence and set of regional interactions? How relevant is China to regional trade flows, investment, currency trading, science and technology standards, and security affairs? Will this alter China's regional or global aspirations, making it either more expansive or more conservative in its desires? U.S. diplomacy needs to be keenly attuned to assessing the ways China is accumulating genuine influence, whether China can operationalize such influence, and how these developments are shaping China's intentions. Although such interactions are not necessarily zero-sum, U.S. policymakers need to be attuned to how they shape the U.S.-China "balance of influence" in Asia and beyond.

Another challenge facing the United States is ensuring regional stability in Asia as three trends converge: China ascends, Japan reemerges as a military power, and India becomes an Asian power. Although this study has focused on China's international behavior, China's diplomatic activism, globally and regionally, is having a profound effect on major power relations in Asia. Historically, China has had territorial conflicts with both Japan and India, and these two states harbor deep concerns about competition with China for regional leadership. These dynamics are a source of enduring suspicions among all three nations, fueling incipient security dilemmas. The relationships among these three powers are rapidly evolving along both cooperative and competitive vectors, often simultaneously. A key task for the United States is to use its role as an external balancer to shape, to the extent possible, relations among these three in a way that reduces suspicions, minimizes the possibilities of conflict, and manages crises.

A Counterfactual Approach

Another analytic approach useful for assessing China's international behavior and the related challenges to U.S. interests is to examine what China is *not* doing. By highlighting the policy choices China has not taken, a better understanding can be gained of China's current perceptions, objectives, and policies.

First, China is not pursuing its core foreign policy objectives through territorial expansion, military intervention, permanent military deployments abroad, creation of client states (including through extensive arms sales), or domination of regional or international institutions. Chinese international behavior could look far more aggressive than it currently does, either regionally or globally. This does not mean that Chinese behaviors do not challenge some U.S. interests, but rather that the challenge is more specific and subtle.

Second, China is not promoting a radically alternative view of global or regional affairs in Asia. It is not promoting a "Beijing Consensus" as an alternative to the "Washington Consensus."[2] Although some states may view China's development approach of authoritarian-capitalism as replicable, these are usually dictatorships with little global appeal. In fact, China's development path validates the core axioms of the Washington Consensus more than it challenges them. The global financial crisis in mid-2008 did more to highlight the limits of free-market policies (especially in the financial sector) than any Chinese

---

[2] The Beijing Consensus was created by an American journalist and has few promoters in China. Cooper, 2004.

diplomacy that advocated state intervention in economic policymaking. Furthermore, China has embraced most of the major global and regional economic and security institutions. Its participation rate in intergovernmental institutions is at an all-time high.

In Asia, it is no longer actively promoting its "new security concept," as Beijing realizes that this does not resonate with Asian countries who seek good relations with both the United States and China. China's effort to grow its soft power is focused on reassuring nations about China's intentions rather than actively peeling them away from the United States based on a Chinese model of development or regional security. Most nations are drawn to China because of its large and growing economy rather than its ideals. China has done well using its hard power softly rather than generating soft power, as Joseph Nye originally defined it. Many of the foreign policy ideas China promotes are broadly consistent with the liberal institutionalist tradition that the United States pursued after World War II (with the obvious exception of political liberalization). In other words, China is focused far more on working within the current rules and institutions to accumulate power and influence than on opposing and revising them.

China's international behavior may have appeared to some like an alternative to the United States during the past eight years of the Bush administration. Many nations viewed Bush as limiting U.S. involvement in international organizations, by-passing the U.N. on key questions, adopting an activist democracy-promotion agenda, and favoring military force. China was effective at implicitly creating a contrast with U.S. foreign policy under George W. Bush. Under Barack Obama's administration, it is less certain that China will have the same opportunity to draw such a stark contrast with U.S. foreign policy.

Third, China has not adopted a confrontational posture with the United States, despite its discomfort with U.S. unipolar status and the U.S. democracy-promotion agenda. Even during the Bush years, Chinese leaders avoided confrontation with the United States (such as on Iraq in 2003), put effort into stabilizing U.S.-China relations (especially after 9/11), and sought to expand areas of practical cooperation (e.g., North Korea). U.S. and Chinese leaders have broadened their channels of diplomatic exchange. These new channels have resulted in limited changes in Chinese behavior on key international security issues such as North Korea, Iran, Sudan, and Burma. China's international behavior reflects a continued recognition that an adversarial relationship with the United States would have a very negative effect on China's security environment and on its ability to accomplish both its long-standing and its more immediate objectives.

Furthermore, China has not sought to create an anti-U.S. coalition to balance U.S. power. Beijing has pursued bilateral ties with nations close to the United States and also those alienated from Washington. China appears to have quietly rejected such approaches by leaders from Venezuela and Iran. China has been embracing multilateral organizations that include U.S. membership and also those that the United States is not a part of. And, in regional organizations such as the SCO and EAS, China has not sought to dominate them and has deferred its advances when they have been met with resistance from regional states, including U.S. allies.

At the same time, China pursues opportunities to challenge U.S. preeminence and freedom of action. Sino-Russian relations have a distinct patina of anti-U.S. sentiment, manifesting in successive actions in the U.N. to constrain U.S. actions. China has been opportunistic in using U.S. foreign policy problems to promote Chinese interests at U.S. expense. China reached out to the EU following the Iraq War to try to exploit trans-Atlantic tensions to push for elimination of the EU arms embargo on China. China reached out to both the Philippines and Thailand in 2004 and 2006 when their ties with the United States frayed. It is instructive that China has either failed or registered narrow success in many of these ventures.

Fourth, in Asia, China is not actively trying to break up U.S. alliances. It is not offering U.S. allies security assurances and military cooperation as a replacement to their security arrangements with the United States. Indeed, military diplomacy and defense cooperation is perhaps the smallest part of China's bilateral diplomacy with Asian nations. China is not promoting itself as an alternative security partner to the United States. Rather, it has focused on growing economic cooperation and reassuring U.S. allies by participating in regional institutions and committing to their norms of behavior, at least for now. Since the beginning of this decade, more Chinese strategists recognize that—official rhetoric aside—U.S. security commitments play a stabilizing role in Asia.

A final cut at this problem is to consider what a distinct Chinese balancing strategy would look like. It could include promoting an alternative concept of global and regional security and pushing Asian nations to choose between the United States and China. Such an approach could also include extensive security assistance—including large-scale joint training and exercises, meaningful intelligence exchanges, and arms sales in an effort to build an anti-U.S. coalition. It could also include technical assistance to internal security agencies in authoritarian regimes to advance one-party rule and entrench the current regime. There is little evidence that these activities are occurring, but these areas merit continued watching.

Will China Change in the Future?

Since the end of the Cold War, China's perceptions and objectives have driven a foreign policy that has, for the most part, accommodated U.S. power, focused on the gradual development of China's economic power and its military capabilities, and sought to minimize external threats. Going forward, a key question will be how the dual processes of China's growing material capabilities and its expanding global interests will transform Chinese foreign policy perceptions, objectives, and policies. Will these trends accelerate ongoing changes in Chinese foreign policy, such as the increasing sensitivity to its reputation and security dilemma dynamics, or will it produce alternative behaviors heretofore unseen? Specifically, as China's national capabilities expand, will its intentions change and will it become more aggressive in confronting the United States?

The analysis in this monograph suggests that this is not likely in the next two decades, barring a major discontinuity in China's current trajectory such as that caused by widespread domestic instability or an armed conflict with the United States or a major Asian nation. Why? Simply put: China's national capabilities will only gradually increase while the internal constraints and external restraints on a revisionist foreign policy will remain substantial.

China's accretion of power and influence in the next two decades will be gradual and limited. China faces numerous constraints on its ability to sustain robust growth. Few growth projections for China in the next two decades suggest that China would have the national resources to meet its substantial developmental needs while simultaneously supporting a breakout international strategy that would allow an easy and cost-free sprint to global parity with the United States. Also, this gradual accretion of Chinese power and influence will occur in a context of the rise of other major regional powers, such as Japan and India, who are watching China and checking its advances. These represent real constraints and restraints on major shifts in China's international strategy.

China's internal challenges will continue to loom large in the foreign policy calculations of Chinese leaders, suggesting that a fundamental reorientation in its foreign policy is unlikely. China's myriad domestic challenges will continue and some will grow in the next two decades, such the demographic constraints on growth and the need to shift to a consumption-based growth model.

For the current fourth generation of leaders and the fifth generation, the long-standing CCP lexicon of using foreign policy to create a stable external environment, to gain access to markets and resources, to minimize external commitments, and to avoid limits on Chinese choices will persist. Chinese leaders will continue to view their foreign policy through the prism of fostering domestic stability and growth. As argued above, China's domestic challenges increasingly function as both drivers and constraints on its foreign policy, and none of these are likely to change radically China's national interests.

In addition, Chinese leaders are mindful of the past mistakes of rising powers and want to avoid repeating them. They have studied the negative experiences of Imperial Japan, Weimar Germany, and the Soviet Union as well as the positive experience of the rise of the United States after World War II. They have concluded from these experiences the importance of not relying on military power to ensure international stature and of not confronting the dominant power. Rather, Chinese leaders are focused on increasing China's comprehensive national power as a way to ensure national revitalization. They realize that this will take time and international space. Western scholars of international relations debate China's ability to avoid such power-transition dynamics, but the international goals of Chinese leaders are clear on this point.[3]

As China pursues its current foreign policy strategy, its stake in the current international system will grow and this will likely provide greater binding influence on China. China will seek to perpetuate the system that has allowed it to gain prosperity and improve its security. This phenomenon has already been at work in the gradual evolution of its positions on North Korea, Iran, Sudan, and Burma. In all these cases, China has been more willing to take actions, previously rejected, in order to manage these problems or at least to prevent their worsening. This modification in Chinese behaviors is a direct consequence of the shifts in China's conception of its national interests, which, in turn, are a direct result of China's internationalization. China may change some of the rules and play a greater role in shaping international organizations (and potentially further constrain the United States), but Chinese-initiated changes in the structure of the current international system are unlikely.

A further consideration is that even as Chinese capabilities and influence grow, the costs of confronting the United States will remain high and the benefits of doing so will remain unclear, if not low. U.S. economic and military power will not remain static over the next 20 years, even if the gap in relative capabilities narrows. And the United States is not likely to take an overtly confrontational strategy toward China, which would fundamentally alter Beijing's cost-benefit calculus in its international behavior. The United States will continue to remain important (but not as central as before) to Chinese perceptions of their external security environment and the structure of the international system. Even assuming that the world becomes distinctly more mul-

---

[3] John Mearshimer, *The Tragedy of Great Power Politics*, New York: W. W. Norton and Co., 2001; Goldstein, 2005; Aaron Friedberg, "The Future of U.S.-China Relations: Is Conflict Inevitable?" *International Security*, Vol. 30, No. 2, Fall 2005, pp. 7–45; and Thomas Christensen, "Fostering Stability or Creating a Monster? The Rise of China and U.S. Policy Toward East Asia," *International Security*, Vol. 31, No. 1, Summer 2006b, pp. 81–126.

tipolar, the U.S. economy and military will continue to cast a long shadow over Asian and global affairs. In such a world, China's awareness of the costs of confrontation with the United States will persist.

These arguments are not meant to imply that China's international behavior will not change in the coming two decades. It will as Chinese capabilities gradually expand, as the international system becomes more multipolar, and as the U.S. role in global affairs changes. Chinese diplomacy will likely reflect a growing confidence and swagger. Other nations will look to China more, and China will become more comfortable using its capabilities to shape nations and institutions. It will also become more comfortable about disagreeing with the United States and more able to resist U.S. pressure.

The resulting policy challenge for the United States lies in monitoring Chinese international behavior to understand its trajectory. U.S. policymakers also need to find novel ways to accomplish several goals: to reduce China's ability to undercut U.S. interests and deter aggressive actions; to reassure China that the United States does not treat it as a strategic adversary in order to short-circuit China's most intense insecurities about U.S. intentions; and to generate opportunities for greater partnership in solving transnational problems that pose a threat to the stability of the international system.

A final implication of this analysis is that U.S. expectations of China's future trajectory should not proceed under the assumption that U.S. actions are autonomous to the evolution of Chinese perceptions, objectives, and policies. U.S. policy toward China will continue to be a major influence on China's future behavior and on the content and character of U.S.-China relations. This should remain a central premise for U.S. policymakers. Even as Chinese interests diversify, the United States will continue to loom large in, but not predominate, China's calculations of its economic and security interests. U.S. policies that take a highly competitive approach to China could make an adversarial relationship an inevitable outcome. On the other hand, U.S. efforts to expand areas of cooperation can reassure China and encourage it to set aside its narrow interests for the sake of regional and global good. U.S. policymakers should use all dimensions of U.S. power to signal to

Beijing the cost-benefit ratios associated with accommodating or confronting U.S. interests.

A related consideration is the unfolding relationship between the Obama administration's foreign policy and U.S.-China relations. A U.S. foreign policy that is perceived as less unilateral, ideological, and coercive than that of the Bush administration will deny China the opportunity to draw a stark contrast with the United States—in effect, it will foster a security environment in which China finds less fertile grounds for constraining U.S. options. A foreign policy that actively and appropriately uses multilateral institutions and emphasizes, in rhetoric and in action, the value of negotiated solutions (including those backed up by the possible use of force) may also make U.S. power appear less threatening to China and other countries, undercutting the intensification of the security dilemma in U.S.-China relations and augmenting the global appeal of the United States.

Policy Recommendations

Several policy recommendations for the United States follow from these conclusions. At the level of national policy toward China, the United States should adopt a "mixed strategy" with both cooperative and competitive elements. Specifically, such a mixed strategy should include the three components of engagement, institutional binding, and security balancing.[4]

---

[4] Technically, this could be referred to as a "hedging strategy," but this term is often misunderstood, in both the United States and China, as emphasizing the security-balancing elements of the strategy rather than its genuinely "mixed" nature.

For discussions of hedging strategies in U.S.-China relations, see Evan S. Medeiros, "Strategic Hedging and the Future of Asia-Pacific Stability," *Washington Quarterly*, Winter 2005–2006, Vol. 29, No. 1, pp. 145–167; and Rosemary Foot, "Chinese Strategies in a U.S. Hegemonic Global Order: Accommodating and Hedging," *International Affairs*, Vol. 82, No. 1, January 2006, pp. 77–94.

For the theoretical foundations of a hedging strategy, see Randall L. Schweller, "Managing the Rise of Great Powers: History and Theory," in Alastair Iain Johnston and Robert S. Ross, eds., *Engaging China*, New York: Routledge, 1999, pp. 1–32; and David Edelstein, "Manag-

The logic of pursuing a mixed strategy toward China stems from two core dimensions of China's international behavior: (1) China's growing centrality to stability and prosperity in Asia and globally and (2) the uncertainty about China's future direction as a rising power and the corresponding belief that either a very weak or very strong China could develop and either one would challenge U.S. interests. The latter aspect of the China challenge is particularly important: The point of adopting a mixed strategy is to hedge U.S. security "bets" against the uncertainty about China's future. Uncertainty is the driver of this approach, not hidden U.S. projections about China's intentions.

Each element of this mixed strategy has policy-specific components. U.S. engagement with China has become an accepted fact of U.S.-China policy over the past three decades. Global economic realities and the deep bilateral economic and financial integration demand it, and increasingly so.[5] There are few global security problems—both traditional and nontraditional—that can be resolved without China's involvement. And as China becomes more involved in regions beyond Asia, it has become central to managing their instabilities as well, such as the Darfur crisis in Sudan.

In pursuing engagement, the United States should seek to both shape and test China's intentions, which is the logic behind the policy approach of encouraging China to be a "responsible stakeholder." Perhaps more important, U.S. policymakers can use engagement to signal to China that the United States does not seek to contain China, does not seek to bring about violent political revolution in China, that a stable and prosperous China is in U.S. interests, and that the United States is willing to accept and accommodate some Chinese interests. Meanwhile, the United States can also signal to China that more is expected of it and that if it wants a greater global role, it has to shoul-

---

ing Uncertainty: Beliefs About Intentions and the Rise of Great Powers," *Security Studies*, Vol. 12, No. 1, Autumn 2002, pp. 1–40.

[5] The United States is China's largest trading partner, and China is the second-largest trading partner of the United States. The United States and China are the largest and third-largest trading powers in the world and China is the world's largest exporter. The United States and China were responsible for nearly half of the global economic growth that has occurred between 2003 and 2008. China holds over one trillion dollars in U.S. debt.

der additional burdens. The United States should expand the breadth and depth of bilateral dialogues on economic, diplomatic, and defense issues to ensure that all the relevant actors in China are engaged. The Obama administration's strategic and economic dialogues with China are important steps in this direction. A challenge for U.S. policy in effectively engaging China is to do so while also pursuing the more competitive aspects of U.S. policy, addressed below.

Beyond *bilateral* engagement, there is more the United States can do on the multilateral front. The United States needs to become more active in regional diplomacy in Asia to bolster the credibility and legitimacy of U.S. presence. China has benefited in the last five years from the perception that the United States is distracted with Iraq and Afghanistan and from a related regional skepticism about U.S. power and ideals. This situation provided an opportunity with which China could shape regional perceptions and expand China's influence. Thus, an important element of a U.S. engagement policy is to be more attentive to and more frequently present at major multilateral meetings in Asia to signal the consistency and quality of U.S. commitments to regional allies and partners. This will shape the regional context of China's rise. A renewed U.S. commitment to multilateralism in East Asia, including joining the East Asia Summit, holding a summit with ASEAN leaders, and always attending major regional meetings, would go a long way toward improving regional perceptions of the U.S. commitment to the region.

On economic questions, U.S. policy should focus on negotiating high-quality regional trade agreements and investment treaties and contributing to regional economic crisis-management mechanisms. U.S. policy needs to reassert itself as central to the economies of East Asia. The tone of U.S. policy toward China and U.S. policy in East Asia is important as well. The United States should pursue this agenda of regional engagement and enhanced multilateralism with confidence, not as a defensive reaction to concerns about China. The United States does not need to participate in every multilateral organization that China joins or establishes. U.S. overreaction to China's regional diplomacy would undermine the ultimate U.S. goals of bolstering the credibility and legitimacy of its existing role as a key provider of public and private goods to Asian nations.

The central premise of a binding strategy is to leverage China's desire to have a seat at the table and to gain access to institutional resources as a way to lock it into commitments. Encouraging China's participation also serves as a way to test China's intentions. Does China accept the prevailing rules or does it seek to rewrite them? Importantly, such binding is done in front of China's peers, which further raises the costs to China of defecting from rules or norms. Binding need not be seen as a coercive approach; binding seeks to create opportunities for China to accept restraint in exchange for both the international community's acceptance of some of its interests and China's access to the resources and stature of regional and global institutions.

For U.S. policy, this means expanding China's participation in major international and regional organizations, such as the International Monetary Fund and the International Energy Agency. This would signal U.S. willingness to give China more "voice opportunities" and help U.S. policymakers gauge China's ability to contribute to global problem-solving. Similar U.S. policies had a defining influence on the evolution of China's trade and nonproliferation commitments since the early 1980s. Looking forward, China's participation will be needed for the success of global negotiations on climate change, energy security, pandemic diseases, and other transnational security challenges.

The final aspect of a mixed state strategy is security balancing. This topic will not be addressed in detail here, given that Chinese military modernization was not a subject covered in this monograph. In general terms, the security balancing component of U.S. strategy involves enhancing U.S. alliance cooperation and the credibility of U.S. security commitments to the Asia-Pacific region. Ensuring regional stability by deterring aggressive actions by any state remains a central goal of U.S. alliances and force deployments in the region. The United States should also improve the quality of its regional security cooperation to ensure that U.S. allies and security partners are not vulnerable to predation by China and that none of them feel as if the United States wants them to choose between Washington and Beijing. The United

States can also use such security cooperation to broaden the legitimacy of its presence by addressing both traditional and nontraditional security challenges. China has been fairly effective at engaging Asian states on the latter, so the United States would benefit from leveraging its superior defense capabilities to do the same.

Last, security balancing should not be pursued in a way that is viewed as ganging-up on China, as that would alienate key allies and partners. Enhanced alliance coordination should occur alongside active military-to-military engagement programs between the United States and China as well as among U.S. allies and China. Such efforts can help to lessen the security-dilemma dynamics while also ensuring that U.S. military capabilities can continue to deter potential threats and reassure U.S. allies and partners.

Bibliography

2006 China Statistical Yearbook, People's Republic of China, Beijing, China: China Statistics Press, 2006.

2007 China Statistical Yearbook, People's Republic of China, Beijing, China: China Statistics Press, 2007.

2007 Nian Yi Dao Shier Yue Zhongguo yu Ouzhou Guojia Maoyi Tongji Biao [2007 January–December Statistics Chart for Trade Between China and European Countries], Ministry of Commerce of the People's Republic of China, January 24, 2008. As of October 8, 2008:
http://ozs.mofcom.gov.cn/date/date.html?2632778198=4194528730

2007 Nian Zhongguo Dui Wai Zhijie Touzi Tongji Gongbao [2007 Statistical Bulletin of China's Outward Foreign Direct Investment], Beijing, China: Ministry of Commerce of the People's Republic of China, September 27, 2008. As of October 9, 2008:
http://hzs.mofcom.gov.cn/accessory/200809/1222502733006.pdf

"2007 Zhongguo Junfang Junshi Yanxi Midu Pinfan Kancheng 'Junshi Nian'" [China's Military Exercises Frequent in 2007; It Could Be Called 'Military Exercise Year'], *Zhongguo Qingnian Bao* [China Youth Daily], December 28, 2007. As of October 7, 2008:
http://www.chinanews.com.cn/gn/news/2007/12-28/1117456.shtml

"Adhere to Peaceful Development Road, Push Forward Building of Harmonious World," *People's Daily,* August 24, 2006, as translated by OSC.

Alden, Chris, *China in Africa,* London, UK: Zed Books, 2007.

Alden, Chris, and Andy Rothman, *China and Africa: Special Report,* CLSA Asia-Pacific Markets, September 2008.

Algieri, Franco, "It's the System That Matters: Institutionalization and Making of EU Policy Toward China," in David Shambaugh, Eberhard Sandschneider, and Zhou Hong, eds., *China-Europe Relations: Perceptions, Policies and Prospects,* New York: Routledge, 2008, pp. 65–83.

Allen, Ken, "China's Foreign Military Relations: 2003–2004," *Chinese Military Update,* Royal United Services Institute, Vol. 2, No. 5, December 2004.

Allen, Kenneth W., and Eric A. McVaden, *China's Foreign Military Relations,* Washington, D.C.: Henry L. Stimson Center, October 1999.

Alterman, John, and John Garver, *The Vital Triangle: The United States, China and the Middle East,* Washington, D.C.: Center for Strategic and International Studies, 2007.

Asian Development Bank, "Greater Mekong Subregion," undated. As of October 6, 2006:
http://www.adb.org/GMS/default.asp

"Backgrounder: Eight Steps China Will Take to Boost China-Africa Strategic Partnership," *Xinhua,* January 30, 2007.

Bai Jie, and Cao Jia, "China's Special Envoy on the Middle East Issue Sun Bigan: China Hopes That Palestine Would Strengthen Internal Unity," *Xinhua,* August 2, 2007, as translated by OSC.

"BBC Monitoring China in Africa Digest 26 January 2005," as translated by FBIS, January 26, 2005.

Bergsten, C. Fred, Bates Gill, Nicholas R. Lardy, and Derek Mitchell, *China—The Balance Sheet: What the World Needs to Know Now About the Emerging Superpower,* New York: Basic Books, 2006.

Blum, Samantha, "Chinese Views of U.S. Hegemony," *Journal of Contemporary China,* Vol. 12, No. 35, 2003, pp. 239–264.

Bowley, Graham, "Cash Helped China Win Costa Rica's Recognition," *New York Times,* September 12, 2008.

Bradsher, Keith, "China and India Vie for Company with Oil Fields in Kazakhstan," *New York Times,* August 16, 2005.

Brahmbhatt, Milan, "Steering a Steady Course—Special Focus: Strengthening the Investment Climate in East Asia," East Asia Update, World Bank, November 2004. As of October 6, 2006:
http://www.worldbank.org.cn/English/content/eap10-04.pdf

Cai Wu, online interview with Vice Minister of the CCP Central Committee's International Liason Department, "Jianchi Fengxing Heping Waijiao Zhengce Tigao Yingdui Guoji Jushi Nengli" [Persist in Pursuing a Peaceful Foreign Policy and Improving Our Ability to Respond to the International Situation], June 21, 2005. As of March 27, 2009:
http://www.idcpc.org.cn/ziliao/wenzhang/0506.htm

Calabrese, John, "The Risks and Rewards of China's Deepening Ties with the Middle East," *China Brief,* The Jamestown Foundation, Vol. 5, No. 12, May 24, 2005.

Cao Huayin, "Shixi Dongbeiya Anquan Xin Kuangjia" [A Humble Analysis of the New Framework for Northeast Asian Security], *Gaige Luntan Xuebao* [China Reform Forum Journal], No. 10, 2004, pp. 27–36.

Cao, Belinda, and Judy Chen, "China Will Expand Currency Swap Accords to Help Trade," Bloomberg News, March 31, 2009.

Carlson, Allen, *Unifying China, Integrating with the World: Securing Chinese Sovereignty in the Reform Era,* Stanford, Calif.: Stanford University Press, 2005.

"Central Foreign Affairs Meeting Held in Beijing; Hu Jintao, Wen Jiabao Deliver Important Speeches; Wu Bangguo, Jia Qinglin, Zeng Qinghong, Huang Ju, Wu Huanzheng, Li Changchun, Luo Gan Attend Meeting," *Xinhua*, August 23, 2006, as translated by OSC.

The Central People's Government of the People's Republic of China, "Zhongguo Weihe Budui" [China's Peacekeeping Forces]. As of January 22, 2009: http://big5.gov.cn/gate/big5/www.gov.cn/test/2005-06/28/content_10554.htm

Che Yuming and Zhou Yingfeng, "China's Central Economic Conference Will Focus on 'Ensuring Economic Growth,'" *Xinhua*, December 8, 2008, as translated by OSC.

Chen Hui, "China's Diplomacy Is Moving Toward All Spectrum—Interview with Professor Wu Jianmin, Director of the Foreign Affairs Institute, and Deputy Secretary General cum Spokesperson of the CPPCC," *Zhongguo Jingji Daobao* [China Economics Daily], July 16, 2005, as translated by FBIS.

Chernyak, Igor, "Interview with Rosoboroneksport General Director Anatoliy Isaykin," *Rossiyskaya Gazeta*, April 10, 2009, as translated by OSC.

"China Agrees to Cancel Iraqi Debt," *China Daily,* June 21, 2007. As of March 23, 2009: http://www.chinadaily.com.cn/china/2007-06/21/content_899679.htm

"China, France Hold Joint Navy Drill," *China Daily,* March 16, 2004. As of October 6, 2006: http://www.chinadaily.com.cn/english/doc/2004-03/16/content_315366.htm

"China Makes More Overseas Investment in 2005 Mainly in Asia," *People's Daily Online,* February 11, 2006, as translated by OSC.

"China Non-Committal on Backing India at UNSC," *Press Trust of India,* April 12, 2005.

"China Quarterly Update," Beijing, China: World Bank Office, April 2005. As of October 6, 2006: http://www.worldbank.org.cn/English/content/cqu04-05-en.pdf

China Relations European Commission Web site. As of May 14, 2009: http://ec.europa.eu/trade/issues/bilateral/countries/china/index_en.htm

"China Signs More Technology Import Contracts in 2005," *Asia Pulse,* January 9, 2006.

"China to Develop Iran Oil Field," *BBC,* November 1, 2004.

"China-Africa Cooperation Forum: Past, Present and Future," December 11, 2003. As of August 2005:
http://www.china.org.cn/english/features/China-Africa/82189.htm

China's Foreign Affairs: 2004 Edition, English ed., Beijing, China: World Affairs Press, 2004.

China's National Defense in 2002, Beijing, China: State Council Information Office, October 2002.

China's National Defense in 2004, Beijing, China: State Council Information Office, December 2004.

China's National Defense in 2006, Beijing, China: State Council Information Office, December 2006.

China's National Defense in 2008, Beijing, China: State Council Information Office, January 2009.

China's Peaceful Development Road, Beijing, China: State Council Information Office, December 2005.

China's Peaceful Rise: Speeches of Zheng Bijian 1997–2005, Washington, D.C.: Brookings Institution Press, 2005.

"China's Sinopec Reportedly Set for 51% Stake in Iran Oil Field," *Market Watch,* September 15, 2006.

Christensen, Thomas, "Chinese Realpolitik: Reading Beijing's World-View," *Foreign Affairs,* September/October 1996.

———, Deputy Assistant Secretary of State for East Asian and Pacific Affairs, testimony before the U.S.-China Economic and Security Review Commission on "China's Role in the World: Is China a Responsible Stakeholder?" August 3, 2006a. As of May 28, 2009:
http://www.uscc.gov/hearings/2006hearings/written_testimonies/06_08_3_4wrts/06_08_3_4_christensen_thomas_statement.php

———, "Fostering Stability or Creating a Monster? The Rise of China and U.S. Policy Toward East Asia," *International Security,* Vol. 31, No. 1, Summer 2006b, pp. 81–126.

———, Deputy Assistant Secretary of State for East Asian and Pacific Affairs, statement before the U.S.-China Economic and Security Review Commission on "Shaping China's Global Choices Through Diplomacy," March 18, 2008.

Christensen, Thomas J., Deputy Assistant Secretary of State for East Asian and Pacific Affairs, and James Swan, Deputy Assistant Secretary of State for African Affairs, statement before the Subcommittee on African Affairs of the Senate Foreign Relations Committee on "China in Africa: Implications for U.S. Foreign Policy," June 5, 2008.

Chu Shulong, "US-China Relations: Stability Overtaking All," *Huanqiu Shibao* [Global Times], April 19, 2006, as translated by OSC.

Collins, Gabriel B., and William S. Murray, "No Oil for the Lamps of China?" *Naval War College Review,* Vol. 61, No. 2, Spring 2008, pp. 79–95.

"Commander Highlights Chinese Peacekeeping Force Role in Lebanon," *China Daily,* October 2, 2006. As of March 27, 2009:
http://www.chinadaily.com.cn/china/2006-10/02/content_701079.htm

Cooper, Joshua Ramos, *The Beijing Consensus: Notes on the New Physics of Chinese Power,* London, UK: Foreign Policy Centre, 2004.

Cui Tiankai, "Regional Integration in Asia and China's Policy," speech delivered at Hong Kong University, Hong Kong, February 4, 2005.

"Daguo de Fuze yu Daguo de Xintai" [The Responsibility and Mentality of a Major Power], *Huanqiu Shibao* [Global Times], August 15, 2005.

Daly, John C.K. "Sino-Russian Split at Regional Summit," *Asia Times Online,* November 15, 2007.

Datan, Merav, "Security Council Resolution 1540: WMD and Non-State Trafficking," *Disarmament Diplomacy,* No. 79, April/May 2005. As of June 12, 2005:
http://www.acronym.org.uk/dd/dd79/79md.htm

"Declaration on Fifth Anniversary of Shanghai Cooperation Organisation," the Shanghai Cooperation Organisation Web site, June 15, 2006. As of October 6, 2006:
http://www.sectsco.org/502.html

De Souza, Amaury, "Brazil and China: An Uneasy Partnership," Miami, Fla.: China–Latin American Task Force, Center for Hemispheric Policy, University of Miami, June 2006.

Dittmer, Lowell, and Samuel S. Kim, eds., *China's Quest for National Identity,* Ithaca, N.Y.: Cornell University Press, 1993.

Dominguez, Jorge I., *China's Relations with Latin America: Shared Gains, Asymmetric Hopes,* China Working Paper, Washington, D.C.: Inter-American Dialogue, June 2006.

Downs, Erica, "The Chinese Energy Security Debate," *China Quarterly,* No. 177, March 2004, pp. 21–41.

———, "China's Energy Requirements and Policies," testimony before the U.S.-China Economic and Security Review Commission on "China's Role in the World: Is China a Responsible Stakeholder?" Washington, D.C., August 4, 2006a.

———, *China*, the Brookings Foreign Policy Studies Energy Security Series, Washington, D.C.: The Brookings Institution Press, December 2006b.

———, "Business Interest Groups in Chinese Politics: The Case of the Oil Companies," in Cheng Li, ed., *China's Changing Political Landscape: Prospects for Democracy*, Washington, D.C.: Brookings Institution Press, 2008, pp. 121–141.

Dumbaugh, Kerry, *China's Foreign Policy and 'Soft Power' in South America, Asia and Africa*, Congressional Research Service, Washington, D.C.: Library of Congress, April 2008, pp. 71–77.

Dumbaugh, Kerry, and Mark P. Sullivan, *China's Growing Interest in Latin America*, Congressional Research Service, Washington, D.C.: Library of Congress, April 2005.

Economy, Elizabeth, and Michael Oksenberg, *China Joins the World: Progress and Prospects*, New York: Council on Foreign Relations, 1999.

Edelstein, David, "Managing Uncertainty: Beliefs About Intentions and the Rise of Great Powers," *Security Studies*, Vol. 12, No. 1, Autumn 2002.

Edgecliffe-Johnson, Andrew, Gillian Tett, John Thornhill, and Catherine Belton, "Wen and Putin Criticise Western Leaders at Davos," *Financial Times*, January 29, 2009.

"Egypt Seeks Stronger Trade Ties with China," *Asia Pulse*, September 11, 2006.

Evans, Peter C., and Erica S. Downs, *Untangling China's Quest for Oil Through State-Backed Financial Deals*, Brookings Policy Brief, No. 154, May 2006.

Fairbank, John K., "A Preliminary Framework," in John K. Fairbank, ed., *The Chinese World Order: Traditional China's Foreign Relations*, Cambridge, Mass.: Harvard University Press, 1968, pp. 1–19.

Fewsmith, Joseph, *Elite Politics in Contemporary China*, Armonk, N.Y.: M. E. Sharpe, 2001.

Fewsmith, Joseph, and Stanley Rosen, "The Domestic Context of Chinese Foreign Policy: Does Public Opinion Matter?" in David M. Lampton, ed., *The Making of Chinese Foreign and Security Policy*, Stanford, Calif.: Stanford University Press, 2002, pp. 151–190.

Finkelstein, David, *China Reconsiders Its National Security: The Great Peace and Development Debate of 1999*, Alexandria, Va.: The CNA Corporation, December 2000.

———, "China's 'New Concept of Security,'" in Stephen J. Flanagan and Michael E. Marti, eds., *The People's Liberation Army and China in Transition*, Washington, D.C.: National Defense University Press, 2003, pp. 197–201.

Foot, Rosemary, "Chinese Strategies in a U.S. Hegemonic Global Order: Accommodating and Hedging," *International Affairs,* Vol. 82, No. 1, January 2006, pp. 77–94.

Foster, Vivien, William Butterfield, Chuan Chen, and Nataliya Pushak, *Building Bridges: China's Growing Role as Infrastructure Financier for Africa,* Washington, D.C.: The World Bank, 2008.

Fox, John, and François Godement, *A Power Audit of EU-China Relations,* Brussels, Belgium: The European Council on Foreign Relations, 2009. As of May 14, 2009:
http://ecfr.eu/page/-/documents/A_Power_Audit_of_EU_China_Relations.pdf

Fravel, M. Taylor, "Regime Insecurity and International Cooperation: Explaining China's Compromises in Territorial Disputes," *International Security,* Vol. 30, No. 2, November 2005, pp. 46–83.

———, *Strong Nation, Secure Borders,* Princeton, N.J.: Princeton University Press, 2008.

Friedberg, Aaron, "The Future of U.S.-China Relations: Is Conflict Inevitable?" *International Security,* Vol. 30, No. 2, Fall 2005, pp. 7–45.

Gao Zugui, "An Analysis of Sino-US Strategic Relations on the 'Western Front,'" *Xiandai Guoji Guanxi,* No. 12, December 20, 2004, as translated by FBIS.

Garver, John, "The Legacy of the Past," *Foreign Relations of the People's Republic of China,* Englewood Cliffs, N.J.: Prentice Hall, 1993, pp. 2–30.

———, "China's South Asian Interests and Policies," testimony before the U.S.-China Economic and Security Review Commission on "China's Growing Global Influence: Objectives and Strategies," Washington, D.C., July 22, 2005.

———, *China and Iran: Ancient Partners in a Post-Imperial World,* Seattle, Wash.: University of Washington Press, 2007, pp. 136–230.

Gill, Bates, "The United States and the China-EU Relationship," in David Shambaugh, Eberhard Sandschneider, and Zhou Hong, eds., *China-Europe Relations: Perceptions, Policies and Prospects,* New York: Routledge, 2008, pp. 270–286.

Gill, Bates, and Yanzhong Huang, "Sources and Limits of Chinese 'Soft Power,'" *Survival,* Vol. 48, No. 2, Summer 2006, pp. 17–36.

Gill, Bates, and Chin-hao Huang, "China's Expanding Presence in UN Peacekeeping Operations and Implications for the United States," in Roy Kamphausen, David Lai, and Andrew Scobell, eds., *PLA Missions Other Than Taiwan,* Carlisle, Pa.: U.S. Army War College, April 2009, pp. 99–126.

Gill, Bates, Michael Green, Kiyoto Tsuji, and William Watts, *Strategic Views on Asian Regionalism: Survey Results and Analysis,* Washington, D.C.: Center for Strategic and International Studies, February 2009.

Gill, Bates, and Gudrun Walker, eds., *China's Rise: Diverging U.S. and EU Perspectives and Approaches,* Berlin: Stiftung Wissenschaft und Politik, August 2005.

Glaser, Bonnie, "Ensuring the 'Go Abroad' Policy Serves China's Domestic Priorities," *China Brief,* The Jamestown Foundation, Vol. 7, No. 5, March 8, 2007.

Glaser, Bonnie, and Evan S. Medeiros, "The Ecology of Foreign Policy Decision-making in China: The Ascension and Demise of the Theory of Peaceful Rise," *China Quarterly,* No. 190, June 2007, pp. 291–310.

Global Policy Forum, "Key U.N. Documents," undated. As of March 27, 2009: http://www.globalpolicy.org/security/issues/sudanarchindex.htm

Glosney, Michael, "Heading Toward a Win-Win Future? Recent Developments in China's Policy Toward Southeast Asia," *Asian Security,* Vol. 2, No. 1, 2006a, pp. 24–57.

———, *Meeting the Development Challenge in the 21st Century: American and Chinese Perspectives on Foreign Aid,* China Policy Series, Policy Brief 21, New York: National Committee on United States–China Relations, August 2006b.

Goble, Paul, "Only Interests Are Permanent: Russian-Chinese Relations as a Challenge to American Foreign Policy," testimony before the U.S.-China Economic and Security Review Commission on "China's Growing Global Influence: Objectives and Strategies," July 21, 2005.

Goldstein, Avery, *Rising to the Challenge: China's Grand Strategy and International Security,* Stanford, Calif.: Stanford University Press, 2005.

Gong Li, "Deng Xiaoping Dui Mei Zhengce Sixing yu Zhong-Mei Guanxi" [Deng Xiaoping's Thoughts on US Policy and Sino-US Relations], *Guoji Wenti Yanjiu* [China International Studies], No. 6, 2004, pp. 13–17.

Goode, Erica, and Riyadh Mohammed, "Iraq Signs Oil Deal with China Worth up to $3 Billion," *New York Times,* August 28, 2008.

Gorst, Isabel, and Richard McGregor, "Kazakh Oil Arrives in China," *Financial Times,* May 26, 2006.

Gries, Peter Hayes, *China's New Nationalism: Pride, Politics, and Diplomacy,* Berkeley, Calif.: University of California Press, 2004.

———, "China's 'New Thinking on Japan,'" *China Quarterly,* Vol. 32, No. 184, December 2005, pp. 831–850.

Grimmet, Richard F., *Conventional Arms Transfers to Developing Nations, 2000–2007,* Congressional Research Service, Washington, D.C.: Library of Congress, October 2008.

"Guoji Nengyuan Anquan Xingshi yu Zhongguo Nengyuan Waijiao," in *Guoji Zhanlue yu Anquan Xingshi Pinggu 2004–2005* [Strategic and Security Review

2004–2005], China Institute for Contemporary International Relations, Beijing, China: Shishi Chubanshe, 2005, pp. 45–62.

Guoji Zhanlue yu Anquan Xingshi Pinggu 2001–2002 [Strategic and Security Review 2001–2002], China Institute for Contemporary International Relations, Beijing, China: Shishi Chubanshe, 2002.

Guoji Zhanlue yu Anquan Xingshi Pinggu 2003–2004 [Strategic and Security Review 2003–2004], China Institute for Contemporary International Relations, Beijing, China: Shishi Chubanshe, 2004.

Guoji Zhanlue yu Anquan Xingshi Pinggu 2004–2005 [Strategic and Security Review 2004–2005], China Institute for Contemporary International Relations, Beijing, China: Shishi Chubanshe, 2005.

Harding, Harry, "China's Cooperative Behavior," in Thomas W. Robinson and David Shambaugh, eds., *Chinese Foreign Policy: Theory and Practice,* Oxford, UK: Clarendon Press, 1994, pp. 375–400.

Harris, Lillian Craig, "Myth and Reality in China's Relations with the Middle East," in Thomas W. Robinson and David Shambaugh, eds., *Chinese Foreign Policy: Theory and Practice,* Oxford, UK: Clarendon Press, 1994, pp. 322–247.

Holtom, Paul, "Russia and China's Defense Industrial Relationship and Arms Sales: Is the Party Over?" unpublished conference paper, April 2009.

Houser, Trevor, "The Roots of Oil Investment Abroad," *Asia Policy,* No. 5, January 2008, pp. 141–166.

Hu Angang, *Daguo Zhanlue Liyi yu Shiming* [Great Power Strategy: Interests and Missions], Liaoning, China: Liaoning Renmin Chubanshe, 2000.

Hu Jintao, "Build Towards a Harmonious World of Lasting Peace and Common Prosperity," speech at the Plenary Meeting of the United Nations' 60th Session, New York, United Nations, September 22, 2005. As of May 14, 2009: http://www.fmprc.gov.cn/ce/cehu/hu/xwdt/t213375.htm

———, "Hold High the Great Banner of Socialism with Chinese Characteristics and Strive for New Victories in Building a Moderately Prosperous Society in an All Around Way," report at the 17th National Congress of the Communist Party of China, October 15, 2007. As of March 26, 2009: http://www.china.org.cn/english/congress/229611.htm

"Hu Jintao Proposes SCO Focus on Security, Economy," *Xinhua,* June 17, 2004.

"Hu Pays State Visit to Saudi Arabia," *Financial Times Information,* April 24, 2006.

Hua Liming, "Yilan He Wenti yu Zhongguo Waijiao de Xuanze" [The Iran Nuclear Questions and the Choices for Chinese Diplomacy], *Guoji Wenti Yanjiu* [China International Studies], Vol. 1, 2007, pp. 58–62.

Huang, Cary, "Record $1 Billion Yuan in International Aid Granted by Beijing in 2005," *South China Morning Post,* January 19, 2006.

Huang Renwei, *Zhongguo Jueqi de Shijian he Kongjian* [Time and Space for China's Rise], Shanghai, China: Shanghai Shekeyuan Chubanshe, 2002.

———, "On the Internal and External Environments for a Rising China," *SASS Papers,* No. 9, Shanghai Academy of Social Sciences, Shanghai, China: Shanghai Academy of Social Sciences Press, 2003.

———, "Guoji Tixi de Gaibian yu Zhongguo Heping Fazhan Daolu" [Transformation of International System and China's Road to Peaceful Development], in Liu Jie, ed., *Guoji Tixi yu Zhongguo de Ruanliliang* [The International System and China's Soft Power], Shanghai, China: Shishi Chubanshe, 2006.

Hunt, Michael H., *The Genesis of Chinese Communist Foreign Policy,* New York: Columbia University Press, 1996.

Inter-American Development Bank, "People's Republic of China and Inter-American Development Bank Sign Memorandum of Understanding for Possible Admission to Membership into the IDB," news release, March 18, 2007. As of April 1, 2009:
http://www.iadb.org/NEWS/articledetail.cfm?artID=3696&language=EN&arttype=PR

International Energy Agency, *World Energy Outlook 2006,* Paris, France: OECD/IEA, 2006, p. 101.

International Energy Forum, "Global Energy Outlook: Issues and Challenges," April 2006. As of September 15, 2006:
http://www.nog.se/files/IEA10thIEF2006.pdf

International Monetary Fund, *Direction of Trade Statistics Yearbook,* 2000, p. 164.

———, *Direction of Trade Statistics Yearbook,* 2004.

———, *Direction of Trade Statistics Yearbook,* 2005.

Jia Qingguo, "Learning to Live with the Hegemon: Evolution of China's Policy Toward the U.S. Since the End of the Cold War," *Journal of Contemporary China,* Vol. 14, No. 44, August 2005a, pp. 395–407.

———, "Peaceful Development: China's Policy of Reassurance," *Australian Journal of International Affairs,* Vol. 59, No. 4, December 2005b, pp. 493–507.

Jiang Zemin, "Build a Well-off Society in an All-Round Way and Create a New Situation in Building Socialism with Chinese Characteristics," report to the 16th National Congress of the Communist Party of China, November 8, 2002.

Jin Xide, "Zhongguo Xuyao Daguo Xintai" [China Needs a Great Power Mentality], *Huanqiu Shibao,* September 12, 2002, p. 4.

Johnston, Alastair Iain, *Cultural Realism: Strategic Culture and Grand Strategy in Chinese History,* Princeton, N.J.: Princeton University Press, 1998a.

————, "International Structures and Chinese Foreign Policy," in Samuel S. Kim, ed., *China and the World,* 4th ed., Boulder, Colo.: Westview Press, 1998b, pp. 55–90.

————, "Is China a Status Quo Power?" *International Security,* Vol. 27, No. 4, Spring 2003, pp. 5–56.

————, *Social States: China in International Institutions, 1980–2000,* Princeton, N.J.: Princeton University Press, 2008.

Kastner, Scott L., and Phillip C. Saunders, "Testing Chinese Diplomatic Priorities: The Correlates of Leadership Travel Abroad under Jiang Zemin and Hu Jintao," unpublished presentation at the American Political Science Association annual meeting, Boston, Mass., August 30, 2008.

Kemp, Geoffrey, "The East Moves West," *National Interest,* No. 84, September 2006, p. 75.

Kim, Samuel S., *China, the United Nations, and World Order,* Princeton, N.J.: Princeton University Press, 1979.

————, "China and the United Nations," in Elizabeth Economy and Michel Oksenberg, eds., *China Joins the World: Progress and Prospects,* New York: Council on Foreign Relations Press, 1999, pp. 42–89.

Kurlantzick, Joshua, *Charm Offensive: How China's Soft Power Is Transforming the World,* New Haven, Conn.: Yale University Press, 2007.

Lee, Don, "China Barrels Ahead in Oil Market," *Los Angeles Times,* November 14, 2004.

————, "China Making Big Oil Moves: The Country's Steps to Secure Reserves Have Prompted Worries about Political Calculations," *Los Angeles Times,* January 23, 2006, p. C1.

Lewis, John, and Xue Litai, *China Builds the Bomb,* Stanford, Calif.: Stanford University Press, 1988.

Li Shaoxian and Tang Zhichao, "China and the Middle East," *Contemporary International Relations,* English ed., Vol. 17, No. 1, January/February 2007, pp. 22–31.

Li Zhaoxing, "Wei Renmin Fuwu de Xin Zhongguo Waijiao" [New China's Diplomacy of Serving the People], *Qiushi* (online), October 2004.

————, "Heping, Fazhan, Hezuo: Xin Shiqi Zhongguo Waijiao de Qizhi," [Peace, Development and Cooperation: A New Period in Chinese Diplomacy], August 22, 2005.

————, "2006 Nian Guoji Xingshi He Zhongguo Waijiao Gongzuo" [International Situation and China's Diplomatic Work in 2006], *Qiushi* (online), January 2007.

Li Zhifei, "Lengzhan Hou de Zhongguo Teshi Waijiao" [China's Special Envoy Diplomacy During the Post–Cold War Era], *Guoji Guanxi Xueyuan Xuebao*, No. 3, May 2008.

Lieberthal, Kenneth, *Governing China: From Revolution Through Reform,* 2nd ed., New York: W. W. Norton and Co., December 2003.

Lieberthal, Kenneth, and Mikkal Helberg, "China's Search for Energy Security: Implications for U.S. Policy," Seattle, Wash.: National Bureau of Asian Research, *NBR Analysis,* Vol. 17, No. 1, April 2006.

Liebman, Alex, "Trickle-Down Hegemony? China's 'Peaceful Rise' and Dam Building on the Mekong," *Contemporary Southeast Asia,* Vol. 27, No. 2, 2005, pp. 281–304.

Loser, Claudio, "China's Rising Economic Presence in Latin America," testimony before the U.S.-China Economic and Security Review Commission on "China's Growing Global Role: Objectives and Influence," July 21, 2005.

Lu Guozeng, Ministry of Foreign Affairs, the People's Republic of China, "Assistant Minister Lu Guozeng Addresses the Seminar on Diplomacy and Economy: Vigorously Strengthen Economic Diplomacy to Serve the Building of a Better-off Society in an All Around Manner," December 18, 2004. As of August 20, 2005:
http://www.fmprc.gov.cn/eng/wjb/zygy/gyhd/t176097.htm

Lum, Thomas, and Dick K. Nanto, *China's Trade with the United States and the World,* Congressional Research Service, Washington, D.C.: Library of Congress, January 4, 2007.

Lum, Thomas, Hannah Fischer, Julissa Gomez-Granger, and Anne Leland, *China Foreign Aid Activities in Africa, Latin America and Southeast Asia,* Congressional Research Service, Washington, D.C.: Library of Congress, February 2009.

Lyman, Princeton, "China Rising Role in Africa," testimony before the U.S.-China Economic and Security Review Commission on "China's Growing Global Role: Objectives and Influence," July 21, 2005.

Lynch, Colum, "Russia, China Veto Resolution on Burma Security Council Action Blocks U.S. Human Rights Effort," *Washington Post,* January 13, 2007, p. A12.

————, "U.N. Zimbabwe Measure Vetoed by Russia, China," *Washington Post,* July 12, 2008, p. A09.

Mao Yufeng, "Beijing's Two-Pronged Iraq Policy," *China Brief,* The Jamestown Foundation, Vol. 5, No. 12, May 14, 2005.

McNerney, Patricia, Principal Deputy Assistant Secretary, International Security and Nonproliferation, testimony before the U.S.-China Economic and Security Review Commission on "China's Nonproliferation Practices," May 20, 2008. As of March 26, 2009:
http://merlin.ndu.edu/archivepdf/china/state/105084.pdf

Mearshimer, John, *The Tragedy of Great Power Politics,* New York: W. W. Norton and Co., 2001.

Medeiros, Evan S., "Strategic Hedging and the Future of Asia-Pacific Stability," *Washington Quarterly,* Vol. 29, No. 1, Winter 2005–2006, pp. 145–167.

———, *Reluctant Restraint: The Evolution of Chinese Nonproliferation Policies and Practices 1980–2004,* Stanford, Calif.: Stanford University Press, 2007, pp. 97–174.

Medeiros, Evan S., and Bates Gill, *Chinese Arms Exports: Policy, Players, and Process,* Strategic Studies Institute, Carlisle, Pa.: U.S. Army War College, 2000.

Medeiros, Evan S., Roger Cliff, Keith Crane, and James C. Mulvenon, *A New Direction for China's Defense Industry,* Santa Monica, Calif.: RAND Corporation, MG-334-AF, 2005. As of June 11, 2009:
http://www.rand.org/pubs/monographs/MG334/

Medeiros, Evan S., Keith Crane, Eric Heginbotham, Norman D. Levin, Julia F. Lowell, Angel Rabasa, and Somi Seong, *Pacific Currents: The Responses of U.S. Allies and Security Partners in East Asia to China's Rise,* Santa Monica, Calif.: RAND Corporation, MG-736-AF, 2008. As of March 27, 2009:
http://www.rand.org/pubs/monographs/MG736/

Men Honghua, *Zhongguo: Daguo Jueqi* [The Rise of Modern China], Hangzhou, China: Zhejiang Renmin Chubanshe, 2004.

Ministry of Foreign Affairs, the People's Republic of China, "Foreign Minister Li Zhaoxing Delivers a Speech to UN General Assembly," 59th U.N. General Assembly, September 28, 2004. As of June 10, 2005:
http://www.fmprc.gov.cn/eng/wjb/zzjg/gjs/gjzzyhy/2594/2602/t163560.htm

Minxin Pei and Michael Swaine, *Simmering Fire in Asia: Averting Sino-Japanese Strategic Conflict,* Policy Brief No. 44, Washington, D.C.: Carnegie Endowment for International Peace, November 2005.

Morphet, Sally, "China as a Permanent Member of the Security Council: October 1971–December 1999," *Security Dialogue,* Vol. 31, No. 2, 2000, pp. 151–166.

Nathan, Andrew J., and Robert S. Ross, *Great Wall and Empty Fortress,* New York: W. W. Norton and Co., 1997.

"The National Security Strategy of the United States of America," Washington, D.C.: The White House, September 2002. As of October 6, 2006:
http://www.whitehouse.gov/nsc/nss.pdf

Negroponte, John D., Deputy Secretary of State, "U.S.-China Relations in the Era of Globalization," opening statement before the Senate Foreign Relations Committee, May 15, 2008.

Niu Jun, *From Yan'an to the World: The Origin and Development of Chinese Communist Foreign Policy,* Steven I. Levine, trans. and ed., Norwalk, Conn.: Eastbridge Books, 2005.

"OAS Accepts China as Permanent Observer," *People's Daily Online,* English ed., May 4, 2004. As of June 23, 2005:
http://english.people.com.cn/200405/27/eng20040527_144506.html

Oresman, Matthew, "Repaving the Silk Road: China's Emergence in Central Asia," in Joshua Eisenman, Eric Heginbotham, and Derek Mitchell, eds., *China and the Developing World,* Armonk, N.Y.: M. E. Sharpe, 2007, pp. 60–83.

Pan Guang, "Shanghai Cooperation Organization: Challenges, Opportunities, and Prospects," *SASS Papers,* No. 9, Shanghai Academy of Social Sciences, Shanghai, China: Shanghai Academy of Social Sciences Press, 2003, pp. 99–109.

Panda, Jagannath P., "The Impact of Sino-India Army Exercise on Bilateral Relations," *China Brief,* The Jamestown Foundation, Vol. 7, No. 15, July 2007, pp. 7–10.

Pang Xingchen, ed., *Zui Gao Juece: 1989 Zhihou Gongheguo Da Fanglue* [Highest Decisions: Important State Strategies After 1989], Beijing, China: Zhongyang Dangli Chubanshe, 2004.

Paramonov, Vladimir, *China & Central Asia: Present & Future of Economic Relations,* Conflict Studies Research Centre, Surrey, UK: Defence Academy of the United Kingdom, May 2005.

Percival, Bronson E., "China's Influence in Southeast Asia: Implications for the US," testimony before the U.S.-China Economic and Security Review Commission on "China's Global Influence: Objectives and Strategies," July 22, 2005.

———, *The Dragon Looks South: China and Southeast Asia in the New Century,* Oxford, UK: Praeger Security International, 2007.

"Philippines, China, Vietnam to Conduct Joint Marine Seismic Research in South China Sea," *Xinhua,* March 14, 2005.

Pillsbury, Michael, *China Debates the Future Security Environment,* Washington, D.C.: National Defense University Press, 2000, pp. 203–258.

"PRC Papers Criticize US over Sept. 11," *Taipei Times,* September 12, 2006, p. 4.

Pye, Lucian W., *The Spirit of Chinese Politics,* Cambridge, Mass.: MIT Press, 1968.

Qian Qichen, "Xinshiji de Guoji Guanxi" [International Relations in the New Century], *Xuexi Shibao,* October 18, 2004.

Ratliff, William, "Pragmatism over Ideology: China's Relations with Venezuela," *China Brief,* The Jamestown Foundation, Vol. 6, No. 6, March 15, 2006a, pp. 3–5.

————, "The Global Context of a Chinese 'Threat' in Latin America," Miami, Fla.: China-Latin American Task Force, Center for Hemispheric Policy, University of Miami, June 2006b.

Ren Xiao, *The International Relations Theoretical Discourse in China: A Preliminary Analysis,* Sigur Center Asia Papers, No. 9, Washington, D.C.: Elliot School of International Affairs, George Washington University, 2000.

Report of an Independent Task Force, *More Than Humanitarianism: A Strategic U.S. Approach Toward Africa,* New York: Council on Foreign Relations, November 2005. As of October 6, 2006:
http://www.cfr.org/content/publications/attachments/Repost%2012_06_05.pdf

Romberg, Alan, "The East Asia Summit: Much Ado About Nothing—So Far," *Freeman Report,* Washington, D.C.: Center for Strategic and International Studies, January 11, 2006. As of March 27, 2009:
http://www.stimson.org/pub.cfm?id=264

Ross, Robert, and Alastair Iain Johnston, eds., *New Directions in Chinese Foreign Policy,* Stanford, Calif.: Stanford University Press, 2006.

Ruan Zongze, "Zhongguo Waijiao Chuangzao Heping Jueqi Pingtai" [Chinese Foreign Affairs: Creating the Peaceful Rise Platform], *Liaowang Xinwen Zhoukan* [Liaowang Weekly], No. 50, December 15, 2003, pp. 14–16.

Saunders, Phillip, "China's America Watchers," *China Quarterly,* Vol. 161, March 2000, pp. 41–65.

————, "China's Global Activism: Strategy, Drivers and Tools," *Occasional Paper 4,* Institute for National Strategic Studies, Washington, D.C.: National Defense University Press, June 2006, pp. 21–22.

Saunders, Phillip C., and Erica Strecker Downs, "Legitimacy and the Limits of Nationalism: China and the Diaoyu Islands," *International Security,* Vol. 23, No. 3, Winter 1998/1999, pp. 114–146.

Schweller, Randall L., "Managing the Rise of Great Powers: History and Theory," in Alastair Iain Johnston and Robert S. Ross, eds., *Engaging China,* New York: Routledge, 1999.

Self, Benjamin, "China and Japan: A Facade of Friendship," *Washington Quarterly,* Vol. 26, No. 1, Winter 2002–2003, pp. 77–88.

Shambaugh, David, "Patterns of Interaction in Sino-American Relations," in Thomas W. Robinson and David Shambaugh, eds., *Chinese Foreign Policy: Theory and Practice,* Oxford, UK: Clarendon Press, 1994, pp. 197–223.

————, "Chinese Hegemony over East Asia by 2015," *Korean Journal of Defense Analysis,* Summer 1997, pp. 7–28.

————, "China Engages Asia: Reshaping the Regional Order," *International Security*, Vol. 29, No. 3, Winter 2004/2005.

————, "The New Strategic Triangle: U.S. and European Reactions to China's Rise," *Washington Quarterly*, Vol. 28, No. 3, Summer 2005, pp. 7–25.

————, ed., *Power Shift: China and Asia's New Dynamics*, Berkeley, Calif.: University of California Press, 2006.

————, "China's New Foray into Latin America," *YaleGlobal Online*, November 17, 2008.

Shambaugh, David, Eberhard Sandschneider, and Zhou Hong, eds., *China-Europe Relations: Perceptions, Policies and Prospects*, New York: Routledge, 2008.

Shen Guofang, "Zhongguo Xin Waijiao de Linian yu Shijian" [The Concept and Practice of China's New Diplomacy], *Shijie Zhishi* [World Affairs], No. 13, 2007, pp. 42–44.

Shichor, Yitzhak, "Israel's Military Transfers to China and Taiwan," *Survival*, Vol. 40, No. 1, Spring 1998, pp. 68–91.

————, "Decisionmaking in Triplicate: China and the Three Iraqi Wars," in Andrew Scobell and Larry M. Wortzel, eds., *Chinese National Security Decisionmaking Under Stress*, Carlisle, Pa.: U.S. Army War College, 2005.

————, "China's Voting Behavior in the UN Security Council," *China Brief,* The Jamestown Foundation, Vol. 6, No. 18, September 6, 2006.

————, "Blocking the Hormuz Strait: China's Energy Dilemma," *China Brief,* The Jamestown Foundation, Vol. 8, No. 18, September 23, 2008.

Shinn, David H., "China's Approach to East, North and the Horn of Africa," testimony before the U.S.-China Economic and Security Review Commission on "China's Growing Global Role: Objectives and Influence," July 21, 2005.

Shirk, Susan L., *China: Fragile Superpower*, Oxford, UK: Oxford University Press, 2007.

Shuja, Sharif, "Warming Sino-Iranian Relations: Will China Trade Nuclear Technology for Oil?" *China Brief,* The Jamestown Foundation, Vol. 5, No. 12, May 14, 2005.

"Sino-Arab Cooperation Forum Is of Milestone Significance: Chinese FM," *People's Daily*, January 31, 2004. As of October 6, 2006: http://www.china.org.cn/english/features/phfnt/85844.htm

Stern, David L., "Security Group Refuses to Back Russia's Actions," *New York Times*, August 28, 2008.

Stockholm International Peace Research Institute, *SIPRI's Arms Transfer Database*, April 2009. As of May 14, 2009: http://armstrade.sipri.org

Storey, Ian, "China's 'Malacca Dilemma,'" *China Brief,* The Jamestown Foundation, Vol. 6, No. 8, April 12, 2006.

———, *The United States and ASEAN-China Relations: All Quiet on the Southeast Asian Front,* Carlisle, Pa.: U.S. Army War College, October 2007, pp. 1–11.

"Students Again Make Beeline to US Colleges," *People's Daily Online,* April 5, 2006. As of October 6, 2006:
http://english.people.com.cn/200604/05/eng20060405_256030.html

Stumbaum, May-Britt, "The Invisible Ban: EU Maintains Weapons Embargo on China," *Jane's Intelligence Review,* December 2008, pp. 52–53.

———, *The European Union and China: Decision-Making in EU Foreign and Security Policy towards the People's Republic of China,* DGAP Schriften zur Internationalen Politik, Berlin, Germany: Nomos Publisher, 2009.

Suisheng Zhao, "China's Periphery Policy and Its Asian Neighbors," *Security Dialogue,* Vol. 30, No. 3, 1999, pp. 335–346.

———, "The Making of China's Periphery Policy," in Suisheng Zhao, ed., *Chinese Foreign Policy: Pragmatism and Strategic Behavior,* Armonk, N.Y.: M. E. Sharpe, 2004, pp. 256–275.

Sun Lei, "China Plans Financial Diplomacy, Seeks Right to Have Say in Economic and Trade Matters," *21 Shiji Jingji Baodao* [21st Century World Economic Journal], April 26, 2006, as translated by OSC.

Sutter, Robert G., *China's Rise in Asia: Promise and Perils,* Oxford, UK: Rowman & Littlefield, 2005a.

———, "China's Rise in Asia—Promises, Prospects and Implications for the United States," Occasional Paper Series, Honolulu, Hawaii: Asia-Pacific Center for Security Studies, February 2005b. As of March 27, 2009:
http://www.apcss.org/Publications/Ocasional%20Papers/OPChinasRise.pdf

———, "Durability in China's Strategy Toward Central Asia—Reasons for Optimism," *China and Eurasia Forum Quarterly,* Vol. 6, No. 1, 2008, pp. 3–10.

Swaine, Michael D., *China: Domestic Change and Foreign Policy,* Santa Monica, Calif.: RAND Corporation, MR-604-OSD, 1995. As of March 11, 2009:
http://www.rand.org/pubs/monograph_reports/MR604/

———, "China: Exploiting a Strategic Opening," in Ashley J. Tellis and Michael Wills, eds., *Strategic Asia 2004–2005,* Seattle, Wash.: National Bureau of Asian Research, 2004, pp. 67–101.

Swaine, Michael D., and Ashley J. Tellis, *Interpreting China's Grand Strategy: Past, Present and Future,* Santa Monica, Calif.: RAND Corporation, MR-1121-AF, 2000. As of March 26, 2009:
http://www.rand.org/pubs/monograph_reports/MR1121/

Swaine, Michael, Zhang Tuosheng, and Danielle F.S. Cohen, *Managing Sino-American Crises: Case Studies and Analysis,* Washington, D.C.: Carnegie Endowment for International Peace, 2006.

Swanstrom, Niklas, "China and Central Asia: A New Great Game or Traditional Vassal Relations?" *Journal of Contemporary China,* Vol. 14, No. 45, November 2005, pp. 569–584.

Tang Shiping, "A Systematic Theory of the Security Environment," *Journal of Strategic Studies,* Vol. 27, No. 1, March 2004, pp. 1–34.

—————, "Projecting China's Foreign Policy: Projecting Factors and Scenarios," in Jae Ho Chung, ed., *Charting China's Future,* Lanham, Md.: Rowman & Littlefield, 2006, pp. 129–145.

—————, "From Offensive to Defensive Realism: A Social Evolutionary Interpretation of China's Security Strategy," in Robert S. Ross and Zhu Feng, eds., *China's Ascent: Power, Security, and the Future of International Politics,* Ithaca, New York: Cornell University Press, 2008, pp. 141–162.

Thayer, Carlyle A., "China's International Security Cooperation Diplomacy and Southeast Asia," *Australian Defence Force Journal,* No. 127, 2007, pp. 16–32.

Tian Chunrong, "2006 Nian Zhongguo Shiyou Jinchukou Gaikuang Fenxi" [Analysis of China Oil Imports and Exports in 2006], *Guoji Shiyou Jingji* [International Oil Economics], No. 3, 2007, pp. 16–17.

"Top Ten Sources of ASEAN Foreign Direct Investment Inflow," ASEAN Secretariat Web site, undated. As of October 22, 2008: http://www.aseansec.org/18144.htm

Traub, James, "The World According to China," *New York Times Magazine,* September 3, 2006, pp. 24–29.

Tsui, Enid, and Francesco Guerrera, "China's CNPC Agrees to Buy PetroKaz for $4.2bn," *Financial Times,* August 22, 2005.

United Nations Peacekeeping, *Monthly Summary of Contributors of Military and Civilian Personnel,* undated. As of January 22, 2009: http://www.un.org/Depts/dpko/dpko/contributors/

United Nations Security Council, Web site, undated. As of May 14, 2009: http://www.un.org/

U.S. Department of State, *Voting Practices at the United Nations,* various years. As of May 14, 2009: http://www.state.gov/p/io/rls/rpt/

U.S. Energy Information Administration, *International Energy Outlook 2006,* June 2006, p. 34. As of March 23, 2009: http://www.eia.doe.gov

Van Kemenade, Willem, "Between Beijing and Paris: From Abnormally Good to More Normal," *China Brief,* The Jamestown Foundation, Vol. 7, No. 15, July 27, 2007.

Van Ness, Peter, *Revolution and Chinese Foreign Policy: Peking's Support for Wars of National Liberation,* Berkeley, Calif.: University of California Press, 1970.

—————, "China as a Third World State: Foreign Policy and Official National Identity," in Lowell Dittmer and Samuel S. Kim, eds., *China's Quest for National Identity,* Ithaca, N.Y.: Cornell University Press, 1993, pp. 194–214.

Vaughn, Bruce, and Wayne Morrison, *China–Southeast Asian Relations: Trends, Issues and Implications for the United States,* Congressional Research Service, Washington, D.C.: Library of Congress, April 14, 2006, pp. 12–13.

"The Vital Triangle: China, the United States, and the Middle East," Conference at the Center for Strategic and International Studies, Washington, D.C., September 14, 2006.

Waheguru Pal Singh Sidhu and Jing-Dong Yuan, *China and India: Cooperation or Conflict,* Boulder, Colo.: Lynne Reinner Publishers, 2003.

Wang Gungwu, "The Fourth Rise of China: Cultural Implications," *China: An International Journal,* Vol. 2, No. 2, September 2004, pp. 311–322.

Wang Hongying, "National Image Building and Chinese Foreign Policy," *China: An International Journal,* Vol. 1, No. 1, March 2003, pp. 46–72.

Wang Jisi, "Meiguo Baquan de Luoji" [The Logic of American Hegemony], *Meiguo Yanjiu* [American Studies], Vol. 17, No. 3, Fall 2003, pp. 28–40.

—————, "China's Changing Role in Asia," in Kokubun Ryosei and Wang Jisi, eds., *The Rise of China and a Changing East Asian Order,* Tokyo, Japan: Japan Center for International Exchange, 2004.

—————, "China's Search for Stability with America," *Foreign Affairs,* Vol. 84, No. 5, September/October 2005, pp. 39–48.

—————, "Reflecting on China," *American Interest,* Summer 2006.

—————, "Guanyu Gouzhu Zhongguo Guoji Zhanlue de Jidian Kanfa" [Some Thoughts on Building a Chinese International Strategy], *Guoji Zhengzhi Yanjiu* [International Politics Quarterly], No. 4, 2007, pp. 1–5.

Wang Meng, "Daerfuer Weiji: Zhongguo Waijiao Zhuanxing de Tiaozhan yu Qiji" [The Darfur Crisis: The Challenge and Turning in the Transformation of Chinese Diplomacy], *Shijie Jingji yu Zhengzhi* [World Economics and Politics], No. 6, 2005.

Wang Yi, "Jiaqiang Huxiang Hezuo, Cujin Gongtong Anquan" [Strengthen Mutual Trust and Cooperation, Promote Collective Security], speech at a conference on East Asian Security, December 15, 2003.

———, "Quanqiuhua Jincheng Zhong de Yazhou Quyu Hezuo" [Asian Regional Cooperation Under Globalization], speech to Foreign Affairs College Conference on "The East Asian Community," April 2004.

"Wang Yi Tan Zhongguo de Guoji Diwei He Waijiao Zhengce" [Wang Yi Talks About China's International Position and Foreign Policy], September 4, 2004. As of October 6, 2006:
http://www.china-embassy.org/chn/xw/t83962.htm

Wang Yizhou, "Forming a State Security Concept at the Turn of the Century," *Liaowang*, September 13, 1999a, pp. 23–24, as translated by FBIS.

———, "Chinese Diplomacy Oriented Toward the 21st Century: Pursuing and Balancing Three Needs," *Zhanlue yu Guanli* [Strategy and Management], December 1999b, as translated by FBIS.

"Washington Draws India in Against China," *People's Daily Online,* English ed., July 7, 2005; also in *Global Times,* July 1, 2005 (Chinese). As of August 24, 2005:
http://english.people.com.cn/200507/07/eng20050707_194676.html

Watson, Cynthia A., "China's Approach to Latin America," testimony before the U.S.-China Economic and Security Review Commission on "China's Growing Global Role: Objectives and Influence," July 21, 2005.

Weisman, Steven, "Politeness of China Talks Can't Disguise the Discord," *New York Times,* December 15, 2007.

Wen Jiabao, "A Number of Issues Regarding the Historic Tasks in the Initial Stage of Socialism and China's Foreign Policy," *Xinhua,* February 26, 2007, as translated by OSC.

Wheeler, Mathew, "China Expands Its Southern Influence," *Jane's Intelligence Review,* June 2005, pp. 40–44.

The White Papers of the Government, undated. As of March 23, 2009:
http://www.china.org.cn/e-white/index.htm

Winning, David, Shai Oster, and Alex Wilson, "China, Russia Strike $25 Billion Oil Pact," *Wall Street Journal,* February 18, 2009.

Wishnick, Elizabeth, *Russia, China, and the United States in Central Asia: Prospects for Great Power Competition and Cooperation in the Shadow of the Georgian Crisis,* Carlisle, Pa.: U.S. Army War College, February 2009.

World Bank, *East Asia & Pacific Update,* April 2007. As of March 31, 2009:
http://siteresources.worldbank.org/INTEAPHALFYEARLYUPDATE/Resources/550192-1175629375615/EAP-Update-April2007-fullreport.pdf

"Written Statement Made by Hu Jintao at Dialogue Meeting Between Leaders of G-8 and Developing Nations," *Xinhua,* July 17, 2006, as translated by OSC.

Wu Jianmin, "A Long Way to Go Before China Abandons Weak Nation Mentality," *Zhongguo Qingnian Bao* [China Youth Daily], March 21, 2006, as translated by OSC.

Wu Xinbo, "The Promise and Limitations of a Sino-U.S. Partnership," *Washington Quarterly,* Vol. 27, No. 4, Autumn 2004.

———, "The End of the Silver Lining: A Chinese View of the U.S.-Japanese Alliance," *Washington Quarterly,* Vol. 29, No. 1, Winter 2005/06, pp. 119–130.

Yahuda, Michael B., "China and Europe: The Significance of a Secondary Relationship," in Thomas W. Robinson and David Shambaugh, eds., *Chinese Foreign Policy: Theory and Practice,* Oxford, UK: Clarendon Press, 1994, pp. 266–282.

Yan Xuetong, "The Rise of China in Chinese Eyes," *Journal of Contemporary China,* Vol. 10, No. 25, February 2001, pp. 33–39.

———, *Guoji Zhengzhi yu Zhongguo* [International Politics and China], Beijing, China: Beijing Daxue Chubanshe, 2005.

———, "The Rise of China and Its Power Status," *Chinese Journal of International Politics,* Vol. 1, No. 1, 2006, pp. 5–33.

Yang Jiechi, "Gaige Kaifang Yilai de Zhongguo Waijiao" [China's Diplomacy Since Reform and Opening], *Qiushi* (online), No. 18, September 16, 2008.

Ye Jiang, "Luelun Gaige Kaifang Yilai Zhongguo Quanfangwei Waijiao de Daguo Waijiao Zhong de Daguo Zhanlue Tiaozheng" [A General Discussion of the Strategic Adjustment of the Big Power Strategy in China's Omni-Dimensional Diplomacy Since the Reform and Opening Period], *Mao Zedong Deng Xiaoping Lilun Yanjiu* [Mao Zedong, Deng Xiaoping Theory Research], No. 8, August 2008, pp. 38–44.

Ye Zicheng and Li Ying, "Zhongguo Suoyi Bixu Jian Daguo Waijiao Xintai" [China Therefore Continues to Establish a Great Power Foreign Policy Mentality], *Huanqiu Shibao,* July 20, 2001.

Yeh, Andrew, "Uzbekistan Signs $600m Oil Deal with China," *Financial Times,* May 25, 2005.

Yong Deng, "Better Than Power: International Status in Chinese Foreign Policy," in Yong Deng and Fei-Ling Wang, eds., *China Rising: Power and Motivation in Chinese Foreign Policy,* New York: Rowan & Littlefield, 2005, pp. 51–72.

———, *China's Struggle for Status: The Realignment of International Relations,* Cambridge, UK: Cambridge University Press, 2008.

Yong Deng and Thomas G. Moore, "China Views Globalization: Toward a New Great-Power Politics?" *Washington Quarterly,* Vol. 27, No. 3, Summer 2004, pp. 117–136.

Yong Dong, "Hegemon on the Offensive: Chinese Perspectives on U.S. Global Strategy," *Political Science Quarterly,* Vol. 116, No. 3, 2001, pp. 343–365.

Yu Bin, "China-Russia Relations: Between Crisis and Cooperation," *Comparative Connections,* Vol. 10, No. 4, April 2009. As of May 14, 2009: http://www.csis.org/media/csis/pubs/0804qchina_russia.pdf

Zaborowski, Marcin, ed., *Facing China's Rise: Guidelines for an EU Strategy,* Paris: European Union Institute for Security Studies, 2006.

Zhang Baijia, "Chinese Politics and Asia-Pacific Policy," in Ezra F. Vogel, Yuan Ming, and Tanaka Akihiko, eds., *The Golden Age of the U.S.-China-Japan Triangle 1972–1989,* Cambridge, Mass.: Harvard University Asia Center, 2002, pp. 38–51.

———, "Chinese Domestic and Foreign Policies in the 1990s," in Ezra F. Vogel, Yuan Ming, and Akihiko Tanaka, eds., *The Age of Uncertainty: The U.S.-China-Japan Triangle from Tiananmen (1989) to 9/11 (2001),* Harvard East Asian Monographs Online, 2005, pp. 61–81.

Zhang Qingmin and Liu Bing, "Shounao Chufang yu Zhongguo Waijiao" [Summit Trips Abroad and Chinese Diplomacy], *Guoji Zhengzhi Yanjiu* [International Politics Quarterly], No. 106, April 2008.

Zhang Wankun Franklin, *China's Foreign Relations Strategies under Mao and Deng: A Systematic Comparative Analysis,* Public and Social Administration Working Paper Series, Hong Kong: City University of Hong Kong, 1998.

Zhang Youwen and Huang Renwei, eds., *Zhongguo Guoji Diwei Baogao 2004* [China's International Status Report 2004], Beijing, China: Renmin Chubanshe, 2004.

———, eds., *Zhongguo Guoji Diwei Baogao 2005* [China's International Status Report 2005], Beijing, China: Renmin Chubanshe, 2005.

———, eds., *Zhongguo Guoji Diwei Baogao 2007* [China's International Status Report 2007], Beijing, China: Renmin Chubanshe, 2007.

———, eds., *Zhongguo Guoji Diwei Baogao 2008* [China's International Status Report 2008], Beijing, China: Renmin Chubanshe, 2008.

Zhang Yunling and Tang Shiping, "China's Regional Strategy," in David Shambaugh, ed., *Power Shift: China and Asia's New Dynamics,* Berkeley, Calif.: University of California Press, 2006, pp. 48–70.

Zhao Huasheng, "Can China, Russia and the United States Cooperate in Central Asia," *Zhanlue yu Guanli* [Strategy and Management], March 2004, pp. 34–107, as translated by FBIS.

Zheng Bijian, "China's 'Peaceful Rise' to Great-Power Status," *Foreign Affairs,* Vol. 85, No. 5, September/October 2005, pp. 18–24.

Zheng Yu, "Strategic Cooperation Between China and Russia," *China Strategy: China's Bilateral Relationships,* Vol. 3, Washington, D.C.: Center for Strategic and International Studies, July 2004, pp. 25–27.

"Zhong-E Guanxi Puxie Xin Pianzhang" [Writing New Chapters in China-Russia Relations], in Zhang Youwen and Huang Renwei, eds., *Zhongguo Guoji Diwei Baogao 2008,* Beijing, China: Renmin Chubanshe, 2008, pp. 214–218.

"Zhong-E Zhanlue Xiezuo Huoban Guanxi de Xin Tisheng" [New Progress in China-Russian Strategic and Cooperative Relations], in Zhang Youwen and Huang Renwei, eds., *Zhongguo Guoji Diwei Baogao 2007,* Beijing, China: Renmin Chubanshe, 2007, pp. 255–264.

"Zhongguo Ziyou Maoyi Qu Fuwu Wang" [China Free Trade Area Service Web site], Ministry of Commerce, PRC, undated. As of October 7, 2008: http://fta.mofcom.gov.cn/